LC

THE KREMLIN

THE
KREMLIN

SYMBOL OF RUSSIA

by

JULES KOSLOW

LONDON
MACGIBBON & KEE
1960

FIRST PUBLISHED BY MACGIBBON & KEE 1960

PRINTED AND BOUND IN GREAT BRITAIN BY
THE GARDEN CITY PRESS LIMITED
LETCHWORTH, HERTFORDSHIRE

To Julian, Jon and Evan

CONTENTS

ILLUSTRATIONS

Forty-eight pages of plates are inserted between pages 96 and 97.

'There is nothing above Moscow except the Kremlin, and nothing above the Kremlin except Heaven.'

—An old Russian proverb.

'There is nothing more cherished by us than the Kremlin. There it stand on the banks of a tranquil river, its crenellated walls hoary with age, the roofs of its faceted tall towers tiled dark green. Behind the walls, its palaces and golden-domed cathedrals on the emerald slope of the hill resemble a heap of jewels lying on the velvet lining of a mahogany casket. . . . In olden times, the Kremlin protected the Russians; now the Russians protect the Kremlin.'

—The Soviet writer N. Mikhailov.

I

Origin and Early History

IN ALMOST every country there is an architectural phenomenon
that symbolizes, to a degree, the national character of that country;
in Russia that phenomenon is the Moscow Kremlin.

Though the Kremlin for centuries has been representative of
Russian state power, its origin is somewhat obscure. According to
legend, at sometime around 882 A.D. when a hermit by the name of
Bookal inhabitated the place where the Kremlin now stands, Oleg,
the regent and uncle of Igor, son of Rurik, upon his return to
Novgorod from Kiev, stopped on a hill that was covered with a
virgin forest and laid the first stone of Moscow.

The Russian Chronicles, various medieval Church annals which
are the native source materials for much of early Russian history,
relate how Oleg and Igor went to Kiev, which Oleg established as
'the mother of Russian cities', but there is nothing in them for that
period that mentions Moscow or the mysterious hermit Bookal.
However, just as in later years attempts were made to link the ruling
line of Russian Czars with the ruling line of Roman emperors, it is
not surprising that, at least in legend, an attempt should be made to
link the founding of Moscow with the first historically recognized
rulers of ancient Rus, the Norseman Rurik and his descendants.

Actually, it was not until more than two hundred and fifty years
later, in 1147, that Moscow is mentioned in the Chronicles, and
here, too, the facts are obscure and contradictory. Nevertheless,
generally speaking, the following is the usually accepted version of
how Moscow and its Kremlin were founded.

In 1147, the Prince of Suzdal, Yuri Dolgoruki, returning from a
visit to his son, Andrew Bogoliubsky, stopped to rest on the pine-
studded banks of a charming, tranquil river. All about him was a
virgin forest, except for a few log huts that dotted the countryside
and, on a hill—a hundred and twenty-five feet above the level of
the river—that dominated the setting, the house of the boyar
Stephen Kutchko, the proprietor of the domain.

Yuri decided to stay there for a while and sent his retainers to

Kutchko to announce that the powerful Yuri Dolgoruki of Suzdal wished to enjoy his hospitality. Kutchko, a surly, suspicious, and arrogant man, received him, but treated him so inhospitably that Yuri ordered his followers to drown Kutchko in a pond. He then took the boyar's beautiful wife as his mistress, gave Kutchko's daughter to his son Andrew, and took possession of the boyar's holdings.

Attracted by the picturesque setting of his new lands, Yuri returned there on numerous occasions, and over the years he ordered a blockhouse and a warehouse to be built on the west corner of the hill. In 1156, to protect the tiny settlement, he enclosed this area with a log stockade, thus making it into a *kremlin*.

The origin of the word *kremlin* is not completely clear, even though it is generally understood to mean a fortress or a citadel. One interpretation of the word *kremlin*, or *kreml*, is that it is derived from the Tartar word *krim* or *krem*, or from the Russian word *krom*, which signifies a fortress; another is that it comes from a Russian root meaning 'flint' and refers to the strength of its fortifications. Still another interpretation is that its derivation is from the north Russian word *krem*, huge timber that was used for structural purposes.

The origin of the word *moscow*, like *kremlin*, has also not been definitely established. One interpretation is that *moscow* has a Finnish origin, for in an old dialect *kva* means water, and though the meaning of *mos* is not decided, it might imply 'the way', and, therefore, the word *moscow* simply means 'the water way' to the trading points reached by the river from the Volga and Oka. Another interpretation is that the name Moscow was derived from Mesech, the son of Japhet. What does seem quite definite, regardless of the origin of the word *moscow*, is that the city itself was named after the Moscow River, upon whose banks the settlement began.

Though most historians agree that Yuri Dolgoruki founded Moscow and its Kremlin (in present-day Moscow, near the City Hall, there is an equestrian statue of Yuri, honouring him as the founder of Moscow), there are many stories about the founding—and naming—of Moscow, and at least one, by Giles Fletcher, an Englishman who lived in Russia in the late sixteenth century and who wrote one of the most intrepid accounts of that country, is of interest.

'The citie of Moskva is supposed to be of great antiquitie, though the first founder be unknown to the Russe,' Fletcher wrote. 'It seemth to have taken the name from the river that runeth on the one side of the town. Berosus the Chaldean in his 5. book telleth that Nimrod (whom other prophane stories call Saturn) set Assyrius, Medus, Moscus, and Magog into Asia and Europe. Which may make some probability, that the city, or rather the river whereon it is built, tooke the denomination from this Moscus.'

Throughout the twelfth century, Moscow remained an insignificant village, consisting, in the main, of the Kremlin, that area within the stockade, and a few holdings near the enclosure, close enough so that in case of attacks by marauders, the inhabitants could take refuge behind the Kremlin's log walls.

To the south was the old, queen city of Kiev, steeped in bloody princely struggles for power and the centre of the Russian medieval Church; to the north lay Novgorod, with its trade-wise merchants and its 'democratic' way of life, which was characterized, among other things, by a *veche*, or city assembly, that could be summoned, by the ringing of the town bell, at any time for any question by any free citizen; and on the Volga, not too far distant from Moscow, was the city of Vladimir, for a while the capital of the Monomakh princes, and destined to be the repository of some of the most beautiful architecture of medieval Russia. While these cities and others, such as Tver and Rostov and Suzdal, vied with each other for power, the sleepy town of Moscow was little more than a resting place for travellers on their way from one point to another.

In the thirteenth century, this situation began to change, for Moscow, advantageously situated astride the east-west and north-south trade routes, became more and more a trading centre, a place where merchants could utilize its warehouses and exchange goods.

As an appanage of the younger sons of the princes of Suzdal-Vladimir, Moscow grew in size and population; had a small church that was situated at the gate of the Kremlin; and was regarded as a defence post by the Suzdal-Vladimir princes. Under the rule of Daniel (1246–52), the youngest son of Alexander Nevsky and the progenitor of the future Moscow princes, Moscow became the seat of a strong principality.

However, it wasn't until the beginning of the fourteenth century that Moscow became relatively powerful. Under Ivan I (1328–40), nicknamed Kalita, or Money Bag, because he always had a money bag instead of a sword hanging from his belt, Moscow became the actual capital, though Vladimir was the legal one. One of the factors that helped to make Moscow a suitable centre of power was the fact that the Church decided that Moscow was a more secure place than Vladimir, which was torn by rival princely factions. The Metropolitan Peter was the first to make Moscow his headquarters, and upon his death, having been judged a saint and being further sanctified by reports of miracles at his tomb in Moscow, his successor, Theognost, definitely designated Moscow as the home of the Church.

Now that both the religious and political centre of Russia was resident in Moscow, the Kremlin became, in fact, the centre of power in Russia.

Until the time of Ivan Kalita, the Kremlin itself was small and mean in appearance, and its wooden walls were inadequate for real defence purposes. In order to make Moscow a truly representative capital, Ivan I ordered the construction of various buildings, churches, and ramparts. During his reign, the Cathedral of the Archangel Michael, the Cathedral of the Assumption, and the Church of Ivan Lestvichnik, the first group of churches in the Kremlin to be built of masonry instead of wood, were erected, as well as other buildings. The rotting, flimsy pine stockade was torn down, and in its place he had massive walls and towers built of strong oak timber, the remnants of which were discovered during excavations in the Kremlin grounds five hundred years later, in the middle of the nineteenth century, when the foundations were being laid for Nicholas I's Grand Kremlin Palace.

The construction of this defence rampart was a favour granted by the Khan of the Tartars, for Ivan I, acting as the collecting agent of Tartar tribute in a good part of Russia, had thoroughly ingratiated himself with his master, as well as using this privilege to build up his own power. Nevertheless, Ivan I's power was limited. Like other princes who ruled before and after him, he exercised his princely power mainly as a vassal of the Khan, a vassaldom that had begun in the middle of the thirteenth century, a hundred years or so before the reign of Ivan I, and continued for a century and a half after his death.

The Tartar-Russian story actually began in the Far East, in the early part of the thirteenth century, when Genghis Khan, 'a man of gigantic stature, with broad forehead and long beard, and remarkable for his bravery', as a Chinese writer of the time described him, united the various Tartar tribes around him. After conquering the Celestial Empire of China, he marched westward, with the avowed purpose of conquering the world. 'As there is but one God in Heaven, so there should be but one ruler on earth', he declared, and he was determined that he would be that ruler. By the time of his death, in 1227, he had realized a good part of his ambition, for he had carved himself an empire that extended from the eastern shores of Asia to the Carpathian Mountains in Europe, and from the Arctic Ocean to the Himalayas—the greatest expanse of land that one man has ever ruled in the history of the world.

Upon the death of Genghis Khan, the Khan of Khans, his empire was divided among his sons, with the Khan of the Golden Horde in control of that part of Russia that included Moscow. During the early years of Tartar rule, many of the Russian princes, after first being confirmed in office by the Khan of the Golden Horde, had to make the many thousand mile journey to Mongolia, to receive the final sanction of the Great Khan. As time went on, internal dissension wrecked the unity of the Mongol empire itself, but the Golden Horde retained its grip over Russia. Various princes of Russia toadied to the Khans of the Golden Horde, but none so successfully as the princes of Moscow, who, in the course of time, became the firmest allies of the Khan of the Golden Horde and, as best exemplified by Ivan Kalita, trusted collectors of tribute for the Mongols from their own people. The cunning Moscow princes, 'who loved the Tartars beyond measure', were his willing servants while the Khan was powerful, but as soon as his power began to wane became his rivals and, ultimately, when the Golden Horde began to disintegrate the Moscow princes became the leaders of the liberation movement.

However, this was later, under the great Ivans; now, in the fourteenth century, the Moscow princes were indeed his lackeys, paying homage to him. When the Khan sent ambassadors to the Moscow princes, the prince was compelled to meet the horsed envoys on foot, present them with a goblet of mare's milk and if, while the envoys drank from the goblet, any drops fell on a horse's mane, had to lick it up. Or at other times, the prince had to stand on one foot in front of the Khan or his emissary and feed his horse oats from his own cap, while the Khan or his envoy sat upon his horse, looking down at the servile prince. This ceremony would take place in the Kremlin itself, as well as in Sarai, the capital of the Golden Horde.

One of the earliest Tartars to rule over Moscow was Batu, the nephew of Ogödai, the eldest son of Genghis Khan. Batu was appointed Khan of the Golden Horde shortly after the death, in 1227, of the Great Khan. In 1237 he laid waste a good part of southern Russia, and at Moscow, which he burned to the ground, he ordered a general massacre, instructing his soldiers that the right ears of the Muscovites be cut off and be brought to him as proof that his orders were carried out. According to some accounts—obviously exaggerated for the population of Moscow was not so large at the time—two hundred and seventy thousand ears were brought in by his soldiers and exhibited to the dictatorial 'Czar Batu', as he was called and of whom it was said 'no dog in the land could bark without first obtaining his permission'.

From 1236 to 1462, Russia was put to the sword forty-eight times by the Tartars. On some occasions the Tartar actions were the result of revolts, and on other occasions were punitive measures. However, there were times, too, when the Tartars were invited by a Russian prince to attack holdings of another Russian prince with whom he was in conflict.

The resistance of the Russians to the Tartars was uneven; at times it was heroic, and at other times it was marked by cowardice and fear. In the winter of 1237–38, when Batu marched on Moscow, the soldiers of Moscow, and the people in general, fled as soon as they heard that the invader was approaching. The Chronicles state bluntly: 'And the men of Moscow ran away, having seen nothing'. At another time, however, at Riazan, when Batu sent two heralds and a sorcerer to the princes of Riazan, informing them that 'if you want peace give us a tenth of your goods', the Riazan princes replied, 'When we are dead, you can take all we have'.

It is not strange that in the first years of the Mongol invasion the Russians, like other people who first came into contact with the fierce warriors of the East, should have been frightened, for their very appearance and their manner of warfare were unusual and awe-inspiring. The chroniclers of the period wrote: 'In those times, there came upon us for our sins, unknown nations. No one could tell their origin, whence they came, what religion they professed. God alone knows who they were, God and perhaps wise men learned in books'. In 1240, when Mangu, the grandson of Genghis Khan, threatened Kiev, the Chronicles state: 'As the main army drew nigh, so loud was the grinding of the wooden chariots, the bellowing of buffaloes, the cries of the camels, the neighing of the horses, and the ferocious shouts of the Tartars, that men could not hear each other's voices in the heart of the town'.

Batu, in his invasion of the eastern areas of Russia, had an army of five hundred thousand horsemen. This huge number of soldiers, outfitted with evil-looking scimitars, hooked spears, bows and arrows, and wearing black helmets was a fearful sight, so much so that one writer, in describing the event, wrote: 'The earth groaned under the multitude of warriors, and the clamour of the troops maddened the wild beasts and birds of the night'. In addition to the frightening size of their armies, the very appearance of the Tartars was awe-inspiring.

Giles Fletcher wrote of their appearance as follows: 'For Person and Complexion, they haue broad and flat visages of a tanned Color, yellow and blacke, fierce and cruell lookes, thinne hayred vpon the vpper Lip and a pit on the Chin, light and nimble Bodied, with short Legges, as if they were made naturally for Horse men: whereto they practice themselues from their Child-hood, seldom going a foot about any businesse. Their Speach is uery sudden and loude, speaking as it were out of a deepe hollow throat. When they Sing, you would think a Cow lowed or some great Ban dogge howled.'

Their manner of life was strict and cruel but admirably suited for a warrior nation. 'From infancy they are wont to ride horses, to shoot their arrows at birds and rats, and thus they gain the courage needful for their life of war and rapine', wrote a Chinese author of the thirteenth century. 'They have neither religious ceremonies or courts of justice. From the prince to the lowest man of the tribe, all feed on the flesh of such animals as they kill, and they dress in skins and furs. The strongest among them have the largest and fattest morsels at feasts; the old men eat and drink the remains. They respect naught but strength and courage; they scorn age and weakness. When the father dies, his son marries the youngest wives.'

A wandering nation, they were accustomed to the hazards of the elements and inured to suffering. Bishop Paulus of Nuceria, in his report to Pope Clement VII, wrote: 'In the stead of houses, they use wagons covered with hides. For cities and towns, they use great tents and pavilions, not defended by trenches or walls of timber or stone, but enclosed with a numberless host of archers on horseback'.

When engaged in warfare, their hardy manner of life contributed markedly towards their success. In winter, for instance, they could ride ten days on end without ever making a fire for warmth. They had no need of regular meals, subsisting on dried mare's milk, which they dissolved in water. When they were out of food they bled their horses and drank the horses' blood, and when they wanted something more solid than their milk paste, they made a sheep's pudding full of blood and put under their saddle, where in time it became coagulated, cooked by the heat of the horse's body.

Carrying a minimum of provisions, the Tartar army travelled light. The horsemen, dressed in a coat of buffalo or other hide, carried little else but their weapons; the horses had to be content with the grass of the plains, for the Tartars carried no fodder of any kind with them. The Tartar army, almost unburdened, could cover incredible distances, often appearing, as if from nowhere, and with their blood-curdling cries and yells, intermingled with their throaty supplication '*Olla Billa! Olla Billa!* [God Help Us! God Help Us!]', threw the opposing army into panic and retreat.

In battle tactics the Tartars were often superior to their adversaries; they were, for instance, masters of doubling and wheeling, which often thoroughly confused the enemy. They were also adept in the ancient battle tactic that Cyrus and Darius Hystaspis, the ancient Persian kings, had used so adroitly: of retreating before an invader, thus luring the enemy farther into the country and then, after closing the avenues of escape, attacking in great numbers. Later, the Russians themselves, during the Napoleonic invasion and during the Second World War, availed themselves of this tactic successfully, too.

Almost all writers on the Tartars agree that they were one of the most ferocious warrior nations of all times. Giles Fletcher, in comparing the Tartar with the Russian and Turkish soldiers, remarked that when all chances of success in battle were gone, the

Tartar still fought on, using his teeth against the enemy swords, if he had nothing else left to fight with. The Russian ran away and, when caught, resigned himself to death; the Turk threw up his hands and begged to be taken as a slave.

The Tartars did not station armies among the people they conquered; instead, they conquered, looted, murdered, and then retreated, exacting tribute, which a local prince was obliged to collect and turn over to them. The payment of tribute, however, was no guarantee that the subject people were safe from Tartar terror. Moscow was repeatedly attacked, looted and burned, and its inhabitants slaughtered during the Tartar period, even though from the time of Ivan Kalita the princes of Moscow were, in the main, the collectors of the Khan's tribute in a large part of Russia and enjoyed privileges and power that princes of other Russian principalities were denied.

For the two hundred and fifty years or so in which Tartar supremacy was at its height in Russia, the Kremlin princes, as well as other Russian rulers, were their vassals—at times faithful ones and at other times restless under their dominance. The effect of Tartar rule upon the rulers and people of Russia was significant, but it was not as deep-rooted as one would imagine would be the case during and after centuries of vassalage.

In some areas, such as religion, the Tartars had no effect whatsoever, nor did they wish to, leaving the Russian Church and the beliefs of its people strictly alone. The Tartar influence on the Russian language, except for the introduction of a handful of words, mostly connected with commerce—'denga' (silver), 'tovar' (goods), and so on—was negligible. They had no effect as well on the artistic and cultural (in the narrow sense of the word 'culture') life of Russia. In the wider cultural sense however they did influence Russian life to a degree, though many of the so-called Asiatic characteristics of the Russians that have often been attributed to Tartar influence were not actually Asiatic in the Tartar sense but were Byzantine.

Though it is true that before the Tartar yoke was imposed on the Russians a greater spirit of independence and forthrightness seems to have been characteristic of the Russians of both the lower and upper classes, and that during and after the Tartar period a spirit of resignedness and servility came over them, the reasons for this cannot be attributed to the Tartars alone. Indirectly, centuries of living under a foreign master had taken its toll of the national spirit, but the influence of the Church, which preached resignation and conformity, and of the Russian rulers themselves, who insisted on absolute obedience, was more profound.

Politically, however, the Tartar yoke produced some meaningful effects. The Russian princes, servile for the most part to the Khans, aped the absolutism of the Tartar masters and introduced a system of absolutism in Russia that differed greatly from that of the pre-Tartar princes, such as the benign and scholarly Prince Yaroslav the Wise, the lawgiver of Russia, under whose rule the ethos of Russia was comparable to most European countries of the time.

The manner in which the princes lived and worked became much different after the Tartar conquest. The pre-Tartar Prince Vladimir Monomakh, for instance, who ruled in Kiev in the early part of the twelfth century (1113–25), like most of the princes of his time, was a warrior-prince who shared the field of battle with his soldiers and lived a rugged and very hazardous life. In his testament to his sons, written shortly before his death, he gave a vivid picture of the life of a grand prince of the time—adventurous, brave, and hard-working. After recounting his own exploits and listing dozens of virtues that an honest ruler and human being should be guided by, he proudly stated: 'In war and at the hunt, by night and by day, in heat and in cold, I did whatever my servant had to do, and gave myself no rest. Without relying on lieutenants or messengers, I did whatever was necessary; I looked to every disposition in my household. At the hunt, I posted the hunters, and I looked after the stable, the falcons, and the hawks. I did not allow the mighty to distress the common peasant or the poverty-stricken widow. . . . Without fear of death, of war, or of wild beasts, do a man's work, my sons, as God sets it before you'. After the Tartar conquest the Czars, with a few notable exceptions, did not subscribe to Vladimir's manner of life, but, instead, lived less adventurously and to an extent isolated themselves within the Kremlin.

The Tartar conquest and occupation also had other repercussions. It helped to turn the face of Russia, which had been towards the West, to the East. The Tartars, however, were not entirely responsible for this new orientation. The Lithuanians, Teutonic

Knights, Poles, and the forces of the Vatican also helped to effect the change. They constantly opposed the heretical Russians, preventing them with an almost crusading fervour from influencing either politically or ideologically the Roman Catholic nations of Western Europe. In effect, this was a blockade, which isolated Russia from the rest of Europe and forced her to turn towards Byzantium and the culture it represented.

Intermarriage between Russian and Tartar was not uncommon, and in time many people in the Russian upper class, as well as among the common people, were partly Tartar. Though the great Moscow princes themselves were treated as conquered people, it did not prevent them from intermarrying with the Tartar nobility if the alliance was mutually advantageous. So it was, for instance, that Yuri III, Grand Duke of Moscow between 1303 and 1325, married the sister of the Khan. It is estimated that by the end of the seventeenth century, seventeen per cent of the upper classes of Moscow were of Tartar or Eastern origin.

Undoubtedly, the most important political consequence of the Tartar conquest was that it, unwittingly, accelerated Russian unification, while at the same time it extinguished whatever free political life there was in Russia. It was responsible, too, in large measure for the extreme autocratic power that developed in Russia, which more than any other single factor characterizes the Kremlin and its history.

II

Early Rulers

IVAN KALITA died in 1340 and was succeeded by his son Simeon, called the Proud. Simeon, like his father, kowtowed to the Tartars, and was rewarded by the Khan, even more so than his father before him, by being designated as the prince over all other princes of Russia. He thus became, except for the Khan, the head of the confused *mélange* of city-states which then comprised the ruling power in Russia.

Assuming the title of Grand Prince of the Russias, Simeon the Proud was anything but proud in his relations to the Golden Horde. No less than five times he made his servile journey to the head-quarters of the Horde, to pay homage to his master the Khan, and each time he was received as a faithful servant and sent home with his master's blessings. To the Khan, Simeon represented Russia as 'your faithful province', though to the other princes of Russia he admonished them to be faithful to him, to regard him as their eldest brother, and give him their unqualified obedience and loyalty, if they wished to throw off the Tartar yoke.

Like his father, he continued to enlarge and embellish the interior of the Kremlin; many bells for the Kremlin churches were cast, much money was spent improving the Kremlin buildings, and Greek artists were commissioned to ornament the Cathedral of the Assumption. After ruling for thirteen years, he died in 1353, a victim of the Black Death, which, having originated in China in 1346, swept over Asia and most of Europe, taking a toll of thirteen million lives.

In Moscow, the toll was particularly severe from the Black Death, which an annalist of the time described thus:

'One felt himself suddenly struck as by a knife plunged into the heart through the shoulder blades or between the two shoulders. An intense fire seemed to burn the entrails; blood flowed freely from the throat; a violent perspiration ensued, followed by severe chills; tumours gathered upon the neck, the hip, under the arms or behind the shoulder blades. The end was invariably the same—death, inevitable, speedy, but terrible.'

The Tartars, rulers over a good part of the area where the Black Death was most prevalent, were particularly affected by it, and there is reason to believe that, in addition to internal feuding and the softening of their national way of life, the horrible disease which decimated the people and their leaders was a contributing factor to the ultimate demise of the Tartars as rulers over a good part of their extensive empire.

The Kremlin itself, during the reigns of Simeon the Proud and his brother Ivan the Debonnaire (1353–59), remained, in spite of the improvements and embellishments of various buildings, essentially the same in outward appearance. However, under Prince Dmitri (1359–89) it did change somewhat, for in 1367 the Prince had the first stone wall erected to enclose the Kremlin. The strengthening of the Kremlin walls without the permission of the Khan would not have been allowed in the time of Batu Khan, but the power of the Moscow princes had become so much greater and the Golden Horde had become so weakened by internal dissension that by now the Tartars could be flouted. The erection of the stone walls provided Moscow with the means of increased defence and were also necessary to protect the Kremlin area from the fires that raged periodically in the wooden-hutted town of Moscow, one of which, in 1365, 'made ashes out of Moscow'.

In addition to replacing the oak-timbered stockade with stone walls, emplacements were built for cannon, which were then first coming into use in Russia. The wisdom of surrounding the Kremlin with stone walls was soon justified, for in 1368 the Lithuanians, under Olgerd, attacked Moscow, burning all the houses outside the Kremlin walls and devastating the countryside, but they were unable to penetrate into the Kremlin itself. Again, two years later, in warfare with the city of Tver, which was aided by the Lithuanians and the Golden Horde, the surrounding areas of the Kremlin were burned, but the walls protected the area within the Kremlin from destruction.

In 1380, at Kulikovo, Dmitri, at the head of a hundred and fifty thousand men, the greatest army ever assembled under a Russian ruler, defeated the armies of the Golden Horde, under Mamai, and once and for all destroyed the myth of Tartar invincibility in battle, as well as breaking, though not destroying, Tartar supremacy. Dmitri himself was carried from the field of battle half dead, but was cheered by the news that the Tartars had lost over a hundred thousand men and that the Russians had captured their chariots, tents, horses, camels, cattle, and priceless treasures of silk.

In spite of this momentous victory over the Tartars, two years later Dmitri, now called Dmitri Donskoi in honour of his victory at the Don over the Tartars, was again confronted by the ancient enemy. Tamerlane, the 'conqueror of the two Bokharas, of Hindostan, of Iran, and of Asia Minor', had Mamai put to death by one of his generals, and insisted that Dmitri Donskoi appear before the Horde, The Russian prince refused, and Tamerlane ordered Tokhtamysh, a descendant of Genghis Khan, to march upon Moscow.

At the approach of the Tartars, Dmitri deserted Moscow, ostensibly to get help from other princes, and the city was left to defend itself—which it did spiritedly. No citizen was allowed to leave the city and the wail of prayers beseeching God for a Russian victory over the Tartars went on night and day. For three days the people of Moscow defied the invaders at the walls; they hurled boiling water down from the towers and dropped stones and baulks of timber on the Tartars deployed in the ditch before the walls, while all the time they shouted violent insults and curses at the assailants. Failing to capture the Kremlin by force, Tokhtamysh tried wile. He sent word to the besieged that he was not at war with the citizens of Moscow but only with their rulers, and that he would allow them to leave the Kremlin and occupy their houses again without being molested. Traitors within the Kremlin convinced the people there to believe him, and bearing presents and preceded by priests, they opened the gates and as friends marched out to meet the Tartars. The soldiers of the Horde immediately fell upon them, killed them, and made their way into the fortress. The remaining defenders, demoralized, made no attempt to save themselves, and in the words of a chronicler, 'cried out like feeble women and tore their hair'. The Kremlin was sacked, irreplaceable documents and early archives were destroyed, and, except for a few stone structures, not a house in Moscow was left standing. According to one account, 'smoke, ashes, the earth covered with blood, dead bodies, deserts and burned churches alone remained'. More than twenty-four thousand Muscovites were killed. The Horde, however, unwilling to face a Moscow winter, suddenly withdrew, firing other Russian cities on its way.

After the Tartars left, Dmitri returned to Moscow, and, while shedding tears, cried, 'Our fathers, who never triumphed over the Tartars, were less unhappy than we!'

The town of Moscow was covered with dead bodies, and Dmitri announced that he would pay anybody willing to bury the dead a rouble for every eighty bodies buried. He paid out three hundred roubles, and in this way the previous-mentioned figure of twenty-four thousand was arrived at, although the number was actually greater, for thousands of people perished in the Moscow river while trying to swim to the other side to escape the Tartars, and other thousands were cremated in the fires that raged throughout Moscow.

After the dead were buried, Dmitri ordered that Moscow, which was literally in ashes, should be rebuilt. Since the walls, towers, and buildings of the Kremlin were undamaged, in the main, little reconstruction was required on the fortress, but the surrounding areas had to be rebuilt from the ground up.

In 1389 the tall, heavy-set, dark-haired, illiterate Dmitri who, as the Chronicles relate, could not read but 'had the holy books in his heart', died, and was succeeded by his son Vasili I (1389–1425).

A year after Vasili became Prince of Moscow, a great fire ravaged the town of Moscow, destroying many houses, but the Kremlin was spared. It was not until 1408, eighteen years later, that the Kremlin was again besieged by the Tartars, under the Tartar general Edigé, who was determined to extort tribute from Moscow which had in recent years more and more defied the Tartars. He gathered together a tremendous army and, after spreading the rumour that he was marching against the Lithuanians, actually marched on Moscow. Vasili, like his father before him, fled. He went to Kostroma, again ostensibly to raise an army, leaving the city of Moscow to be defended by his uncle, Vladimir the Brave. Vladimir ordered thousands of houses in the suburbs of Moscow to be burned to the ground, so that the Tartars wouldn't be able to gather *primeta* (combustible material) to fire the Kremlin walls. The inhabitants of Moscow upon the approach of the Tartar army rushed to the Kremlin and, praying before its locked gates, begged to be admitted, so that they could have protection behind its walls.

They were refused entrance, the reason being given that if all the people who asked for admission were admitted a famine within the Kremlin would result.

The Kremlin walls were now mounted with cannon, and the defenders put up a stiff resistance. Edigé tried to capture the fortress by starving out the Muscovites, but before this plan was put to the severe test, he was recalled by his superior, the Khan Temir-Kutlu of the Golden Horde who was having his own troubles. Edigé forced the people of Moscow to pay him three thousand roubles in tribute and left.

Upon the death of Vasili I, in 1425, a violent civil war broke out between members of the Moscow princely family. Before it was ended, Vasili Cross-Eye, a claimant to the throne, was blinded by Vasili II, who in turn was later blinded by Vasili Cross-Eye's brother Shemyaka, and for the last twenty years of his reign was sightless.

In 1451 during the rule of Vasili the Blind, the Tartars once again tried to capture Moscow. Vasili fled the Kremlin, leaving the defences to others. This time the Tartar defeat was an ignominious one. They were defeated so decisively that they disappeared in the course of a single night, leaving behind them all their heavy equipment.

It was during the reign of Vasili the Blind that for the first time, and the last, the Latin cross appeared within a cathedral in the Kremlin. Isadore, Metropolitan of Moscow, at the urging of the Greek emperor John Paleologus, who hoped to get the help of the Pope against the Ottoman Turks, had attended the Council of Florence in 1439, which had been called by Pope Eugenius IV with the express purpose of reuniting the two Churches. Isadore signed the act of union, though it was rejected by the Greek world. Upon his return to Moscow he announced that he had signed the pact, and in his prayers spoke of the Roman Pope and in the Cathedral of the Assumption displayed the Latin cross. Vasili attacked Isadore for his actions, and Isadore fled to Rome, to save his life.

Towards the end of his reign, Vasili the Blind became seriously ill with consumption. Fearing that he had only a short while longer to live, he had his son Ivan crowned co-ruler, in order to prevent a repetition of the difficulties he had had to establish his right to the throne. Curiously enough, however, Vasili did not die of his illness but from trying to cure it. In 1462 the Prince, convinced that he could overcome his sickness by the excruciatingly painful remedy of having his body scorched with burning amadou, underwent the diabolical treatment. As a result of the horrible burns which covered a good portion of his body, gangrene set in, causing the blind ruler's death.

III

Ivan the Great

IVAN III (1462–1505), called the Great, was twenty-three years old when he ascended the throne. Physically, he was an unattractive man—tall, lean, and so stooped that he was nicknamed *Gorbaty*, or hump-backed. Cold, imperious, shrewd, stealthy, and, above all, cautious, he was a born despot, whose very glance it was said caused women to faint. Even when he took his nap after the usual large Russian meal, the boyars who surrounded him were unable to lose their frightened respect for him, and gazed upon their lord with awe-struck expressions. Cruel to his enemies and a believer in torture, he spared no one who opposed him, and though he publicly wept for his victims, he was not averse to putting to death nobles, relatives, and even the highest authorities of the Church. There is reason to believe that if his grandson, Ivan IV, had not surpassed him in cruelty, Ivan III would have gone down in history as 'the Terrible' instead.

From early boyhood, Ivan was given certain court responsibilities by his father, Vasili II, and at the age of twelve he was married to Maria, the daughter of Boris, the Grand Prince of Tver. The marriage, however, was a brief one, for within a few years Maria died an unnatural death, possibly the result of being poisoned.

Two years later, in 1469, an ambassador from the Pope appeared in Moscow with a letter from Cardinal Bessarion, offering Ivan the hand of Zoe Paleologus, the niece of Constantine, the last emperor of the Byzantine empire, who died fighting the Turks when they captured Constantinople in 1453. At the time, Zoe's father, Thomas, had fled to Rome, where he died, leaving in addition to two sons the aforementioned daughter Zoe, who became a ward of the Pope. The Vatican's envoy assured Ivan that the Pope was honouring Ivan by this offer, since other monarchs, notably the King of France and the Duke of Milan, had wanted to marry Zoe. But their proposals had been refused. The intention of the Vatican was obvious; it hoped that by this marriage a reunion of the two Churches could be effected.

Ivan was not particularly intrigued by the idea of unifying the two Churches, but he was definitely interested in having Russia allied through marriage to the erstwhile glorious Byzantine empire. With this in mind, he dispatched an envoy to Rome to secure further information, as well as a portrait of Princess Zoe. In a short while the envoy returned with not only the picture of Zoe but also the Pope's promise that Russian ambassadors could travel freely throughout all lands adhering to the Roman faith. The picture of Zoe obviously did not displease Ivan, for he ordered his envoy to return to Rome to sign the marriage bond.

In 1472 Zoe, accompanied by Cardinal Antonio, crossed the Russian frontier. The story is told that the Cardinal carried before him at every town in Russia he entered the Latin cross, but when he and his party approached Moscow, Philip, the Metropolitan, objected. He is supposed to have said to Ivan, 'If you, wishing to do him honour, permit him to do this, when he enters the city by one gate, I, your father, shall go out by another. It is an outrage for us to think of such a thing, since he who dallies with a false faith is recreant to his own'. Ivan acquiesced to the Metropolitan's objections that the Latin cross should be displayed, and a noble was dispatched to the Cardinal's party. The Cardinal, upon receiving the message from the noble that both the Metropolitan and the Prince objected, reluctantly agreed to bury the cross in a sledge. For all intents and purposes the Pope's grandiose idea to unite the Eastern and Western Churches was buried with it.

Zoe, who took the name of Sophia Fominichna after her marriage, was a proud, forceful woman, shrewd in politics and cunning in court intrigue. She was determined to introduce into the colourless and austere Kremlin the pomp and circumstance of Byzantium. In this she was singularly successful, and as time went on the ceremonies of the court became more and more elaborate.

Owing to his own ambitious nature, as well as to the constant prodding of the proud and ambitious Sophia, Ivan's actions over the years became more and more autocratic and secretive, isolating him from the counsels of his boyars but increasing his personal prestige and power as the unchallenged ruler of all Russia. At the same time that he was concentrating more power in his own hands, he was through negotiations, intrigue, and, occasionally, arms adding more territory to the sovereignty of Moscow, which by now had virtual undisputed dominance over all of the other city-states. Even stubborn Novgorod, the proudest of Russian cities, fell under his suzerainty. To convince the residents of that city that times had indeed changed in Russia, he took away their famous bell, which had been used to call the people together in assembly and was a symbol of Novgorod's particular form of 'democracy', and had it installed in the Kremlin.

No longer, too, could he be challenged by one group of Tartars, the Golden Horde, which in 1480 lost control over its Russian protectorate. In this struggle the cautious Ivan was continuously badgered by the Grand Princess Sophia, who insisted that her husband defy the Tartars, even as her father and uncle had defied the Turks. 'My father and I lost our patrimony sooner than submit', she told him.

Ivan finally agreed to stand firm against the Tartars refusing to meet their envoys. As a result, Ahmed, Khan of the Horde, decided to punish the rebellious Grand Prince and with a large army marched on Moscow. Ivan, following the tedious Russian pattern so characteristic of its rulers, fled at the approach of the enemy. The people of Moscow were furious and accused him of cowardice. A bishop, Vassian, even had the courage to call him a betrayer of Christ and a runaway. 'You are not immortal', he told Ivan. 'Fear you, too, shepherd! Will not God exact this blood of your hands?'

After a series of incidents, in which Ivan left and rejoined the army, he was saved from the dangers of actual combat when the Tartars themselves decided to retreat because of the unusually severe Moscow winter. During the retreat in the steppe, Ahmed was killed by his enemy, the Khan of the Shaban and Nogai Tartars, and shortly thereafter his sons were overthrown by the Tartar Khanate of Crimea. The end of the rule of the Golden Horde over Russia came to an inauspicious end.

Ivan was the first ruler of Russia to be fired with an imperial vision—the unification of all Russia under one prince. Though he did not succeed completely in accomplishing this during his lifetime, he gave such an impetus to it and contributed so much towards this goal that he has gone down in history as *Sobiratel Rusi*, or Collector of the Russian Lands.

In addition to his vision of uniting under one ruler all of Russia, Ivan dreamed of making Moscow the Third Rome. While Con-

stantinople had been the religious and political centre of the Holy
Roman Empire and the Patriarch had had his headquarters at St.
Sophia, there had been a strong bond between the Rome of the
East and Moscow. Now, however, with Constantinople under the
Turks, the situation was changed and Ivan envisaged Moscow as
the centre. His thinking was echoed in the words of a Russian monk
who, writing to Ivan, said: 'Know now, pious Caesar, that the
sovereignty of all Christendom hath been united in thine own, for
the two Romes have fallen, but the third doth endure, and fourth
there shall never be, for thy Christian Empire shall last for ever!'

Taking steps towards this goal, Ivan had the court at the Kremlin
patterned after the Byzantine model. The Church was subjected to
a greater discipline and its hierarchical lines were fashioned in the
Greek manner and, significantly, Ivan adopted the Byzantine
imperial arms—the two-headed eagle—as Russia's own.

Moreover, to strengthen his claim as the inheritor of Byzantium,
the legend was promulgated that Rurik's ancestry, by direct
descent traceable for fifteen generations, went back to the Roman
Emperor Augustus, who it was claimed had a son by the name of
Prus from whom the Lithuanian Prussians and Rurik were descended. The Church, too, contributed its bit to making Ivan's
claim valid by insisting that the royal cap, sceptre, and mantle
which were preserved in the city of Vladimir were actually given to
Vladimir Monomakh by the Greek Emperor Constantine Mono-
machus, when he invited the Russian prince to share jointly with
him in ruling the Greek Empire. This fiction was spread even
though the Greek emperor had died fifty years before Vladimir
became Grand Prince of Kiev.

Ivan's successes in bringing under one ruler vast territories provided the Moscow régime with power; and Sophia's success in
bringing to the Kremlin not only the court customs of Byzantium
but its priests, scholars, artists, and architects, as well as Greek and
Latin books and *objets d'art*, provided the régime with a culture it
had never before known. It was now imperative that the Kremlin,
which housed the headquarters of the aspiring Third Rome, be
made magnificent, to symbolize the new glory.

2—TK

IV

The Exterior Kremlin

BY AND LARGE, the Renaissance had no effect on Russia, which since the Tartar conquest had been virtually isolated from the mainstream of European affairs. However, under Ivan III, though Russia did not participate in the Renaissance, it did benefit by it, for it was to Renaissance Italy that Ivan sent his envoys with orders to bring back the artists and artisans who were to plan, build, and embellish the new Kremlin.

One of the most important Italian masters whom Ivan III's envoys cajoled into coming to Russia was a native of Bologna named Ridolfo Fieravanti Aristotele, who had worked for Cosmo de Medici, Francis I, Gian Galeazzo of Milan, Matthias Corvinus, and Pope Sixtus IV among others. At the same time that Ivan's envoys approached Aristotele to come to Moscow, the Turkish Sultan Mohammed II was trying to obtain his services too. Aristotele's fame had spread far and wide, for he had among other feats performed the magnificent task of moving the campanile at Bologna from one place to another and had strengthened the leaning tower of Cecato. A typical Renaissance man, Aristotele, in addition to being an outstanding architect, was well known as an engineer, military expert in fortifications, and metal caster. Though the boyar Simeon Tolbuzin, the head of Ivan's delegation, did not bid as high for Aristotele's services as the Sultan's envoys, Aristotele decided to go to Christian Russia rather than Mohammedan Turkey.

In January, 1475, at the age of sixty, accompanied by Tolbuzin, Aristotele came to Moscow. With him, also, were his son Andrei and an assistant named Pietro. The salary agreed upon for the Italian master's services was ten roubles a month.

During the latter part of the fifteenth century, other Russian envoys were sent to Italy, mainly to the northern part, to recruit artisans. Soon a large number of Italian masters were resident in Moscow, among them the main architects of the Kremlin—Solario, Alevisio, Marco Ruffo, and Antonio Friazin.

All through the reign of Ivan III and his son Vasili III (1505–33)

34

work continued at a furious pace on the battlements and buildings of the Kremlin, and by the end of the rule of Vasili, in 1533, the general appearance of the Kremlin was established.

Undoubtedly, it is the unique construction of the walls, towers, and escarpments of the Kremlin that upon first glance give it its exotic appearance. Circling the sixty-five-and-a-half-acre enclosure for a mile and a quarter, in the form of an irregular triangle, the walls vary in height from thirty to seventy feet and vary in thickness from fourteen to twenty feet. For the entire length of its crenellated walls there is a nine foot wide rampart and, on the inner side, a low parapet. Nineteen towers, all different in design though possessing certain basic architectural similarities, rise from the walls, and five gates, no two of them alike, allow for entrance to the grounds.

'How am I to describe the walls of the Kremlin?' wrote the mid-nineteenth-century Frenchman Marquis de Custine. 'The word *wall* gives an idea of quite too ordinary an object; it would deceive the reader: the walls of the Kremlin are a chain of mountains. This citadel, reared on the confines of Europe and Asia, is, as compared with ordinary ramparts, what the Alps are to our hills; the Kremlin is the Mont Blanc of fortresses.'

To construct this 'chain of mountains', with its watchtowers, required fourteen years, from 1485 to 1499. Aristotele—though there is no definite record of this—was probably the original designer of the walls, or at least a chief consultant, since the beginning of work on them coincided with his stay in Moscow. It is definite that his technical knowledge of construction and manufacture of bricks played a large part in the successful erection of the walls. The bricks that were made under his direction, some of them still extant, measured thirty-one by fourteen by eighteen centimetres, and it has been remarked that they were far superior to those of a much later day with respect to hardness and durability. He organized a brick-manufacturing plant near Moscow, which was the source for the tens of thousands of bricks used on the lofty walls, and also taught the Russians how to prepare the necessary mortar. Other architects who helped build the Kremlin walls were the aforementioned Ruffo, Friazin, Alevisio, and especially Solario, whom the Chronicles refer to as the chief 'architecton' of the Kremlin.

In 1485 when construction began in earnest on the walls and

towers, which had been neglected since the time of Dmitri Donskoi and were now in a deplorable condition, the first walls and towers to be erected were on the south side of the Kremlin—the side most exposed to enemy attack. Piecemeal, over the next fourteen years, walls and towers were built on the east, west, and north side, and by 1499 the last section of the wall and towers was finished, forming an unbroken triangle of brick and mortar around the Kremlin area.

Solario, the chief architect of the Kremlin, died in 1492, probably of overwork, while working on the fortress. The year before an inscription was carved on one of the towers that the celebrated Milanese architect built which read:

'Joannes Vasilii Dei gratia Magnus Dux Volodimeriæ, Moscoviæ, Novogardie, Tiferiæ, Plescoviæ, Veticie, Ongarie, Permiie, Buolgarie, et alia totius Q Raxiæ dominus, anno tertio imperi sui has turres condere fet. statuit Petrus Antonides Solarius Mediolanensis, anno not. Domini 1491, K. Julii.'

Prior to his death, Solario seemed to have suggested that Alevisio of Milan should succeed him as chief architect, and in 1493 Ivan III appointed him to continue Solario's work. His tenure of office was not a tranquil one, and he continuously ran into difficulties. A succession of fires, which had always been the most plaguing of problems in the wooden-structured city of Moscow, broke out. The most serious one was in 1493. A good part of Moscow and the suburbs was levelled, and the Kremlin itself was so severely damaged that Ivan had to leave. He took up residence in the village of Podkopaevo, where he lived in a peasant hut near the town church. Merchants and priests, who had continually fulminated against the new constructions which necessitated a widening of the Kremlin area and thus the removal of existing buildings, including mansions, graveyards, and churches, now claimed that the fire was God's vengeance for the sacrilegious actions of the Grand Prince and his Italian artisans in destroying religious centres and disturbing the remains of the dead.

In spite of this strong opposition, Ivan, constantly prodded on by Sophia, ignored the critics and insisted that the work be continued as planned. Though 1499 (some authorities insist, however, it was 1516) is often given as the year that the walls and towers were completed, this date is somewhat misleading, for the superstructures of the towers were in the main added over a period of many years. Since the Italians fell into disfavour early in the six-teenth century, owing to fear of Latin influences, and were replaced when the occasion arose by artisans from other countries, mainly Protestant Germans, English, and Dutch, the style of the tower superstructures differs, often quite radically, from the Italian-inspired bases upon which they rest, and, for that matter, from each other.

Over the centuries, the nineteen towers and five gates of the Kremlin assumed a special importance, owing to events that happened in or near them. Though some of the occurrences, it is true, were based more on fancy than fact, nevertheless the towers and gates did take on historic significance—oftentimes meaningful personal ones, too, for the Russian people—as well as being interesting architecturally.

It is generally agreed that the best overall picture, from the outside, of the Kremlin can be had by starting at the Forest Gate (*Borovitskaia*—'*bor*' meaning 'wood'), and making a complete circle of the walls. In Czarist days, as well as in the early nineteen-thirties when the Soviet government was proud to show the intriguing Kremlin to foreign visitors, guides often began the tour of the Kremlin walls from this point.

The Forest Gate, near the south-west corner of the Kremlin and close to the mouth of the Neglinnaia River, is the spot where the first settlement of the Kremlin was made. The river itself now runs underground through a conduit alongside the western wall, where the popular Alexander Gardens are situated, and is therefore concealed from view. In olden days, however, the Neglinnaia's swampy banks afforded added protection to the fortress and there was a drawbridge that spanned the river and led to the gate. The holes where the chains of the drawbridge were attached are still visible in the gate. The Forest Gate, built by Solario in 1490, unlike other gates of the Kremlin, is not surmounted by a tower. On the gate for many years was the image of Our Saviour Not Made with Hands, and on the west side was an image of the Virgin Mary surrounded by prophets and saints. However, they were not easy to distinguish even in the olden days because, as one nineteenth-century traveller complained, the glass enclosing the images was so dirty. It was through this gate that Napoleon, in 1812, entered the Kremlin.

Slightly to the south of the gate is the Forest Tower, a hundred
and ninety-six feet high and noted for its particularly impressive
stairformed superstructure, built in the seventeenth century and
resembling the famous Sumbeka Tower in Kazan, which is a
striking example of Oriental architecture.

At the south-west corner of the Kremlin is the Water-Pumping
Tower (*Vodovsvodnaia*), which, as its name implies, contained the
necessary machinery for collecting water. The tower that Antonio
Friazin built in 1480 had little resemblance to its present appearance, for in 1805 it was torn down and rebuilt, only to be destroyed
again seven years later by order of Napoleon. When it was reconstructed in 1817, it was done in Empire style.

Following the wall along the Moscow River, the next tower is the
Annunciation (*Blagoveshchenskaia*), named after the cathedral of
that name, and characterized by a cross at the top instead of, as in
former days, the usual imperial double eagle or weathercocks.

The Secret Tower (*Tainitskaia*) and Gate were built by Antonio
Friazin in 1485, and is so named because of a hidden passageway
that connects it with the Moscow River, but again, like so many
other Kremlin towers, it is today not in its original form. Catherine
the Great, who had ambitious plans to change the face of the
Kremlin, had it torn down to make room for a contemplated palace
she wished to build there. The palace was never built, ostensibly
because of the unfavourable condition of the Kremlin soil and a
lack of money in the royal treasury at the time. The tower and the
gate were subsequently rebuilt, and the present squarish gate has
practically no resemblance to the Friazin original. It is the only one
of the five Kremlin gates that is no longer used.

The next two towers are the First Nameless and the Second
Nameless, the former a hundred and twelve feet high and the latter
a hundred feet—each of them having a four-storeyed superstructure. The First Nameless, like the Secret Tower, was torn down by
Catherine, rebuilt, later destroyed by Napoleon, and again rebuilt.

The Peter Tower (*Petrovskaia*), with its bonnet-shaped roof, is
one of the shorter towers, only eighty-eight feet high. It, too, was
destroyed and rebuilt several times.

At the south-east corner of the Kremlin is the hundred and sixty-
eight-foot-high Beklemishev Tower (*Beklemishevskaia*), which was
built in 1487 by Marco Ruffo. During the bombardment of the

Kremlin in 1917, its spire was destroyed, but five years later the Communists restored it. Except for this loss and other minor changes made over the centuries, it and the Annunciation Tower are the only two towers on the Moscow River side of the Kremlin which can be considered to be, more or less, in their original state.

As one turns north along the Kremlin wall, the first tower there is the Konstantin Tower (*Konstantinovskaia*), named after the church that is behind it. It was built by Solario at the same time that he built the Forest Gate. Originally it had a gate, but today only the upper part of it is still in existence.

The next tower is the Alarm Tower (*Nabatnaia*), which contained the bells that clanged a warning to the people of Moscow of approaching enemy troops.

Following the Alarm Tower is the slender Czar Tower (*Czar-skaia*), the shortest tower along the Kremlin walls, measuring only fifty-six feet in height and having but two floors in its superstructure. The Czar Tower was built much later than the others—in 1680. Prior to this time a wooden pavilion was on this spot, and Ivan the Terrible, it is reputed, used to sit there and watch the executions take place below in the Red, or Beautiful, Square, the *Krasnaia Ploshchad* (in Russian *krasnaia* means either 'red' or 'beautiful').

At the Red Square, opposite St. Basil's Cathedral, stands the most famous of the Kremlin towers and gates, the Saviour (*Spas-skaia*). It is the highest of all the towers, rising to a height of two hundred and thirty-eight feet and having ten storeys. It is named the Saviour because of the picture of Christ that is painted on the wall over the entrance, and for centuries it was the custom for all males, from the peasant to the Czar himself, to uncover their heads and cross themselves before His image. 'Should a stranger, either ignorant of the custom, or through inadvertency, attempt to pass with his head covered, he will be reminded immediately of his duty by a military sentinel, who is stationed here night and day', an English traveller wrote in 1821. 'Should he refuse to take off his hat or cap, he will be forced to the measure, or be prevented from continuing his route.' It was not unusual that such an obstinate man would be forced to kneel down before the image of Christ fifty times as a punishment. It was here, in front of the image of the Saviour, that criminals before their execution were permitted to say their last prayers. It was customary, too, for the Czar to pass through this gate on the way to his coronation at the Cathedral of the Assumption within the Kremlin walls.

The lower part of the Saviour Tower and Gate was built by Solario in 1491, and Latin and Russian inscriptions on the wall attest to his work. The Russian inscription reads:

'In the year 6599 [i.e. 1491 A.D.], in July, by the grace of God, were erected these towers for archers, by order of Joann Vassilie-vitch, Sovereign and Autocrat of All Russia, Great Duke of Vlodimer, Moskva, Novgorod, Plescof, Perm, Bulgaria, &c., in the 30th year of his reign; executed by Peter Antonius, from the town of Milan.'

The Gothic upper part of the Saviour Tower was constructed in 1625 by Christopher Halloway, an Englishman, who also made the mechanism of the clock bells in the tower, which strike on the hour. The tunes that have been played by the chimes, which were installed under the direction of Peter the Great, afford an interest-ing glimpse into the various changes that have occurred in Russia from the eighteenth century to the present. In the eighteenth cen-tury the chimes rang out the German folk song 'Ach, du Lieber Augustin'; later, it was the Russian hymn 'Kol' Slaven' and the 'March of the Preobrazhensky Regiment'. After the Revolution of 1917 they chimed 'The Internationale' and, at three and nine o'clock, the 'Russian Revolutionary Funeral March'. In more recent years they have played the 'Soviet Hymn'.

The Saviour Gate, the main entrance to the Kremlin and the most imposing one, has had many anecdotes told about its sacred Russian character. One story that old-time Russians swore by was that when Napoleon occupied the Kremlin in 1812, every time he tried to pass through the Gate of the Saviour, his horse pranced and reared, and then fell down with Napoleon still on his back, always on the same spot by the gate. The horse's frantic pawings and strokings of the pavement caused a hollow in it, which a nine-teenth-century visitor attested to seeing there as late as 1823. The Russians claimed that the violator of Russian soil, Napoleon, was considered unworthy of passing through the Gate of the Saviour, and that his horse, like Balaam's ass, was inspired and thus rebuked him.

On the Red Square, too, is the Senate Tower (*Senatskaia*),

named after the Senate Building which is behind it inside the Kremlin walls.

Opposite the Historical Museum, north of the Saviour Tower and Gate, is the Nicholas Tower and Gate (*Nikolskaia*), which was built by Solario at the same time as the Saviour Gate. It was named after St. Nicholas the Miracle Worker, the guardian saint of Russia, who has always been revered more than any other saint by the people. Above the crown of the arch was a picture of the saint, now removed, in a small gilt frame, and beneath it was an inscription in gilt letters which read:

'In the 1812th year from the incarnation of God the Word, during the time of invasion by the enemy, almost all this strong tower was demolished by a mine; but by the wonderful power of God, the holy image of the great favourite of God, here designed upon the same stone, and not only the holy image, but the pane of glass covering it, and the lantern with the candle, remained uninjured. Who is greater than God, our God? Thou art the God, the marvellous God, who doest wonders by thy saints.'

In 1820 the superstructure that Napoleon destroyed was rebuilt by Beauvais. In addition to being the patron saint, St. Nicholas was looked upon as the dread of perjurers, and thus, in front of the gate bearing his image, oaths were administered to litigants in the olden days in the hope that the presence of the sacred image would persuade them to speak the truth.

The Kremlin walls become lower near the northern corner, where the Corner Arsenal Tower (*Uglovaia-Arsenalnaia*) stands, and turn south-westward, following the course of the concealed, conduit-covered Neglinnaia River. This tower is strategically the strongest of the Kremlin towers, and has massive dimensions. The perimeter of the base is a hundred and sixty-eight feet, and it rises to a height of two hundred and three feet, with more than half of it (a hundred and five feet) being the substructure.

After the Middle Arsenal Tower (*Sredniaia-Arsenalnaia*)—a hundred-and-twenty-nine-foot-high tower, behind which is the Kremlin Arsenal Building—is the Trinity Tower and Gate (*Troitskaia*), which closely resembles the Saviour Tower. A bridge across the former bed of the Neglinnaia connects the Trinity Gate with the Kutafia Tower, a short (only sixty-three feet high) but massive structure that is surmounted by battlements and embrasures. The word *kutafia* means 'awkward', and the tower was so named because of its bulky, sprawling design.

The last two towers are the Commandant Tower (*Komendant-skaia*) and the slender Armoury Tower (*Oruzheinaia*). In front of the latter tower are mounds that are remnants of fortifications Peter the Great had built around the Kremlin in 1707 in anticipation of an attack by the Swedish King Charles XII.

Though the Kremlin has all the appurtenances of a gigantic medieval fortress, there are some observers who do not think of it as cold and forbidding. To them it seems rather as something magical, with its 'grace and light and the aroma of adventurous years', as one writer expressed it when visiting the Kremlin just prior to the First World War.

The cupolas and roofs and bulbous towers of many colours glittering in the sun, together with the variegated architectural amalgam that fascinates because of the constant presence of the unexpected, can in fact make it seem more dreamlike than real. A twentieth-century American writer stated that it has 'the appearance of a fairy-tale town', and a nineteenth-century Frenchman, upon seeing the Kremlin from the Stone Bridge (*Kamennyi Most*), the most advantageous spot to view the fortress, wrote that he fancied he was 'gazing upon one of those magical cities which the imagination of the Arabian story-tellers alone can build, an architectural crystallization of the Thousand and One Nights'.

If the exterior of the Kremlin captivates the imagination of some people, then certainly the interior of this city within a city, with its magnificent cathedrals and palaces, does too. For within the walls the visitor comes face to face not only with architectural marvels but senses the hundreds of years of Russian history—with its drama, violence, and intrigue—that have taken place there.

V

The Interior Kremlin

OVER the centuries there were many changes made on the various structures within the Kremlin, some of them being completely razed and new buildings erected in their stead and others undergoing 'modernization', each generation feeling that it could improve the appearance of this or that cathedral or palace. As a result there are today few buildings that are actually in their original state. Nevertheless, in an overall sense, the late fifteenth- and sixteenth-century appearance of the Kremlin can still be visualized by the visitor. Though there are certain relatively modern structures within the grounds, such as the Grand Kremlin Palace of Nicholas I which was built during the middle of the nineteenth century, that are out of keeping with most of the other buildings, other structures have maintained enough of their original design to give the illusion of its medieval grandeur.

Invasion and revolution, too, have taken their toll of the buildings, though the destruction that occurred, for instance, during the occupation by Napoleon or the Bolshevik Revolution of 1917 resulted surprisingly enough in minor damage. Fires, on the other hand, which were a periodic occurrence in Moscow, did more damage, often destroying a good part of the Kremlin. Still, it was undoubtedly the renovating zeal of various Czars that, more than any other single factor, accounted for the various major changes which took place over the years in the Kremlin, and resulted so often in architectural incongruities which, though often interesting in themselves, prevented the Kremlin from having a 'oneness' of form and, according to many observers, made it somewhat offensive aesthetically.

The Kremlin was—and is—a functional centre, where the rulers of a great nation have lived and worked, and where administrative orders were conceived and executed. As such, convenience often took precedence over the desire to preserve inconvenient historic structures.

In addition, the lack of a strong nationalism in Russia before the nineteenth century made the Russians negligent of their historic past. Time after time famous works of art would be painted over by succeeding artists; irreplaceable architectural structures of earlier periods would be wantonly destroyed to make room for a newer structure, without regard to its historic and artistic significance; and at the whim of a Czar a medieval church would be razed, because it interfered with the view from his palace window. The opinions of artists and intellectuals had little weight in autocracy-ridden Russia, and, even when protests were made concerning the destruction of irreplaceable historic treasures, they were given scant attention by the rulers, especially with regard to the Kremlin, the seat of their imperial, autocratic power. When architects were called in to rework or design Kremlin buildings, the most conservative ones were usually asked—leaders of this or that acceptable school of architecture, who too often designed the buildings not with the overall unity of the Kremlin in mind but with a desire to monumentalize their own particular school of architectural theory.

It is necessary to remember, though, that the Kremlin is not a building but a miniature city within a city and, like cities everywhere, was destined to change radically over the centuries. What similarity exists, for instance, between modern London and ancient Londinium, or present-day New York and Peter Stuyvesant's New Amsterdam? Thus, if this is borne in mind, it is remarkable that the Kremlin has maintained so much of its original form. The Kremlin, hemmed in behind its formidable walls, could not expand like the rest of the city of Moscow and, therefore, in spite of carelessness, lack of national pride during its earlier history, and autocratic whim, represents, to a degree at least, a continuum of that phenomenon called Russia.

The various existing structures within the Kremlin span a period of six hundred years, from the Church of the Saviour in the Wood (*Spas na Boru*), built in 1330, to the erection of office buildings by the Communists several years ago. Since the basic large-scale construction of the Kremlin was entrusted to the Italians by Ivan the Great and his successor Vasili III, it is not surprising that it has an Italianate appearance. However, this is true more of the walls and towers than of the buildings within the Kremlin. Relying upon the Italians' genius for fortification, Ivan III and Vasili III allowed them freedom of design and execution of the battlements. When it came to the erection of cathedrals within the walls, the Czars, fearful of Papist influence, insisted that Russian architects be consulted and Russian models be used. As a result the fortifications are of Italian inspiration and design, while the churches within are not. Even though it is true that in certain cases, such as the Cathedral of the Assumption, there are Renaissance features, the structures are in the main akin to Russian models, and are more or less a continuation of native influences that can be traced historically to Kiev, Novgorod, and Vladimir. The Italians were given more leeway in building non-church structures, and the Palace of Facets (*Granovitaia Palata*), for instance, is quite typical of early Italian Renaissance architecture.

Around Cathedral Square (*Sobornaia Ploshchad*) a group of church structures were erected in the late fifteenth and early sixteenth centuries that has made that square the heart of the Kremlin as well as its most picturesque area. Three large cathedrals face the square here, in addition to other churches in other parts of the Kremlin. That the Kremlin within its three score acres has over a dozen churches may be surprising to non-Russians, but it must be remembered that the erection of a church by a Czar was considered an act of great devotion, and they vied with each other in the number and magnificence of the churches they ordered to be built.

The first of the cathedrals in the Kremlin, at Cathedral Square, that was built under Ivan the Great was the Cathedral of the Assumption (*Uspenskii Sobor*), the most famous of all the Kremlin churches. Here ever since the sixteenth century the Russian Czars were crowned and the Metropolitans and patriarchs of the Church were buried. The original Cathedral of the Assumption was built in 1326 under Ivan Kalita, but by the time of the reign of Ivan the Great it had fallen into a state of decay and Ivan ordered that a new church should replace it.

Aristotele was given the commission by Ivan, and was instructed to visit the Cathedral of the Assumption in Vladimir, built in 1158, so that he could use it as a model. Work began on the Assumption in 1475 and was completed in 1479. Years later, in 1515, the frescoes ornamenting it were completed. They were so skilfully executed that it was written in the annals of the period that when the Great Duke, bishops, and boyars entered the church and saw them they exclaimed, 'We see Heaven!'

Architecturally the Cathedral of the Assumption is similar to the one in Vladimir, and the interior has been compared to St. Mark's, in Venice. Other historians, however, believe that Aristotele was more influenced by the temples of Egypt and the East. Rambaud, for instance, mentions that the upper part of the church which is partly enveloped in shadows is 'like the crypts of the Pharaohs'. Another writer states that one could very well imagine the Assumption to be 'the work of some Byzantine architect, whose mind was filled with memories of Santa Sofia'.

The nineteenth-century French writer Théophile Gautier was particularly impressed with the colossal columns that support the central dome and the four satellite cupolas, all of them embellished with murals that gleam with beaten gold. 'Nothing could be more astounding than this decoration', he wrote, 'where thousands of figures surround you like a mute assemblage, ascending and descending the entire length of the walls in files of Christian pana-thenaea, standing alone in poses of hieratic rigidity, bending over to the pendentives and draping the temple with a human tapestry swarming with motionless beings that look at you with fixed eyes and seem to threaten you with hands outstretched in benediction. . . . The iconostase, a lofty screen of silver-gilt with five rows of figures, like the façade of some golden palace, dazzles the eye with its fabled magnificence.' And then writing of the gleaming filigree from which peer Madonnas and saints, their aureoles ablaze with thousands and thousands of precious stones, he commented, 'The madness of religious extravagance can go no further'.

It is little wonder that Gautier was so impressed by the magnificence of the church that he considered it to be 'the madness of religious extravagance', for to ornament the Assumption, artists executed two hundred and forty-nine full images and two thousand and sixty-six half lengths and heads, many of them much larger than life. Pillars were overlaid with solid gold, and two hundred and ten thousand gold leaves were used throughout the cathedral.

In addition to its interesting architecture and decorations and its importance as the 'Rheims Cathedral of Russia', the Assumption was famous for its collection of miraculous things. Over the centuries, at one time or another, it contained, according to the Church, the robe of Jesus Christ (*Riz Gospodnya*), sent to Czar Michael by Abbas, the Shah of Persia, in 1625; the nail of the Lord (*Gvozd*

Gospoden), which was sent from Georgia to Moscow in 1686 and was considered by the Church as invaluable; a section of the robe of the Virgin Mary; part of the remains of John the Baptist; the right hand of Andrew the First, called Apostle; the head of Gregory the Theologian; and the chains of the apostle Peter, which was supposed to have been obtained in Jerusalem by Eudokia, wife of Theodosius the Little, in 431.

Napoleon, however, when he occupied the Kremlin in 1812, had little regard for the holy objects in the Assumption and ordered that the cathedral be used to house one of his cavalry troops. The French then built a furnace at one end of the cathedral, collected together various precious objects such as candlesticks, icons, and so on, and melted them down. Altogether it is estimated that they stripped the church of over five tons of silver and several hundred pounds of gold. Before the French could complete their work, Napoleon ordered his army to retreat. Thereupon, the Cossacks entered the Kremlin and recovered much of the treasure, most of it now molten silver and gold.

The second of the three cathedrals in Cathedral Square to be built under Ivan III was the Cathedral of the Annunciation (*Blagovesh-chenskii Sobor*), which was built on the site of the original Annunciation, constructed in 1416, under Vasili I. Pskov architects instead of Italian ones were commissioned to build the new cathedral, and using the Vladimir Uspenskii Cathedral as their model, they built the new Annunciation in eight years, between 1482 and 1490. The Annunciation, which is the smallest of the cathedrals on the square, is considered by most authorities to be in better taste than other Kremlin cathedrals, as well as having a more intimate character. It is here, across its agate and jasper mosaic floor, that the Russian princes walked to the altar to be married and where christenings were held. Like other Kremlin cathedrals, it is richly decorated; the gold enclosure of the image of the Annunciation alone contains more than eighteen pounds of pure gold, in addition to pearls and other precious gems. Here, too, many relics were preserved, such as the relic of Elizabeth, the mother of John the Baptist, relics of St. Luke, St. Matthew, and others. Part of the cathedral was damaged in the fire of 1547, and when it was repaired open porches, used for the first time in Russian churches, were added to three of its sides.

The Cathedral of the Archangel Michael (*Arkhangelskii Sobor*), on the south side of the square, was originally built of wood in the middle of the thirteenth century and later, in 1333, was rebuilt of stone. In 1505 Ivan III commissioned the Italian Alevisio to erect a new cathedral, and in 1509 it was completed, featuring for the first time in church construction in Russia basic Italian features in the exterior design of the church, though the interior was still based on characteristic Russian Orthodox models.

From the fourteenth century on, the princes of Russia had been buried in the Cathedral of the Archangel Michael, and when the new cathedral was finished, Ivan III had the tombs of the princes that had preceded him removed to it. From the time of Ivan III to the time of Peter the Great, all the Russian sovereigns were buried here, with the exception of Boris Godunov whose remains were buried in the Trinity Monastery of the Holy Sergius (*Troitsko-Sergievskaia Lavra*). Often referred to as the St. Denys of the Czars of Russia, forty-seven Russian rulers were buried in the cathedral. (Princesses and Czarinas were buried elsewhere—in nunneries.) After Peter the Great, the Czars were buried in St. Petersburg in the fortress of St. Peter and Paul, with the exception of Peter II who, too, was buried in the cathedral at Moscow. The tombs, still in existence, are arranged in genealogical order, from the founder of Moscow to the predecessor of Peter the Great, with the coffins of Ivan the Terrible and his two sons in the most sacred spot of all—next to the altar.

By 1487 it became clear to Ivan III and his zealous wife Sophia that the magnificence that they planned for the Kremlin, the 'Vatican' of the Third Rome, would not be complete without a splendid palace where native and foreign dignitaries could be impressed. Before the introduction of the Italian architects, the Kremlin was a wooden city, and the Czar's palace was made of timber too. However, now with the greater utilization of masonry, Ivan gave orders to Marco Ruffo to build a palace of stone to replace the wooden palace. The Palace of the Facets was the result, so-called because of the facet-shaped stones that adorn the wall facing Cathedral Square. It was finished in 1491 by Pietro Solario, who took over the job from Marco Ruffo. Like his compatriot Ruffo, he attempted to simulate the walls of the Castello in Ferrara and the Pitti Palace in Florence.

One of the most remarkable features of the Palace of the Facets is the single gigantic pillar in the centre of a seventy-seven by seventy foot vaulted chamber. The pillar, highly gilded, flows into arches, and with them supports the ceiling. There are four vaults, each of them crossed by a twisted gilt stucco cord. In the early eighteen-hundreds an English visitor noted that the walls were covered with crimson velvet, the floor overlaid with red cloth, and bronze chandeliers and gilded ornaments were profusely scattered throughout the chamber. Around the base of this central pillar there are shelves which on grand state occasions were weighted down with a display of the court's gold and silver plate and vessels.

In this immense room, over the years, court balls were given, grand receptions were held for foreign ambassadors, Metropolitans were installed, and national assemblies were formally opened. Here, too, on the south side of the room, the throne was situated, and on the west side, close to the ceiling, there was an opening, screened by a curtain, behind which the female members of the royal family, forbidden to attend various ceremonies, could watch the proceedings from an upper-level chamber without being observed.

Eight years after the Palace of the Facets was completed work was begun on the Terem Palace (*Teremnoi Dvorets*), which was to be the new living quarters of the royal family. Under the supervision of Alevisio, the palace was completed in 1508, three years after Ivan the Great's death. Since it was customary for members of the royal family to have separate quarters, throughout the sixteenth and seventeenth centuries various additions were made to the palace. However, after a fire in 1682 which destroyed a good part of the palace, it was restored to approximately its original condition.

In the Terem Palace (the word *terema* in Greek means 'repose') there were two apartments in the upper storeys in which were the bedchambers of the sovereign and where, too, were the rooms in which the boyars awaited the pleasure of the ruler.

From the early sixteenth century, when the main structures of the Czar's Palace were erected, until the middle of the nineteenth century, when Nicholas I ordered a part of it torn down to make room for his new, gigantic Grand Kremlin Palace, the Czar's Palace underwent many alterations. Some of the changes were undertaken because of the need for more space, others because of damage by fires. However, even after the erection of the Grand Kremlin Palace, a good part of the old palace was left untouched, and many visitors in the later nineteenth century have written glowing accounts of its magnificence. Gautier, for instance, described the old Czar's Palace as 'a chimera of sumptuous and barbaric imagination', and its chambers and passages seemed to him 'like a labyrinth excavated in some cyclopean block of stone. . . . We walk through them as in a dream, at times stopped by a grille which opens mysteriously, at times forced to follow a narrow, dark passage in which our shoulders almost brush both walls, emerging after our intramural journey into a hall with a rich and riotous wildness of ornamentation, at the end of which we are surprised at not seeing the Grand Khan of Tartary seated cross-legged upon his carpet of black felt'.

Many of the Russian rulers, often for long periods of time, did not use the palace for their sleeping quarters. With the enigmatic quality that characterized so many of the sovereigns of Russia, they would often desert the palace and reside for weeks, or even months, in the most squalid of peasant huts or in inelegant monasteries. Even Ivan the Great, one of the most regal of rulers, chose a peasant's hut to reside in when he fled the Kremlin after the fire of 1493, and Olearius, a seventeenth-century visitor to Moscow, remarked in his account of his stay in Moscow that 'there is lately built a very fair place of stone, according to the Italian architecture for the young Prince, but the Great Duke continues still in his wooden palace, as being more healthy than stone structures'.

Still, despite the fact that some of the princes sought from time to time the simple life, for the benefit of foreigners they always put on the most lavish show possible, a show that would have made Gautier truly believe that he was in the court of the Grand Khan of Tartary. Richard Chancellor, the Englishman who opened Russia to British merchants, wrote an account of the dazzling riches of the Great Duke's court, which he saw when he and his companions were invited there by the sovereign. Of one of the feasts, he wrote:

'The Emperor sitting upon a high and stately seat, apparelled with a robe of silver, and with another diadem on his head; our men, being placed over against him, sit down. In the midst of the room stood a mighty cupboard upon a square foot, whereupon stood also a round board, in manner of a diamond, broad beneath, and towards the top narrow, and every step rose up more narrow than the other. Upon this cupboard was placed the Emperor's plate, which was so much that the very cupboard itself was scant able to sustain the weight of it. The better part of all the vessels and goblets were made of very fine gold; and amongst the rest, there were four pots of very large bigness, which did adorn the rest of the plate in great measure, for they were so high, that they thought them at least five feet long. There [were] also upon this cupboard certain silver casks, not much differing from the quantity of firkins, wherein was reserved the Emperor's drink. . . .

'For goodly and rich plate we never saw the like or so much before. There dined that day in the Emperor's presence above 500 strangers and 200 Russians, and all they were served in vessels of gold, and that as much as could stand one by another upon the tables. Besides this there were four cupboards garnished with goodly plate, both of gold and silver. Among them were twelve barrels of silver containing about twelve gallons apiece, and at each end of every barrel were six hoops of fine gold. This dinner continued about six hours.'

Such was the magnificence of the Russian court at the time of Chancellor's visit in 1553 during the reign of Ivan the Terrible. Sophia's and Ivan the Great's vision of making Moscow the Third Rome had indeed—at least in ornate display—become a reality.

VI

Vasili III

BETWEEN the reigns of Ivan III, the Great, and Ivan IV, the Terrible, or the Dread as the Russian word *grozny* is often translated, was the reign of Ivan III's son and Ivan IV's father, Vasili III (1505–33). Though he is often referred to as the sovereign who reigned between the two 'Terrible Ivans', his reign was no less brutal than his father's, and there were times during his rule when the boyars looked back with nostalgia to the reign of Ivan III as being more tolerant and Ivan the Great himself as being more accessible to them. A fierce autocrat, Vasili brutally crushed those who opposed him and, like his father before him, was a 'collector of Russian lands', so that by the time of his death the Russian empire extended from the Gulf of Finland to the Ural Mountains.

Like most of the Moscow Grand Princes, he had a cold, forbidding, mirthless countenance and conducted himself, as did the others, in such a manner that Heberstein, the knowledgeable Austrian Ambassador to his court, declared that 'in the authority which he wields over his subjects, the Grand Prince of Moscow easily surpasses all the monarchs of the known world'. As for the subjects themselves, they accepted the Grand Prince's omnipotent position. Heberstein revealingly related that when the average Muscovite was questioned about various matters he had little knowledge of the stock reply was 'I know not. Only God and the Czar know'.

The opulence of Vasili's court would have made Princess Sophia proud indeed, for under her son the life in the Kremlin was as lavish and spectacular as ever the Byzantine Princess had dreamed of. When foreign envoys arrived at the Russian frontiers they were met with great pomp by Vasili's officers, were conducted to Moscow through the richest districts, in which all the natives were instructed to appear on the streets of the towns attired in their most expensive clothes. Shops and inns were closed, and a holiday spirit was officially prepared, complete to officially decreed smiling faces.

At the Kremlin itself, at the Palace of the Facets, the envoy would finally be taken before the richly robed and bejewelled Vasili, who sat on his throne surrounded by his nobles, dressed in sky-high fur caps, *kaftans* of white satin, and armed with gleaming silver hatchets. At the customary feast the very boards would groan under the weight of silver and gold vessels. The guests and their hosts would dine for hours, first drinking brandy, then eating roast swan served with sour milk, pickled cucumbers, and stewed prunes, which was followed by various kinds of meats served with all manner of wines, especially imported Greek ones. Somewhere during the feast the Grand Prince would drink to the health of the envoy, immodestly saying, 'Thou art come from a great sovereign to a great sovereign. After receiving our favour and seeing the lustre of our eyes, it shall be well with thee. . . .'

After the dinner, in which time after time the envoy and the Prince turned their cups upside down over their heads to show that the vessels were empty, the envoys would be dismissed with gifts heaped upon him. Heberstein, for example, mentioned that his gifts from Vasili included eighty sables, three hundred ermines, fifteen hundred squirrel skins, and a fine horse and sledge with white bearskin trappings.

Under Vasili Russia continued to be somewhat less isolated from Western Europe since he, like Ivan the Great, adopted the policy of permitting a few Europeans to enter the country. But, like most rulers throughout the history of Russia, he was suspicious of their intent and influence and was quite willing to close the 'open door' if his suspicions were too greatly aroused.

On the diplomatic front, Vasili was extremely active; he concluded a sixty-year peace treaty with Sweden; formed alliances with Livonia and the Hanse cities; and managed to keep on good terms with the Turkish ruler, Sultan Selim, and his successor, Solyman the Magnificent, and with Tamerlane's descendant, Baber, the Great Mogul of India.

Throughout his twenty-eight-year reign, Vasili continued the reconstruction work on the Kremlin, begun by his father, Ivan III. A few years after he became ruler, he commanded Alevisio that a ditch be dug along the eastern side of the Kremlin wall, had its banks faced with brick and stone, dammed up the Neglinnaia River, and had reservoirs built around the Kremlin. Along the Red Square, extending from the Neglinnaia to the Moscow, a moat, thirty-one to forty-two feet deep and a hundred to a hundred and twenty feet wide, was constructed, which could be filled with water, thus connecting the two rivers. Drawbridges were built at the Saviour and Nicholas gates to connect both sides of the moat, alongside of which walls were erected. With the construction of the moat, the Kremlin became in effect a fortress surrounded on all sides by water.

Moreover, Vasili ordered other constructions, to strengthen the defences of the Kremlin. Along the Moscow River, an additional wall made of brick was erected, and additional towers were constructed opposite the Secret, Trinity, and Konstantin towers. Most of these structures were removed in 1801, when it became obvious that owing to advances and changes in military defences they were of little use.

Inside the Kremlin, too, Vasili continued to build new structures and add new decorations to already existing ones. One of the new buildings was the Church of St. John the Baptist, and another was the Ascension (*Voznesenskii*) Convent, which was originally founded in 1389 by the Grand Princess Eudoxia, wife of Dmitri Donskoi. About thirty nuns were usually domiciled there, and within the convent were various churches dedicated to the martyr Catharine, to the 'Joy of All the Afflicted', to the Mother of God of Kazan, to the Assumption of the Virgin Mary, and so on. The fame of the convent rests upon the fact that, until the middle of the nineteenth century, the Grand Princesses and Czarinas were entombed here.

Besides his interest in the physical aspects of the Kremlin, Vasili, like his father before him, instituted many rigid court and royal family customs that gave the Russian imperial court its particular flavour. One of the customs that Vasili introduced, and which was to prevail for many years, was the manner of selecting a wife for the ruler. Vasili was convinced that the sovereign's wife should not be a foreigner but a Russian, and so when he decided to marry he notified the various towns and provincial governors that they were obliged to send to the Kremlin the most beautiful and sensible of the unmarried daughters of the locality, particularly those of noble birth.

Upon arriving at the Kremlin the girls were given sleeping quarters and were told to prepare for their reception. As many as five hundred girls were brought to the court, where they all ate at one common table and where various forms of entertainment were provided for their amusement. The Russian antiquary Boltin wrote that 'the monarch observed them privately and listened to their conversations. It is affirmed by some that he even visited them by night, in order to see which of them slept quietly or unquietly. After reiterated visitation and observation of their understandings, tempers and dispositions, and having made up his mind in consequence, he came and sat down at table with them, where he presented her on whom he had fixed his choice for a bride with a handkerchief and a ring. On the same day he dismissed the rest from his house with presents consisting of several articles of dress. The name of the bride-elect was then publicly declared, and the title of grand princess was conferred upon her'.

Doctors and midwives were busy examining the girls, whose number constantly dwindled from the original batch of five hundred, as the Grand Prince, for one reason or another, disapproved of them and ordered that they should be sent home, with the customary presents. Some of the rulers systematically reduced the number of girls from five hundred to three hundred, then to two hundred, then to a hundred, and finally to ten. These ten then underwent the most rigid physical examination by doctors and midwives to make sure they were healthy.

The competition for the Grand Prince's favour by the families of the girls was fierce, often involving poisoning of one of the girls by the family of another, and there were several instances where the chosen virgin did not succeed in becoming the Grand Princess, having died from some mysterious ailment before the wedding could take place. It is little wonder that the competition was so fierce that if often ended in murder, for the advantages were inestimable not only to the chosen girl but to her family. The bride's father, for instance, often became the closest companion to the Grand Prince and a powerful figure at court, in some cases second only to the ruler himself.

Nevertheless, in spite of the elaborate system of choosing the Grand Princess, and the thoroughness of the physical examination, which a foreign diplomat at Vasili's court wrote was so thorough that 'no part of them is unsearched', Vasili's wife, Solominia Saburov, was unable to bear him a son. Therefore, after twenty years of marriage, Vasili decided to send her to a convent, and prepared to marry Helena Glinsky. Upon hearing of Vasili's intention, Mark, the Patriarch of Jerusalem, refused to approve the marriage and prophesied that if Vasili should go ahead with the union 'thou shalt have a wicked son; thy states will become prey to terrors and tears; rivers of blood will flow; the heads of the mighty will fall; thy cities will be devoured by flames'. In spite of the dire predictions of the Patriarch, Vasili married for the second time. From this marriage, he had two sons, Ivan, the crown prince, and Yuri.

In 1533 Vasili III died, and his son Ivan IV (1533–84), then three years old, became Grand Prince. His mother, Helena, a Russian from Lithuania, ruled Russia in the name of her young son, guided by her uncle Michael Glinsky and her lover Prince Oblensky. The two advisers vied for power, and Helena finally chose the ruthless and self-seeking Oblensky and had Michael Glinsky thrown into prison where he died.

Helena was a capricious woman who ruled in an arbitrary manner, and her five years as regent were filled with court intrigues, mal-administration, and struggles with powerful boyars, who felt insulted and disgraced that they should be ruled by a woman. Domestically, her regency was little more than a bitter battle for control, in which, among other events, the uncles of the young Ivan were imprisoned. In foreign affairs an inconclusive war was waged with Lithuania, and what was more important, the Kazan and Crimean Tartars, emboldened by the apparent weakness of the throne, ravaged large sections of the Muscovite empire.

In 1538 Helena died under mysterious circumstances, presumably having been poisoned by her enemies. The situation now became even more unbearable. Two princely families, the Shuiskys and the Belskys, vied with each other for power, during which time vodka and blood flowed freely. The court was plunged into a riot of debauchery and drunkenness, and murder upon murder was committed in the ensuing struggle for control of the government.

During the time that Helena was regent and later, when the Shuiskys who had emerged victorious were in power, little was done to continue the work on the Kremlin that had been so vigorously pursued by Ivan the Great and Vasili. No new structures were built and, with the fierce and bloody struggle for power going on, little thought was given to enhancing the beauty of existing ones.

VII

Customs and Character

MOSCOW in the sixteenth century was already a very large city, with more than forty thousand dwellings and a population that various authorities have estimated was between one and two hundred thousand inhabitants. Giles Fletcher, late in the sixteenth century, wrote that Moscow was even larger than London, and other travellers in Russia reported that it was twice the size of Florence or Prague and that the circuit of the walls of Moscow was more extensive than the city of Paris.

There were four parts to the city: the Kremlin area itself, where the Grand Prince, his family, and relations lived, as well as a few of the richest and most powerful boyars; the Kitaigorod, the area closest to the Kremlin, where the traders, wealthy boyars, and the few foreigners lived; the Bielgorod, the living quarters of privileged citizens and merchants; and an outer ring, or suburbs, where the artisans and labourers lived.

Next to the Kremlin area, the most important section of Moscow was the Kitaigorod, which, in addition to being the dwelling place of the better-off citizens, was the trading centre of Moscow. In the seventeenth century, Olearius described the Kitaigorod as always being full of people during the day, '. . . especially slaves and idle persons. All the market-place is full of shops as also all the streets abutting upon it: but every trade hath a station by itself, so as that mercers intermingle not with linen or woollen drapers, nor goldsmiths with saddlers, shoemakers, tailors, furriers, and the like, but every profession and trade hath its proper street: which is so much the greater convenience in that a man does of a sudden cast his eye on all he can desire'.

The word 'Kitaigorod' has been variously interpreted as meaning 'Chinese City'; 'middle town', from the Tartar, because the Kitaigorod was in the middle between the Kremlin and Bielgorod; and Rambaud suggests that it was 'perhaps derived from Kitaigorod in Podolia, the birthplace of Helena, mother of Ivan IV, foundress of the Kitai-gorod of Moscow'. Whatever its origin, it was given its specific dimensions by the wall enclosure that Helena ordered to be built. In 1534 she instructed that a deep ditch from the Neglinnaia be dug, embracing the merchants' quarters to the Moscow River through the *Troitskaia Ploshchad*, the area used for duels, and the Vasiliovskoi Meadow. Helena ordered that everyone should participate in the construction, and it appears that even the servants of the court, the Metropolitan himself, and the boyars, as well as ordinary inhabitants of the city, were recruited for the job. The walls surrounding the Kitaigorod were finished about 1538.

Sixteenth-century Moscow was as filthy and unsanitary as most European cities of that period. One writer of the time commented that the streets were 'so dirty, after rain hath ever so little moistened the ground, that it were impossible to get out of the dirt, were it not for the great posts, which set together make a kind of bridge, much like that of the Rhine, near Strassburg, which bridges, in foul weather, serve for a kind of pavement'. The streets themselves were for the most part crooked and winding, forming a veritable maze, and the few main streets where an attempt was made to conquer the mud were paved with logs.

As for the houses, they were almost all made of wood, having large courts and outhouses. The dwellings of the poor were, except for a table and a few chairs and a few cooking utensils, barren and uncomfortable, having, as Voltaire remarked, 'none of the accommodations or pleasures of life. . . . These people might have passed for Spartans, had they been sober'.

Voltaire's observation on the inordinate amount of drunkenness among the Russians was not an original observation. Practically all writers on Russia, both native and foreign, could not help but note that from medieval days to recent times excessive drinking was one of the most common, and vicious, habits of the Russians. Rambaud wrote that 'debauchery and drunkenness were the national sins. Rich and poor, young and old, women and children, often dropped down dead drunk in the streets, without surprising anyone. The priests, in their visits to their sheep, got theologically drunk. "Even at the houses of the great lords", says M. Zabiéline, "no feast was gay and joyous unless every one was drunk. It was precisely in drunkenness that the gayety consisted. The guests were never gay if they were not drunk".'

As early as the fourteenth century, a Venetian traveller named

Contarini, who toured Russia, wrote: 'Here the men and women alike are comely, yet have a beastlike air. And a hideous plague ravageth all, of every degree, and that plague is drunkenness, so that Moscow's familiar spirit would indeed seem to be the spirit of the bottle. One meeteth here even nobles in liquor. And those nobles do boast of the same, and, to boot, maltreat them who remain temperate'.

A popular Russian tale is that when God created the world He made various nations and endowed them with many good things such as land, corn, and fruit. Upon completion of His work, He asked the various nations if they were satisfied, and all of them said yes except the Russians who had received the same as the rest. They replied, 'Please, Lord, some vodka'.

Still it must be noted that the Russians, and especially the Russian nobility, were not unique for drunkenness; it was a characteristic of most courts of Europe. For instance, John Drinkwater, in writing of English royalty, remarked that 'there was scarcely a sober man at the Court of Charles I'. Nevertheless, it did exist to excess in Russia, and was such a common feature of daily life, in and out of the courts, that one observer of Moscow life at the time remarked that 'travellers were disgusted by the drunkenness and general bestiality of the Muscovites'.

Another feature of Russian life that has been commented on over the years is the Russians' penchant for cruelty. As recently as the nineteen-twenties, the writer Maxim Gorky remarked: 'It seems to me that to the Russian people belongs peculiarly—just as a sense of humour belongs peculiarly to the English—an instinct of extraordinary cruelty, cold-blooded and seeming bent on testing the limits of human endurance, as if to watch the tenacity, the power of resistance, of life. In Russian cruelty, a diabolical refinement may be perceived. There is something subtle and almost fastidious about it'.

Gorky's view is not peculiar to him, for writer after writer stresses this aspect of the Russian character, whether in Czar, commissar, or in the plain, simple Ivan Ivanovich. The admirable qualities of the Russians, such as their sincere hospitality, openhandedness and deep-seated pity and piety, have often been overlooked or ignored, and many Russians and Russophiles have quite justly complained that the negative aspects of Russian life and character have been stressed while the positive values have been slighted over.

Dostoevsky pleaded that the Russian people should be judged 'not by the degrading sins which it often commits, but by the great and holy things to which, in the midst of its degradation, it constantly aspires. . . . Judge the people not by what it is, but what it would like to become'.

Still, Dostoevsky notwithstanding, a people must be viewed by its acts not by its aspirations which, though noble as they may be, do not, unless put into action, determine its character. Though, too, the history of all countries is the history of violence rather than the history of peace and kindness and consideration, Russia, while not a special case apart from other nations, is a prime example of the violence, cruelty, and inconsideration that a people and its rulers are capable of committing. Whether in Russia this violence originated among its rulers and permeated down to the mass of people, or whether, as Gorky believed, it was an inherent characteristic of the Russian people themselves, is a moot question, which various writers, historians, politicans, sociologists, and psychologists have tried for years to unravel.

The Tartars, themselves not a kindly people, often viewed the Russians as being extremely cruel and violent, while characteristically enough ignoring their own perverse perfection in the art of committing horrors. Abu Al-Ghazi, a Tartar, wrote of the Russians that though they had 'wit and sprightliness of imagination', were 'industrious and good at invention, yet at the same time slothful', still with whatever good qualities they have 'it must be owned they are Thieves, Robbers, Drunkards, and harden'd beyond any thing that can well be imagined. If a Russian peasant has once resolved to conceal a thing, there is no getting him to speak, tho he should be cut Limb from Limb; of which I have my self seen very remarkable Instances. The greatest Criminals among them suffer the most cruel Death, with an Unconcernedness enough to shock the most insensible Spectators, and one would be apt to attribute that great Indifference with which they shew for Life to some exalted stoical Sentiments, if it was not well known that they have no Notion of those sorts of sublime Opinions, and that tis nothing but a Desire of seeing an End to their Miseries which makes them face Death, if not with Pleasure, at least with a very visible Tranquillity'.

Among the most severe critics of the Russians, as far as their shortcomings as a people and a nation were concerned, were the

British who wrote about the Muscovite state—although most Western European observers, especially the Germans, have been harsh
too. The English poet John Milton, for instance, in his *A Brief
History of Moscovia* wrote that the Russians 'have no Learning . . .
their greatest friendship is in drinking: they are great Talkers,
Lyars, Flatterers and Dissemblers'. Giles Fletcher observed that
'the Russe neither believeth anything that an other man speaketh,
nor speaketh any thing himself worthie to be believed'.

Dr Edward Clarke, an Englishman who visited Russia at the end
of the eighteenth century and who violently despised most things
Russian, wrote that 'the picture of Russian manners varies little,
with reference to the prince, or the peasant. The first nobleman in
the empire, when dismissed by his sovereign from attendance upon
his person, or withdrawing to his estate in consequence of dissipa-
tion and debt, betakes himself to a mode of life little superior to that
of brutes. You will then find him throughout the day with his neck
bare, his beard lengthened, his body wrapped in a sheep's hide,
eating raw turnips, and drinking *quass*; sleeping one half the day,
and growling at his wife and family the other. The same feelings,
the same wants, wishes, and gratifications then characterize the
nobleman and the peasant; and the same tyranny which extends
from the throne downwards, through all the bearings and ramifica-
tions of society, even to the cottage of the lowest boor, has entirely
extinguished every spark of liberality in the breasts of a people who
are all slaves. They are all, high and low, rich and poor, alike servile
to superiors; haughty and cruel to their dependants; ignorant,
superstitious, cunning, barbarous, dirty, mean. The emperor canes
the first of his grandees; princes and nobles cane their slaves; and
slaves, their wives and daughters. Ere the sun dawns in Russia,
flagellation begins; and throughout its vast empire cudgels are
going, in every department of its population, from morning until
night'.

The historian Mirsky has attempted to explain the Western European antipathy to the Russian, as well as attempting an explanation
of the Russian himself.

'All Western accounts of Muscovy are patently hostile, due in
part to political hostility especially in the case of German writers,
who never forgot the horrors of the Muscovite invasion of Livonia,
and to the profound incompatibility of the Puritan and Muscovite

standpoints (this applies particularly to the English travellers), but also to the fact that even judged by its own standards Muscovite behaviour fell short of the Muscovite ideal. Its crudity was largely due to the very low general standard of life, and also to the lack of those influences that tend to soften and refine human relations. The lack of respect for human personality was inherent in the Muscovite outlook. Absolute obedience took the outer form of servility and was not necessarily inseparable from genuine loyalty. The Muscovite more frequently displayed unquestioning loyalty to an idea or to a cause, especially to one sanctioned by religion, than the personal loyalty fostered by European feudalism and by the Turanian clan system. The small stress laid on worldly ethics by the Church found reflection in the low standard of common morality prevalent in Muscovy. . . . The absence of recognized personal rights tempted people to prefer roundabout to straightforward ways, except in dealing with inferiors and dependents.'

This 'absence of recognized personal rights' that 'tempted people to prefer roundabout to straightforward ways' often led them to thievery, which according to many observers was almost a national characteristic. While on the one hand the Russian was capable of great liberality, such as his proverbial hospitality, in which he would insist on giving away food or goods that he could ill afford to spare, on the other hand he had a lack of respect for private property and an urge for expropriating the belongings of others.

Masson, a courtier in the time of Catherine the Great, wrote that 'next to drunkenness, the most prominent and common vice of the Russians is theft. I doubt whether any people upon earth be more inclined naturally to appropriate to themselves the property of others—from the first minister to the general office, from the lackey to the soldier, all are thieves, plunderers, and cheats. In Russia theft does not inspire that degrading contempt which stigmatizes a man with infamy, even among the lowest of the populace. What the thief dreads most is being obliged to return his booty, for he reckons a caning as nothing; and, if detected in the act, he cries, with a grin: "*Vinavat gospodin! vinavat*; I have done wrong, sir", and returns what he has stolen, as if that were a sufficient amends'.

Another aspect of Russian life that was widely commented on by visitors and writers was the boorishness of the people, both in high and low stations of life. The Russian was described by one writer as being 'filthily dirty, clad in long, cumbersome garments which prevented all free movement, with their unkempt hair down to their shoulders and matted beards, they behaved haggishly at table, dipping their black and greasy fingers indiscriminately into plates and dishes, always eating too much and drinking noisily and greedily out of unwashed vessels'. Another writer, noting their wild, unkempt hair and beards, wrote that they had a 'ridiculous appearance, like wild men of the woods'.

Like drunkenness, the boorishness of the Russian was not confined to the lower classes, but was a feature of life among the wealthier classes, extending to the court and the highest officials of the government. The early seventeenth-century Danish king, Christian IV, was reported to have said of the Russian officials who spent some time at his court that 'if these people come again we must build them a pigstye, for nobody can live in any house that they have occupied till six months afterwards because of the stench they leave behind them'.

Even as early as the time of Ivan the Terrible, there were Russians who were aware of the primitive manners of the people and attempted to correct what they considered a serious shortcoming. One of these people was Sylvester, the court chaplain and a man of great dignity, who wrote down a series of precepts, called the *Domostroy* (*The Good Householder*), with the view to reforming the personal habits of the people. In these rules of conduct he promulgated, he advised the citizens on manners, the women on how to keep their household in order, how to secure salvation, what foods should be eaten and on what days, and even listed various recipes for preparing food and beer. He advised the husband how to treat his wife and children, and he wrote that the people should, at all times, 'please God, honour the Czar'. He went into details of how one should conduct oneself at the table and, among other specific instructions, said that a person should 'blow his nose, and spit without noise, taking care to turn away from the company, and put his foot over the place'. This last precept obviously was put into effect, for as late as the early nineteenth century an English visitor in Russia remarked, 'There is another custom very prevalent among the Russian nobility, which is extremely disagreeable—that of spitting upon the floor. Neither fine inlaid floors, nor even Wilton carpets, oppose any obstacle to this detestable practice. The Russian

noble will spit immediately before you, and rub the saliva with his
foot. It is but just to say, however, that he, sometimes, retires to a
corner of the room, to conceal his deposit'.

Cleanliness, or lack of it, has always been a favourite subject of
comment among foreigners who have written about Russia. While
some were greatly impressed by the Russians' penchant for taking
scorchingly hot steam baths, which were followed in the winter by
the steam-bather running out of the bathhouse and rolling around
naked in the snow, other commentators insisted, steam bath or not,
that the Russians were indescribably filthy. In fact, one commen-
tator insisted that in Russia little had changed since the early tribal
days, when the Russians were said to have performed ablutions, or
had ablutions performed on them, only three times in the course of
their lives—at birth, at marriage, and after death. Clarke categoric-
ally stated that the Russian people 'are filthy, full of vermin', and
that it was well known that Potemkin, the famous minister of state at
the time of Catherine the Great, had the habit of taking vermin from
his head and killing them on the bottom of his plate while dining. A
number of foreign visitors to Russia complained bitterly of certain
habits of Russian servants, one of them being that the servant in
order to clean a plate would spit on it and then wipe it clean with a
dirty napkin.

All in all, the comments of visitors and even the comments of
Russians themselves on the personal mannerisms of the people in
old-time Russia rarely reveal a kind word or a flattering remark
about their personalities or character. Even the day-to-day relationship of the common man seemed to be filled with complaining and
bickering, as if the tedium of their lives could be relieved only by
abusing each other; a type of conduct, it may be observed in passing,
common among extremely poor and oppressed people in many
areas of the world.

Bored and defeated in life, they quarrelled frequently and violently, so that, as one writer observed, 'even in the open streets, you
may hear them rail and abuse one another, like fish-women, and
that with such animosity in outward appearance, that a stranger
would think it impossible they could part without fighting. They
have one good quality, which is that they seldom or never swear,
blaspheme, or curse in their anger; but on the other hand, they use
the most horrible and reviling expressions, accusing one another of

sodomy, buggery, and all other enormous crimes they can think of, and that, very often, without any respect of persons, nay, even betwixt parents and children'.

However, it must have been an intrepid child who would dare to revile his parents, for the laws of the land, say, in the seventeenth century, were such that a child had no rights and was expected to give unlimited reverence and obedience to his parents. One law stated that 'when children insult their parents, or even strike them with their hand, and the parents make complaint of it, the children shall be knouted'. Another law stated that 'a child that brings a formal process against his parent shall not be heard, but punished with the knout, and then delivered up to the parents'.

For hundreds of years the knout was the favoured form of punishment, being used, as the above laws testify, even on children. The knout has been described as 'a whip made of parchment cooked in milk and so hard that its strokes were like those of a sword. Practised executioners could kill a man with three strokes. There were few instances of any one surviving thirty'.

A Frenchman named de la Motraye has given a detailed description of the knout used for punishment. As quoted by John Mottley, an eighteenth-century writer, in his book on Peter the Great, de la Motraye wrote the following:

'The Patient strips himself to his Waste, taking off his Shirt, and leaves nothing on but his Breeches; or if a Woman, nothing but her Petticoat: This done he ascends a Sort of Scaffold, where his Feet are fastened to the Floor; his Hands are put over the Shoulders of a strong Man, who with his Hands holds him fast to his Breast, so that he cannot stir; then the Executioner advances three or four Steps, as if he was running till he comes within Reach of the Offender, and gives him his first Stroke on the Middle of his Back; then he retreats three or four Steps, and comes forward again, always with such Dexterity, that he never gives two Strokes, upon the same Place: He repeats this Motion as many Times as there are Blows ordered to be given by his Sentence, the Blood running in Abundance all this while from the Patient's Back. This is the moderate Knout. When the Sentence orders the Knout between the moderate and the severe, one may see small Pieces of Flesh taken off at every Stroke of the Executioner; when it is ordered to be given with the utmost Severity, it is often mortal; for then the Executioner striking the Flanks under the Ribs, cuts the Flesh to the very Bowels'.

Crime and punishment in the sixteenth century and for years after was a welter of confusion. Even though Ivan III and Ivan IV did codify the laws to some degree, the laws were so uncertain that Giles Fletcher, after eyewitnessing the laws' application, stated bluntly that 'there is no written law in Russia'.

The punishment for debt was most severe, as violent, for instance, as that of the Twelve Tables of Roman law. Rambaud has described it thus:

'The insolvent debtor was subjected to the pravège; that is, tied up half-naked on a public place, and beaten three hours a day. This punishment was repeated for thirty or forty days. If by that time no one was moved by his lamentations and cries to pay his debt for him, he was allowed to be sold, and his wife and children let out to hire; if he had none, he became the slave of the creditor. . . .

'In cases of accusation of theft, murder, or treason, the accused was subjected to tortures worthy of a Spanish Inquisitor. The punishments were infinitely varied: a man might be hung, beheaded, broken on the wheel, impaled, drowned under the ice, or knouted to death. A wife who had murdered her husband "was buried alive up to her neck"; heretics went to the stake; sorcerers were burned alive in an iron cage; coiners had liquid metal poured down their throats. We must not forget the death of "ten thousand pieces", the torment in which the sides were torn away by iron hooks, and all the varieties of mutilation. On the other hand, a noble who slew a mougik was only fined or whipped. The noble who killed his slave suffered no penalty; he could do what he liked with his own.'

Though crime, especially stealing, was widespread in old Russia, most travellers there stated that they were almost always treated with the utmost hospitality and that, as Masson wrote—and this is borne out by others writing of their experiences in Czarist Russia—'you are in less danger of being assassinated than even in England'.

However, while this feeling of safety was felt by travellers in Russia, the citizenry were not so fortunate. Life was cheap, and the taking of it by the authority of the Czar, which was unchallenged, was a commonplace. From medieval times on, the structure of Russia can be compared to a pyramid, with the absolute master at the apex and the nobles and the bureaucracy forming its extreme upper section, resting upon and being supported by a docile mass of common people.

Numerous explanations have been offered for this docility, such as the two centuries of Tartar rule, which destroyed the independent spirit of the people; the isolation of Russia for so many years from the mainstream of various European movements that whipped the people into action on various fronts—religious, political, social; the lack of participation of Russia in the mind-liberating Renaissance and other stimulating intellectual movements that swept Western Europe; and the hundreds of years of Eastern orientation, where absolutism was even stronger than in Europe.

Turgenev, for instance, claimed that the root of much of the evil that existed in Russia was a result of the lack of will power in the people themselves. 'We Slavs are badly off for that commodity [will power] and we grovel before it. . . . We want a master in everything and everywhere.'

And certainly in the sixteenth century, they had their wish in a high-handed, authoritative despot who was, indeed, a 'master in everything and everywhere'. His name was Ivan Grozny, or Ivan the Terrible, who became Grand Prince of Russia in 1533, at the age of three.

VIII

Ivan the Terrible: Early Years

IT SEEMS as though the first four hundred years of effort expended in building, rebuilding, fashioning, and refashioning the Kremlin, from the time of Yuri Dolgoruki, the reputed founder of Moscow, to the vigorous efforts of Ivan the Great and Vasili III, was a preparation for the reign of Ivan the Terrible, who more than any other Russian ruler was the human complement of the brick, mortar and stone fortress he inhabited for fifty years.

If the Kremlin was mysterious, so was Ivan; if it was cold, forbidding, austere, so was Ivan; if it was a confusion of intention and execution, so was Ivan; if it was 'a tyrant's ideal, a city of assassins that looked on a city of victims . . . a fortress, abattoir, seraglio, acropolis and necropolis in one . . . with an infernal heart', then certainly Ivan was its ideal occupant; if the Kremlin alarmed and menaced, so did Ivan: in short, the Kremlin, though it was not the creation of Ivan, was his image.

Ivan was born on August 25, 1530, in Moscow, and while his mother, Helena, 'that remarkable woman, who had the passion of a Spaniard and the ferocity of a Tartar', ruled as regent, Ivan was treated with respect and awe by the court. However, Helena died when Ivan was eight, and from then on his boyhood was filled with bitterness, frustration, and neglect. The nobles, as mentioned previously, struggled for power among themselves, and Ivan and his younger, feeble-minded brother Yuri were left to shift for themselves. Many years later, in a letter to Prince Kurbsky, Ivan described his boyhood thus:

'After the death of our mother, Helena, we were left with our brother Yuri absolute orphans; our subjects did their own will, carried on the government lawlessly. They took no care of us, their sovereign, but busied themselves only in the gain of wealth and power, and began to war with one another. And what evil things they did! How they killed boyars and captains, the friends of our father! The houses, villages and domains of our uncles they took for themselves. . . . They treated us and our brother Yuri like strangers, like beggars. We were ill-clothed, cold, and often went hungry.'

Nevertheless, in spite of being neglected and abused, Ivan had an education that was far superior to the customary one of young noblemen in Russia at that time. Mostly through his own efforts and desire for learning, he became the most literate, cultured, and articulate ruler, with the possible exception of Catherine the Great, that royal Russia has ever had. Described by one of his contemporaries as a 'rhetorician of lettered cunning', he was extremely adept in arguing theological matters, possessed a prodigious memory for Holy Writ, was widely acquainted with Greek history, and in his letters, especially those he wrote to Kurbsky, the renegade general and critic of his régime, evidenced a great deal of erudition.

Kluchevsky, the Russian historian, analysing the famous Kurbsky letters, wrote that Ivan's 'letters to Kurbsky constitute political treatises on the authority of a Czar and polemical pamphlets against the boyars and their political claims. . . . [In them there is a] diversity of the literary material which the author must have painfully collected before scattering it with so lavish a hand over these never-ending pages. What, indeed, do they not contain in the way of names, texts, and examples cited? Long and short excerpts from Holy Writ and the Fathers of the Church; verses and whole chapters from the Old Testament Prophets—from Moses, David, Isaiah and the rest, as well as from Church expositors of the New; passages from Saints Basil, Gregory, and John Chrysostom; types derived from classical mythology and epic literature, such as Zeus, Apollo, Antinous, Aenaes, and so forth; Biblical names, such as Jesus of Nazareth, Gideon, Abimelech and Jephtha; detached episodes from Jewish, Roman and Byzantine history, as well as from histories of some of the Western European nations; medieval names, such as Genseric, the Vandals, the Goths, the Sarmatians and the Franks—names which Ivan must have read in the Greek chronicles referred to; unexpected quotations from Russian chronographical works'.

In addition to an unusual, mainly self-pursued acquisition of knowledge, Ivan's education consisted, too, of training in brutality, cruelty, and torture. The age in which he lived, the sixteenth century, was a hard and ferocious one, not only in Russia but elsewhere—viz. Henry VIII and Bloody Mary, the St. Bartholomew Massacre, Catherine de Medici, the Inquisition, and so on—and his tutors made sure that he should be brought up according to the temper of the times. Thus, when he was a young boy, he was taken to the torture chambers, where he witnessed the inhuman devices used upon prisoners, heard the shrieks of agony, and saw the flow of blood, so that within him there would be awakened the lust for cruelty, that he would not grow up to be a weakling, disgusted at the sight of blood and horror.

He was encouraged not only to witness cruelty but to engage actively in it. Wild animals, such as bears and tigers, were captured and then taken to special enclosures in the Kremlin, where Ivan and other children of the nobility tormented them. One of the favourite sports of the children was to climb to the top of the Kremlin wall and from the heights drop a cat or dog on to the ground below, and then, urged on by their teachers, climb down again to look at the splattered remains of the animal.

Ivan, it seems, according to one of his early biographers, needed little urging to engage in such educational activities, and was an eager and apt pupil, unmoved by the sight of blood, and showed no sign of remorse or pity when he witnessed the most brutal of tortures; in fact, according to a contemporary, he was 'delighted' at what he saw.

In spite of the fact that Ivan indulged himself in these excesses—such as riding through the streets of Moscow with other young boyars and, when the urge to inflict pain possessed them, striking any citizen who crossed their path with a whip or charging their horses headlong into a group of passers-by—these acts of brutality were not confined to the Prince and the nobility. Heberstein described the activities of other boys, commoners, and what they did for 'fun', and the conclusion is that violence and brutality were traits that extended from those in high places to those in low.

'The youths and boys', Heberstein wrote, 'usually have a large open space in the city, where they assemble on holidays and can be seen and heard by the people. They assemble at a given signal, which is a certain sort of whistle; after which they run off and fight among themselves. First they strike and punch one another with their fists; but soon with their knees and feet, too, striking at random, as hard as they can, in the throat, the chest, the belly, and the genitals or wherever else they can. In the struggle for victory one will fling another down in such a way that they are often carried off half-dead.

The one who is most often victor, remains last on the spot, and the one who most bravely bears blows, carries off the glory. They have this sort of competition so that the boys may get used to giving blows and receiving punches.'

Even though Ivan complained in later life that he was neglected as a child and that the high officials of the government treated him as though he were a menial instead of the Grand Prince of Russia, there was little opposition, or outward complaints, when, after the Christmas fêtes of 1543, he decided to put his power to the test. Ordering the boyars to appear at court, he admonished them sternly about their ways of governing, and threatened them that if they did not mend their ways he would punish them severely. To illustrate the seriousness with which he issued the warning, he ordered one of the boyars to be seized and handed over to the kennel keepers of the Kremlin. Then, stating that the boyar was not the only guilty one, but that he would be used as an example to the others, he ordered him to be, literally, thrown to the dogs, who tore him to pieces.

At the time he carried through this piece of administrative instruction to his subordinates, Ivan was thirteen years old.

At sixteen years of age, Ivan advised his counsellors that he wished to be crowned not as Grand Prince of Russia, the customary title, but with the new title of Czar and Autocrat of All Russia. His counsellors were astonished at this, but they offered no opposition, and, consequently, in January 1547, Ivan ordered the Metropolitan, Macarius, to make the necessary arrangements for his coronation, and to make sure that at the coronation he would be crowned, according to his wishes, as Czar Ivan IV.

The title 'Czar' had always intrigued Ivan much more than the more modest title 'Grand Prince'. In the books that Ivan had read as a very young man about the kings of Egypt, Babylonia, Assyria, Judea, and the rulers of Rome and Constantinople, the Slavonic language, which was what Ivan read, used the word 'czar' for them. It was a high-flown title, with an air of mystery, and time-honoured among the 'greats' of history. Like his grandfather Ivan III, the sixteen-year-old ruler was acutely conscious of his tie to the glory that was Byzantium, which was a result of Ivan III's marriage to Sophia Paleologus; in addition, he believed, too, like his grandfather, that he was not only porphyrogenitic through his ancestor Vladimir Monomakh but that through Constantine the Great his lineage could be traced directly back to the great Czar of Czars, Caesar himself.

The word 'czar' has often been traced to a contraction of 'Caesar', which in itself must have intrigued Ivan. However, the actual origin of the word is not clear. It has been suggested that it is of Eastern origin, meaning in Persian 'throne' or 'supreme power', and that the Assyrian and Babylonian kings' names often ended with 'czar', such as in Nebuchadne*zzar* or Belsha*zzar*. 'Czar' was also used by certain Tartar rulers, and it is possible that Ivan got the idea of using the title from them. Nevertheless, whatever the origin of the word, no Russian ruler had presumed to use it as his title as head of Russia until Ivan the Terrible, intrigued by the magnificence and power that the title seemed to imply, insisted that in the Kremlin coronation he be officially crowned 'Czar', as well as Prince of Vladimir, Moscow, Novgorod, and so on.

At about the same time he decided to be crowned Czar Ivan IV, the boy ruler decided to marry. He called the boyars and high churchmen together, and addressed them as follows:

'By the mercy of God, and his all-pure Mother, by the prayers and grace of the great wonder-workers, Peter, Alexis, Sergei, and all the Russian wonder-workers in whom I put my trust, and with thy blessing, Holy Father, I propose to marry. At first I thought to marry a foreign princess, the daughter of some king or czar, but afterward I gave up the thought. I have no wish to marry a foreign princess, for if I marry a wife from a strange land we may not agree, and life would be hard for us. Therefore, I wish to marry in my own realm and God will bless it.'

A circular letter was sent to the nobles throughout Russia stating, 'When these, our letters, reach you, it shall be your duty instantly to repair with your unmarried daughters, if such you have, to our lieutenant in the city for inspection. Conceal not your marriageable daughters under any pretext. Whoever shall conceal a marriageable daughter and not bring her to our lieutenant, on him shall be our great disfavour'.

Then, in the traditional manner, the girls from all over Russia were assembled and fêted in the Kremlin, where Ivan observed them. His choice fell upon Anastasia Romanov, the daughter of a well-known and popular family among the Muscovites.

The marriage was an extremely happy one, and Anastasia was

probably the only one of his seven wives (two of them were never officially recognized by the Church) that Ivan really loved deeply. How he felt about his mistresses, who numerically were said to rival Solomon's, there is no record. The Czarina Anastasia was described by a contemporary English traveller as 'wise and of such hollyness, vertue, and government as she was honnored, beloved and feared of all her subjects. He being yonge and riotous, she ruled him with admirable affabillitie and wisdome'.

With Ivan's marriage to Anastasia began Ivan's 'good period', in which, with regard to the times, he could be considered an enilght-ened ruler. Scholars, artists, printers, physicians, and apothecaries were invited to come to Russia, mainly from Germany, and, in the daily conduct of government, an attempt was made to conduct public affairs with moderation and understanding. Ivan himself, during this period, appeared to be happy and content, showing few signs of the cruel, hypocritical, suspicious, unrestrained, proud, lecherous, moody man he became in later life.

In addition to his happy marriage, another event that had a pro-found effect on Ivan, causing him to forgo the cruel ways charac-teristic of his youthful period, was a catastrophic fire that broke out in Moscow in 1547. Moscow periodically had its great fires, and almost daily its small ones, being a wooden-structured city and thus especially susceptible to conflagrations. Through ukazes, the authorities constantly ordered certain precautions, under penalty of severe punishment, such as that all fires had to be extinguished by dusk, that in the summertime no lights were allowed in houses, and that cooking had to be undertaken in the open air. In spite of the precautions, horrible fires constantly broke out, often destroying a good part of the city. There was little if any fire-fighting equipment, and the only recourse to put out the flames was to obtain water from the river. Usually, however, nothing was done, and the Muscovites regarded the fires with passive fatalism, their only activity in com-bating the flames being fervent prayers.

The fire that broke out in 1547 was one of the worst that had ever occurred in Moscow. At the time, a fierce wind was blowing, which spread the flames to all points of the city. Soon, all of Moscow was in ashes, presenting as one historian described it, 'an immense funeral pile, over which was spread a pall of thick and black smoke. The wooden edifices disappeared entirely. Those of stone and brick presented a still more gloomy aspect, with only portions of their walls standing, crumbling and blackened. The howling of the tempest, the roar of the flames, the crash of falling buildings, and the shrieks of the inhabitants, were all frequently overpowered by the explosions of the powder magazines in the arsenals of the Kremlin. To many people it seemed that the day of judgment had actually arrived, that the trump of the archangel was sounding, and that the final conflagration had arrived'.

The frenzy of the inhabitants, surrounded on all sides by the roaring flames, was unbounded. They rushed by the thousands to the Moscow River, hoping to find safety in the water. But many of them, their clothes in flames, were consumed before they could reach the river, and the streets became littered not only with the debris of the burned-out buildings but with blackened bodies of dead Muscovites. Thousands of people were burned to death, the exact figure never known, since children were not included in the figures issued later by the government.

The damage to the Kremlin was particularly severe. The strong winds blew embers over the crenellated walls into the fortress itself, and by the time the fire was over the Cathedral of the Assumption was partially destroyed and great damage was done to the Czar's Palace and the Cathedral of the Annunciation. The armoury buildings were destroyed, as were the house of the Metropolitan and the dwellings of many of the boyars who lived within the Kremlin. Irreplaceable sacred relics, frescoes, holy screens, and treasures of all kinds were consumed.

Ivan, his brother, Anastasia, and various nobles fled the Kremlin and went to the Czar's palace on the Sparrow Hills. As soon as the fire burned itself out, Ivan gave orders for the restoration of the Kremlin. During the next two years, 1548–49, not only was the fortress city restored but the city of Moscow rose again from its ashes, as it had so many times before and so many times in later years. Perhaps no city of comparable size, with the exception of Constantinople, has so often been burned to its very foundations, and has so often risen again.

Almost from the moment the fire started there were rumours throughout Moscow that the city had been set on fire by magic, that members of the nobility had taken human hearts, soaked them in water, and with this water had sprinkled the houses and streets of

Moscow, thus casting an evil spell over them. The Russians, from the Czar to the humblest peasant, were extremely superstitious, believing in, as Rambaud pointed out, 'horoscopes, diviners, sorcery, magic, the miraculous virtues of certain herbs or certain formulae, the evils produced by "lifting the footmarks" of an enemy, in bewitched swords, in love philtres, in werewolves, ghosts, and vampires', and the rumours that were thus spread were taken very much to heart.

Five days after the fire began, some nobles, led by Prince Skopin-Shuisky, taking advantage of the agitated feelings of the Muscovites, and possibly having been responsible for starting the rumours about evil spirits, gathered a huge crowd before the square in front of the Cathedral of the Assumption, and asked them pointedly, 'Who set fire to Moscow?' The cry went up that it was the Glinskys, the enemies of the Shuiskys, and the mob, urged on by the nobles, killed Yuri Glinsky who was in the square at the time. Three days later, a mob appeared at Ivan's residence in the suburbs and demanded that other members of the Glinsky family be executed. The mob was dispersed but only after much difficulty.

The threatening mob and especially the horror of the fire had a marked effect on Ivan, and he decided to assemble the boyars, the clergy, and some of the common people in the grand place of execution at the Kremlin, and address them there. Focusing his attention on the Metropolitan, Ivan said:

'Holy Father, your zeal for virtue, your love for my country are known to me, second my good intentions. I lost my parents too young; the boyars and the nobles, who only aspired to domination, took no care of my person; they have usurped in my name wealth and honours; they are enriched by injustice, and overwhelm the people, so that no one dares to hinder their ambition. I was, as it were, deaf and dumb; I heard not the lamentations of the poor, and my words did not sweeten their woes.'

Then, turning his attention to the nobles, he continued: 'You, you are delivered then to your caprices, you rebellious subjects, you corrupted judges; how can you now justify yourselves? What tears you have caused, what blood you have shed, which falls upon me! But fear the judgment of God'.

Ivan then turned to the common people, saluted them, and went on: 'Oh, you! a people that the Almighty has confided to me, I invoke today your religion and your love for me; show yourselves generous. It is impossible to repair the past evils, but I shall in the future wisely preserve you from apprehension and pillage.

'Forget the sorrows that shall never be renewed, scatter every subject of hatred and discord, let a Christian and brotherly ardour embrace all your hearts. From this day forward, I, I will be your judge, your defender!'

Shortly thereafter, Ivan called together the clergy to have them approve a code of laws that he had ordered drawn up, and also asked them to condemn him for his sins. Impassionedly, he begged them to 'convict me in them, thunder the Word of God, that my soul may live!' The clergy, fearing that his new-found resolve to govern benignly might be short-lived, were afraid to condemn, and refused. They did, however, dutifully approve the new civil code.

Since the days of the great fire and the resulting mob action that threatened Ivan, the Czar had confided in and trusted the advice of an extremely intelligent priest, Sylvester, who became his confessor and adviser. As time went on, Sylvester became, together with Alexi Adashev, an obscure clerk Ivan had become extremely fond of and had elevated to the position of chamberlain, the administrative heads of the government, with the power of ministers. Bypassing the boyars whom he mistrusted, believing that they were blocking the forward march of power by insisting on their hereditary rights, Ivan boldly handed the business of government over to two obscure men, who he felt were both loyal to him as well as being aware of the possibilities of Russia becoming great, strong and unified. His letter of appointment to Adashev points up his intentions as Czar, at least during his 'good period'.

'Alexi, I have raised thee up from among the ranks of the humble and the most insignificant of the people. I had heard of thy good deeds and have therefore chosen thee above thy degree, for the aid of mine own soul. Though it was not thine own wish, yet I have desired thee, and not thee alone, but others also who are like thee and think like thee, who assuage my grief, and, like thee, are able to take care of the men who are entrusted to me by God. I therefore enjoin upon thee to receive petitions from the poor and injured and to read them through with care. Have no fear of the strong and famous, who worm their way into places of honour and oppress and destroy the poor and weak by their superior powers. . . .'

With the affairs of state entrusted to two loyal and intelligent advisers, happily married to the comforting and loving Anastasia, and crowned with the imposing title of Czar and Autocrat of All Russia, the young, ambitious Ivan was ready for adventures that would unify the country and extend its borders.

The choice for the first adventure was the traditional enemy of Russia—the Tartars. And the place he sought them out was at their stronghold—Kazan.

IX

Ivan the Terrible: Middle Years

F ew events in Russian history have added such stature and prestige to the Kremlin in the eyes of the Russian people as Ivan's campaign and subsequent victory over the Kazan Tartars. Although for years the Golden Horde had been defeated and scattered, Tartars still ruled in Kazan, Astrakhan, and in the Crimea, and though they no longer menaced the power of the Russian state as they had in the past, their very presence as rulers reminded the Russians of the centuries of oppression and vassaldom.

The successful campaigns against Kazan in 1551, and in Astrakhan in 1556, took on a grandeur of accomplishment that filled the Russian nation with a sense of power. Among the ruling group, and especially to Ivan himself, it meant that he was now a full-fledged autocrat, in vassaldom to no one and complete master over the magnificent wide expanse of Rus. Once and for all the fear of the East was over. Except in the Crimea, which was not then part of Russia, where the Tartars were still powerful, the Russians now had destroyed the last vestiges of the greatest of all Oriental military machines, the descendants of the power that had been Genghis Khan's and Tamerlane's.

The campaign against Kazan started badly, for though the Russians were the aggressors they made inadequate preparations and were ill-equipped, and as a result severe defeats were initially inflicted upon Ivan's forces. The Czar reorganized the army, making it into a more efficient fighting force, and equipped it with more and better weapons, including a hundred and fifty cannons, a tremendous number for the time. With the reorganized, well-equipped troops, the Russians set out once more for Kazan, and soon the Tartar city was besieged. With the aid of a Danish engineer who organized the mining and breaching of the high walls, Kazan was finally stormed and taken.

Ivan himself, like most Russian rulers, kept away from the actual battlefield, preferring to stay in his tent, praying endlessly. Even at the very moment that the walls of Kazan were being mined and

Muscovites were mounting the breached sections with the cry 'God
be with us!' Ivan fearfully remained in his tent. The story was told
that at the time of the explosions messengers came running into
Ivan's retreat, shouting, 'Come, O, Ivan! Thy troops wait for thee!
Come at once, O, Ivan! to sustain the hearts of thy servants!' Ivan,
however, insisted that he could not come until he had finished his
prayers and then, before the icon of St. Sergius, performed such
long, drawn-out devotions that by the time he finished the main
battle was over, and by the time he finally arrived at the walls of
Kazan, the banners of the victorious Russians were already flying
over the city.

Unabashed at his own cowardice, Ivan, nevertheless, rode triumphantly through Kazan as the conquering Czar, attended Mass
at the Kremlin in Kazan, and then, turning his back on his troops,
hurried back to Moscow where his wife Anastasia was about to have
a child.

Flushed with victory, Ivan ordered that the various monuments
of the Tartars be destroyed and that churches and monasteries be
erected to show his faith in God and the 'triumph of the Cross over
Islam'.

The most magnificent and imposing structure that Ivan ordered
erected to monumentalize the victory is the Cathedral of St. Basil
the Blessed (*Vasili Blazhennyi*) on the Red Square in Moscow,
which received its name from a Moscow holy beggar of that name
and was erected on the very spot where St. Basil the Blessed was
buried. Though St. Basil's, or the Pokrovsky Cathedral as it is sometimes called, is not in the Kremlin area proper—adjoining it outside
the walls—it actually can be considered part of it—like the Red
Square itself—owing to its proximity and its historic ties to the
fortress.

Work on St. Basil's began in 1553 under the direction, significantly enough, not of Italian architects but of Russian ones—the
Pskov masters Barma and Posnik Iakovlev. The cathedral was completed and consecrated in 1560. Although it is quite definite that
it was the Pskov architects, called 'very wise and eminently fit for
this marvellous work', by a chronicler of the times, and not a
foreigner who designed the cathedral, the legend has persisted to
this very day that it was, indeed, an Italian. This unnamed Italian
architect, so the legend goes, when he had finished the cathedral

was called before Ivan, who asked him if he could design another church as beautiful as St. Basil's. The architect replied that he could. Whereupon Ivan had his guards seize the architect and blind him, so that he would not be able ever again to create for another potentate a church to rival the magnificence of St. Basil's.

In the city of Moscow, with its 'forty times forty' number of churches, none is as remarkable at St. Basil's. It has caught the fancy not only of Orthodox Russians but of the present-day anti-Church Communists, who in 1923 converted it into an anti-religious museum. One contemporary Russian writer, for instance, proudly wrote that 'this shrine with its numerous domes, a riot of colours and shapes, is a festive ensemble of Russian architecture. Gone are meagreness and restraint—in its stead flamboyant imagination—a great explosion of Russian genius—wide-open greeting, the crimson peal of bells'.

Foreigners, too, upon observing the cathedral on the Red Square, run riot in their descriptions of it. A few of their comments are:

'You might take it for an immense dragon, with shining scales, crouching and sleeping.'

'Conceive the most brilliant bird of tropical forests suddenly taking the shape of a cathedral, and you have *Vassili Blagennoi*.'

'A powerful imagination has defied all symmetry. From the base to the summit, the church is covered with colours, which are glaring, and even crude. This many-coloured monster has the gift of stupefying the most blasé traveller.'

'The most fantastic and astonishing of all earthly churches is *Vassili Blagennoi* (St. Basil the Blessed) in Moscow. . . . It stand as the climax of ecclesiastical architecture from the tenth to the sixteenth centuries.'

'Its design is bizarre; its colour is motley; the two both harmonise and contrast—the whole fascinates. It is at once both a nightmare and a revelation. . . . It cannot be forgotten, yet it repels by its egregious fatuity. It is the over-inflated frog at the instant of explosion.'

The exterior of St. Basil's has many of the features of the wooden-structured churches of the north of Russia, with the square superstructure and the main octagonal tower. It has eleven steeples, which resemble exotically shaped plants, and eight bulbous cupolas all of different design, resembling Eastern turbans, pineapples, and so on, many of them with interlacing designs and many of them faceted. The colouring of the cathedral is truly exotic, consisting of various shades of red, orange, yellow, green, blue, violet, gold and silver. In contrast to the exterior of the cathedral, which has so often been compared to a colossal tropical plant, the interior is cold, sombre and darkly mysterious, like an immense cave, with gloomy, almost inaccessible labyrinths; dark, brooding corners; strange openings, like caeca; doors so low that one has to crouch almost double to get through them, and which lead nowhere; and precipitous stairways that descend into what appear to be unplumbed depths. Throughout the cathedral are images, which Gautier has described as seeming to be 'in their archaic Byzantine and constrained appearance to have been translated awkwardly into gold by the childish devotion of a primitive race. These images that you view across the carved and silver-gilt work of the iconostas, where they are ranged symmetrically upon the golden screen, opening their large fixed eyes and raising their brown hand with the fingers turned in a symbolic fashion, produce, by means of their somewhat savage, superhuman and immutable traditional aspect, a religious impression not to be found in more advanced works of art. These figures, seen amid the golden reflections and twinkling light of the lamps, easily assume a phantasmagorical life, capable of impressing sensitive imaginations and of creating, especially at the twilight hour, a peculiar kind of sacred awe'.

About the same time that St. Basil's Cathedral was finished and consecrated, in 1560, Anastasia, Ivan's beloved wife, died. Probably no single event in Ivan's life had such a profound effect upon him; he was completely distraught, almost insane with grief, and anger too, for Ivan, having the suspicious nature so characteristic of Russian rulers, which expressed itself among other ways in a plaguing suspicion that every one of his supporters were traitors, believed, or let on that he believed, that his devoted Czarina had been poisoned. Years before when he had been ill and the boyars had refused to take the oath to support his son in case of the Czar's death, his suspicions had reached a fever pitch, and now unable, or unwilling, to believe that it was possible for Anastasia to die a natural death, he cried out against almost all of his advisers, accusing them of treachery. Sylvester was imprisoned in the remote Solovetsky Monastery, and Adashev, knowing that his days were numbered, committed suicide by taking poison while under arrest in Dorpat.

But the punishment of Sylvester and Adashev, his two closest advisers, did not, could not, mollify the embittered Czar; nothing could, it seemed, now that Anastasia was dead, for, as von Eckardt, a biographer of Ivan, stated, 'the centre of his life was dead . . . the light went out in his heart; and with it, Czar Ivan's will for good'.

The Czar now became Ivan Grozny—Ivan the Terrible—God's scourge on earth as he has been called, and for the next twenty-four years, until his death in 1584, terror and executions were the order of the day.

The Kremlin itself, now that the reign of terror had begun, became in fact as well as in appearance a forbidding place. In the underground dungeons, victims wasted away in chains. In the houses of the nobles, both within the Kremlin area and elsewhere, the aristocracy lived in a constant state of anxiety; no one was safe from Ivan's wrath. Periodically someone would be summoned before the Czar, accused of treachery, and killed, for, since Ivan saw treachery everywhere, sooner or later he put to death almost every person who at one time or another had been a member of his council.

Although the execution of his associates stemmed from Ivan's pathologically suspicious nature, Prince Kurbsky, a leading Russian general and early supporter of Ivan who later fled to Poland and became Ivan's severest critic, believed that the executions were also the result of a Machiavellian ideology that Ivan embraced, partly as a result of a conversation the Czar had had with an old anchorite in a remote monastery.

'How can I govern really well and keep my great and powerful subjects in submission?' Ivan had asked.

'If thou dost wish to be an autocrat, keep no adviser who is wiser than thyself; for thou art greater and better than them all', the old man had replied. 'Only thus wilt thou remain firmly established in sovereignty and hold all things in thy hand. But if thou hast men about thee who are wiser than thou art, then of necessity thou must be obedient to them.'

This advice was certainly not alien to Ivan's nature, and it is little wonder that Ivan was extremely pleased by the anchorite's remarks. Kurbsky, who was present at the meeting between the Czar and the monk, reported that the Czar, after the advice had been given, kissed the hand of the old man, thanked him for his counsel, and said, 'If my own father were still alive, he might have spoken such profitable and just words to me'.

One of the places where the executions took place was right outside the Kremlin walls. In the Red Square, on the north-east side, was a stone execution block, and as the victims were placed upon it, Ivan, from a vantage position on the Kremlin wall, watched the executioner at work. Executions were public and the Muscovites were urged—often compelled—to witness them as an object lesson in good citizenship.

In the summer of 1570 one of the largest mass executions occurred. Various instruments of torture were placed in the square, such as bundles of faggots for burning; huge cauldrons of water for scalding alive; ropes for pulling limbs from bodies; wild bears in cages; and hangman's gallows. The spectacle of so many instruments of death frightened the people who, concerned with their own necks, fled from the execution site. Ivan ordered his guards to circulate around the city and round up spectators. They rode all through Moscow but were unsuccessful, for the people hid when the guards approached. Ivan, enraged, mounted his horse and together with some soldiers rode around Moscow, crying, 'Come, good people! There is nothing to be afraid of. No harm shall overtake you'. Assured of their safety by the Czar himself, the inhabitants flocked to the site in such numbers that not a single spot was unoccupied. When the crowd finally assembled, Ivan asked them if he was right or wrong in condemning the victims to torture and death. The mob answered with loud shouts, 'Long live Your Majesty!'

The macabre show lasted for four hours, during which time Ivan forced his young son to witness the horrors from beginning to end. The bodies were left to rot in the hot sun, where for days dogs could be seen gnawing on the stinking corpses.

Court life within the Kremlin was a curious *mélange* of heavy quietude, brooding piety, exaggerated court formalism, and fearful excesses. Church services were held constantly, and Ivan, extremely pious, attended them for hours on end. In fact, as the terror grew, Ivan became more and more pious, convinced that he was God's servant on earth and that he had been called upon by the Almighty to carry out His will. And Ivan was a faithful and willing servant, who fully believed that the extermination of his enemies was a righteous religious act.

Ivan's predilection for combining extermination of his foes with the will of God had at times a gruesomely humorous aspect to it. There is the story that one of the people Ivan had condemned to death had fled and had hidden in a monastery. Ivan found him there, and turning to his soldiers said, 'He is seeking God. Let us help him to get to Heaven more quickly'. Whereupon, he had the man seized and blown up in a cask of gunpowder.

Though there was little gaiety in the normal course of court life, there were on occasion large, festive, and, oftentime, boisterous feasts, during which times Ivan was wont to play practical jokes, some of them resulting in the mutilation or death of the victim. One famous story is about his court jester, who when Ivan in a playful mood poured hot, boiling soup on his head, cried out in pain. Ivan asked the jester if the pain was unbearable, and the jester answered that it was. Whereupon, Ivan plunged a knife into the clown's heart, putting an end to his pain.

On another occasion while the Czar was dining, the Voivode of Slavitza, Boris Titov, presented himself to the Czar, bowing to the floor and giving Ivan the usual greeting. 'May God preserve you, my dear Voivode!' the Czar said. 'You deserve a favour from me', and he took up a knife, approached the kneeling Titov, and cut off one of his ears. Titov, so the account goes, did not express the least sign of pain or resentment and without changing expression thanked Ivan for his gracious punishment, and wished him a long and happy reign.

Titov's reaction was not an unusual one, for there are innumerable stories, quite similar in nature, in which, after a particularly horrible action had been perpetrated on an individual by the Czar, the victim would fall to the feet of his oppressor and cry out something to this effect, 'May you reign long and happy, O illustrious prince, who honours your faithful subjects with such favours, and who condescended to punish them for the generous purpose of improving their conduct'.

Ivan's 'pranks' were not limited to his own subjects, for there were occasions when he played them on foreigners. On a certain festival day, for example, Ivan had indulged himself in some vagary or other which caused some Dutch and English women who were present to laugh. Shocked at their insolence, he had them sent to his palace, where he had them stripped stark naked before him in one of the large rooms. Ivan then ordered that four or five bushels of peas be thrown on the floor, and the offenders were compelled to pick them up. When they had finally finished, he had them served generously with wine, and lectured them on how to behave when they were in court, especially warning them to think twice before laughing at a Czar.

Another story, probably apocryphal, concerned the French Ambassador. It appears that the Ambassador, when he was ushered into Ivan's chamber, refused to take off his hat. Ivan, enraged, ordered that it be nailed to his head. A sequel to this story is the one related to Alexander Gordon, who was in the service of Peter the Great. He wrote that the story was still current in his time that when the Ambassador of Queen Elizabeth of England appeared before Ivan with his hat on his head, the Czar asked him if he had heard what had happened to the French Ambassador who, too, had refused to uncover his head before His Majesty, and then proceeded to inform Elizabeth's envoy of the Frenchman's fate. The English Ambassador replied that he had not heard the story before, but if he had, he still would not uncover his head, since he would not put in the balance his life against the dignity of the crown he had the honour to represent. Also, he knew very well that his sovereign, the great Queen of England, would certainly resent any injury committed on her Ambassador, even though it was undertaken by the most powerful ruler in the world. Whereupon, Gordon wrote, 'the Czar looked sternly about amongst his nobles. "Observe", says he, "how this man stands up for the honour of a woman. Is there any one of you who durst undertake so much for me?" ' The English Ambassador was allowed to wear his hat, sans nail, and was wined and dined by the Czar.

What caused Ivan to be 'terrible' is a question that has been asked many times, and the answers have varied. Most historians agree that he was not unique in his cruelty—that it was an age of cruelty in other countries besides Russia. And in each country where terror reigned, certain economic, social, political and religious factors can be found to be the cause. Thus, in Russia too, Ivan's terror can be and has been traced, for instance, to a definite political policy— the breaking down of the power of the boyars, uprooting them from their positions of power and thus impoverishing them, so that they could never become, singly or in groups, a serious threat to the power of the throne. Certain Marxist historians, like Pokrovsky, practically ignore the evil that Ivan perpetrated on rich and poor alike, and hold him up to adulation as the Czar who broke down feudal relations. Calling the hated *Oprichniki* 'warriors', Pokrovsky wrote, 'The "warrior's" road lay over the dead body of old Muscovite feudalism, a fact which made the "warriors" progressive, whatever the motives that immediately guided them'.

Stephen Graham, a modern biographer of Ivan, believes that, among other things, a reason for Ivan's terror can be found in Anastasia's death, which, he says, was a great shock and may even have affected his mind. And then he ventures the hypothesis that Ivan's abnormal mania for cruelty may have been the result of 'some mental disease, possibly some syphilitic infection of the brain'.

Von Eckardt traces his cruelty to the inherent cruelty of the Russian people, reflected in its leaders. 'Ivan's inhumanity is no exception in Russian history. . . . Russian cruelty has something gloomy and dreary about it. It is hard to say whether this is due to the influence of the Tartar period or whether the East Slavs were always this way inclined; but however this may be, hardly any other people in Europe has so often practised, tolerated and discussed cruelty of such a type, repeating itself century after century.'

Florinsky, the historian and economist, believes that Ivan definitely suffered from 'the mania of persecution', and that his excesses can to an extent be traced to his seeing treason everywhere around him, so that he 'ruthlessly eliminated, one after another', his 'real and imaginary enemies'.

Whatever the reason for his becoming 'terrible', and the answer is probably a combination of the above hypotheses, one of the most amazing, and incomprehensible, facts about the terror was the Russian people's reaction to it. As long ago as the sixteenth century, Richard Chancellor attempted to explain the inexplicable attitude of servility that the whole nation seemed to have. He wrote: 'I compare them to a young horse that knoweth not its strength, whom a little child ruleth and guideth with a bridle for all his great strength; for if he did, neither childe nor man could rule him . . . thus, if they knew their strength, no one man were able to make match with them'.

Perhaps the deepest analysis of the indifference of the Russian to what went on about him, even the horrors of Ivan's rule and the apparent senseless killing of poor people who certainly, unlike the boyars, did not at the time threaten him, may be found in Gorky's analysis of the Russian peasant:

'The boundless plain upon which the log-walled, thatch-roofed village huts stand huddled together, has the poisonous property of desolating a man's soul and draining him of all desire for action. The peasant may go beyond the limits of his village, take a look at the emptiness all about him, and after a while he will feel as if this desolation had entered into his own soul. Nowhere are lasting traces of toil to be seen. The estates of the landlords? But they are few, and enemies live there. The cities? But they are far away, and culturally not much more important than the village. As far as the eye can see stretches an endless plain, and in the midst of it stands an insignificant wretched little man, cast away upon this dreary earth to labour like a galley-slave. And the man is overwhelmed by a feeling of indifference which kills his capacity to think, to remember past experience, and to draw inspiration from it.'

From the common man, at least, there was no danger of opposition to the Czar's brutality. And so the reign of terror continued, while the mass of the nation, filled as one historian put it 'with a multitude of superstitions, and no ideas whatever', looked on apathetically—if they bothered to look at all.

X

The Terror

IN DECEMBER, 1564, Ivan abandoned the Kremlin. Together with the new Czarina, his two sons, and some members of his court, he got into a sleigh and drove off, leaving no word where he was going or for how long he would stay away. Hundreds of sleds, laden with the Czar's prized possessions, the state's treasury, and provisions, followed behind him. A month later he sent the city a message which read: 'Unable to brook the treachery by which I was surrounded, I have forsaken the state and taken my way whither God shall direct'. In this letter as well as in another he wrote, he complained that he had taken the step with deep sorrow in his heart. He also complained bitterly that throughout his life, even as a child as well as during his time as ruler, he had always been betrayed and robbed, especially by the boyars. Thus, he wrote, unable to bear the heathen boyars who had forsaken God, he himself would now reside in the wilderness and go wherever 'God shall direct'.

From the moment of his departure, Moscow was thrown into turmoil. Shops closed, commerce ceased, and speeches were made against the boyars. The people felt deserted, helpless, and leaderless. Taking advantage of their feelings, Ivan dispatched a letter to the 'black' people, the lower classes of Moscow, as well as to the merchants and others of non-noble stock, telling them that he was not angry with them and they should not be afraid.

Interminable and violent discussions took place over what was to be done. Finally it was decided that the Metropolitan and several of the oldest boyars should go to the Czar at his country place, which was now an armed fortress, and beg him to return. When the emissaries arrived there, they saw an aged, grey-haired, pathetic-looking man, who apparently was on the verge of a mental and physical breakdown. For weeks Ivan had been having fits of rage, had been visited by terror and hallucinations, and had been living the life of an ascetic, in an attempt to calm his 'anguished soul'. The Metropolitan and the boyars approached him with the following petition:

'If, Sire, thou dost despise what is temporal and transient, and wilt take no thought for thy great land and its cities, nor for the countless masses of thy devoted people, be mindful at least of the holy, miracle-working pictures and of the one Christian faith, which through thine abdication is faced with utter ruin or the revilings of heretics. But should treason and malice in our land cause thee, O Sire, affliction of which we have no knowledge, it is for thee to punish the guilty ones severely or to show them mercy; thy wise laws and ordinances shall set all things right again.'

This was just what Ivan wanted—a completely free hand from both the representatives of the clergy and, especially, the boyars themselves. He replied: 'I do agree to take back the throne, but on the following conditions: I shall be free to execute which traitors I desire, free to visit with my displeasure, be it by death, arrest, the confiscation of estate, without incurring an anathema or demur on the part of the clergy'.

Thus, two months after forsaking the throne, Ivan rode triumphantly back into the Kremlin. By tens of thousands, the people of Moscow kneeled in the snow blessing their Little Father and praying for him, thanking God that the Czar had returned to protect and lead them. And the few who dared to lift their eyes saw in the sleigh a stranger, for the Czar, according to a description of him at the time, now looked like a completely different person; he was unkempt, with long hair and a beard that was awry, his mouth was twisted, his brow was furrowed, and his eyes had the look of a demented man.

From the moment of his return, Ivan acted as a man possessed. Even as he had cried before the Metropolitan and the boyars at his retreat that 'they [the boyars] killed our meek and pious consort Anastasia Romanovna, and had not God protected us by disclosing to us men's evil intentions, they would have exterminated us, too, and our children', he now cried that all traitors, no matter who they were or where they were, would be exterminated. What followed was a reign of terror that made the previous excesses of the Czar seem trivial and mild. He was not content only to kill, but he insisted that torture precede execution and that the torture be done by the most cruel means possible—red-hot needles, the rack, the knout, to name but a few.

In his personal life, too, Ivan now indulged in excesses that made his previous actions seem pale indeed. With wild abandonment he

had women abducted and brought to the Kremlin, where he indulged himself in orgies. Or, sometimes, tiring of the Kremlin, he
went, accompanied by his jesters, to one of his country estates near
Moscow and gave himself completely to wild revelries. The four-
foot-long wooden staff, with its carved handle and deadly iron tip,
that he now carried with him at all times was often in use. He got
into the habit of striking people at random with it, often killing them
in fits of rage.

One day at dinner a courtier had the temerity to criticize Ivan,
saying that the mead that was served at Ivan's table was mixed with
blood. Ivan answered his criticism by plunging his staff through his
critic's heart. In discourse with a boyar he would often drive the
staff through the man's foot, and if he did not flinch or cry out, Ivan
would compliment him and favour him. He poured spirits over the
heads of companions, and then set their hair on fire. In his walks
around the city, if he saw a man whose face he did not like, he would
use his staff, wounding or killing him, and there were cases in which,
seized by a whim, he ordered the first man he met in the street to be
seized by his guards and killed. He ordered the town of Vologda to
send him a pot full of fleas, for some reason or other, and when the
town did not send the measure full, he fined the inhabitants seven
thousand roubles.

In his fury, Ivan constantly averred that he was merely carrying
out God's will as His personal servant to cleanse the land of sin and
evil. He prayed more fervently than ever and attended church services more diligently than he had in the past. He viewed God as the
wrathful, avenging God of the Old Testament, and himself as His
scourge. An articulate man, probably the most articulate man of his
time in Russia, Ivan knew what he was doing and often wrote down
the ideological reasons for his actions. On one occasion, attempting
to explain his actions, he wrote: 'It is the function of the sovereign to
show graciousness and mildness to the good, but wrath and destruction to the evil. If he neglects this, then he is no Czar. Therefore,
good works have nothing to fear from the Czar, but only those that
are evil'.

And to help him rid Russia of evildoers, he organized the *Oprichnina* (meaning 'the apart'), which he claimed would sweep the
country clean of sinners and traitors. Actually, the formation of this
picked body of men, with loyalty sworn only to him, the head

Oprichnik, created a state within a state. Ivan expropriated almost half of the state's realms for his personal possession, to be ruled by him through the *Oprichnina*, and even Moscow itself was divided into two. The laws of the land did not apply to the *Oprichnina*, which had its own courts, own laws, own police, own administration. The *Oprichnina* police were a fearful sight to see: they had black horses, they themselves were dressed in black, and they carried a dog's head and a broom at their saddle bow, symbols of their intention to hunt down rebels and to sweep Russia clean.

The stories of the terror that the *Oprichnina* spread throughout Russia are legend: they killed without fear of punishment; they carried off women; they expropriated land, houses, personal possessions at will. Responsible only to the Czar, by the oath they had sworn to him, they became, like Ivan, the scourge of the land. But in all this terror there was method in Ivan's formation of the black-uniformed bullyboys—he was determined to break down the power of the boyars, of all hereditary feudal groups, and to establish himself as the undisputed, supreme autocrat of Russia, sharing power and authority with no one.

Perhaps no single incident more clearly brings out the role of the *Oprichnina* and its methods than Ivan's campaign against Novgorod. Suspecting a plot against him from the proud city of Novgorod, Ivan ordered a campaign unleashed against the north Russian trading centre. The *Oprichniki* preceded him to the city. On their way this advance guard killed all in their path. Whole villages and towns were destroyed, together with their inhabitants. When Ivan and his troops finally arrived in Novgorod, preceded by the *Oprichniki*, he called together the city's leaders at a banquet. Then in the midst of the festivities, at a given signal, the *Oprichniki* pounced upon the Novgorod leaders and slaughtered them, while Ivan and his son went to an enclosure especially reserved for the torture of their victims and personally watched the horror. The townspeople were then rounded up, and from five hundred to a thousand of them were killed every day. Some of the inhabitants were burned, others racked to death, and still others drowned in the Volkhov River. Whole sleighs full of bound captives were run into the water; others were thrown into the river from bridges, while Ivan's soldiers, in boats, speared those who tried to swim to safety.

The slaughter, unbelievable in its ferocity, went on for weeks. A chronicler of the period wrote:

'And so great was the disaster and our agony of fear before the untamable savagery of the Czar, so terrible was the wrath of God at our sins, that for five weeks, or even more, a thousand persons a day, and at times even fifteen hundred, were cast into the water; but we were thankful for every day on which no more than five or six hundred persons were thrown into the river.'

Finally, Ivan grew weary of it all; he gave orders that the male survivors should be rounded up and brought before him. Only seventeen men could be found alive in all Novgorod. Ivan then spoke to them without remorse, without shame, without pity, in what must be one of the most remarkable speeches of all times by an annihilator of an entire city to its few wretched survivors.

'Seventeen men of Novgorod,' Ivan said, 'surviving through the grace of the Almighty Lord God and the spotless Mother of God and all the saints, pray for our God-fearing rule as Czar, for our sons Ivan and Feodor, and for our Christian army, that God may grant us victory over all our enemies and adversaries, visible and invisible. But may God judge him who has betrayed us and you. . . . May all the blood that has been shed fall upon them, and may the traitors be held accountable for it. But as for you, lament no more over all this, but live thankfully in this city.'

It is estimated in the Pskov Chronicle that sixty thousand persons were killed in Novgorod and other nearby towns. Novgorod, once the most advanced city in all of Russia, never recovered from Ivan's terror, and from then on became little more than a small, unimportant provincial town.

A year or so after Ivan's destruction of Novgorod, Moscow itself was subjected to one of the most calamitous events in its entire history—not from the hand of its own Czar, as had been the case in Novgorod, but from the ancient enemy of Russia, the Tartars, who were still rulers in the Crimea.

A horde of two hundred thousand horsemen suddenly descended upon Moscow in a predatory raid. Though this raid was of gigantic proportions, raids by the Tartars for booty and slaves were not unusual. The slave trade by the Tartars of the Crimea, in alliance with the Ottoman Turks, was one of their main sources of income. Russians, Lithuanians, and Poles were constantly being captured

by them, and then sold as slaves from Kaffa, the principal seaport
for the slave traffic at the time.

Heberstein wrote that he had heard that as many as eight hundred
thousand slaves were carried off by the Tartars over a period of only
a few years, most of them being sold to the Turks at Kaffa. 'Those
whom they could not sell', he wrote, 'they beat to death. For the
old and sick, for whom not much was paid, and who are not good
for work, are given by the Tartars to their young men, just as they
give hares to young hounds, to make them savage; they stone them
to death, throw them into the sea or over a precipice, or do whatever
they like with them. But those whom they sell or keep can work out
their freedom in six years' time; but they are not then allowed to
leave the country. They become servants or see in what other way
they can manage to provide for their own food.'

Russian girls, especially the blonde, fair-skinned ones, were especially desirable for the harems of the East, and they were the most
valuable slaves on the market. There is the story that the Sultan of
Constantinople asked his eldest son and heir, 'My son, wilt thou
conquer Crete for me?' His son replied, 'What have I to do with
Crete? I will conquer the land of the white Russian girls'.

So it was that in 1571, at the height of the Tartar-Turk slave
trade, which did not end until the nineteenth century, that the
Tartars, who were said to carry baskets with them on their horses
so as to kidnap Russian children, particularly girls, made their
greatest raid—and their boldest—against the very capital of the by
now powerful Russian state.

Ivan fled at their approach, taking with him his family and his
treasure from the Kremlin, leaving the city leaderless in its moment
of greatest crisis. He barricaded himself in the Troitsky Monastery,
but when the Tartars approached to the very gates of the city, he
fled still farther away to a hiding place in the far north more than
three hundred and fifty miles from Moscow.

The leaderless Russian army offered no resistance, and the
Tartars entered the defenceless city. The people of Moscow
panicked and fled towards the Kremlin to seek sanctuary there
behind its immense walls. But the Kremlin gates were closed to
them, the dignitaries within claiming that if they opened the gates
to the people of Moscow all of them would starve to death. Denied
refuge in the Kremlin, the inhabitants tried to escape the city.

However, most avenues of escape were closed, either by the Tartar soldiers themselves or by the great fires that had resulted from the Tartar torch. At the gates farthest away from the invading Tartars, the crush of people was unbelievable. Giles Fletcher wrote that people tried so desperately to get away that at those gates which were the farthest distance away from the enemy, the inhabitants were so wedged between the gate and certain streets leading to it that 'three ranks walked one upon the other's head, the uppermost treading downe those that were lower: so that there perished at that time (as was sayd) by the fire and the presse, the number of 800,000 [sic] people or more'.

Sir Jerome Horsey, the English envoy to Russia, wrote: 'The city and the suburbs, thirty miles compass, built most of fir and oak timber, was set on fire and burnt within six hours' space, with infinite thousands of men, women, and children, burnt, smothered to death . . . very few escaping both without and within the three walled castles. The river and ditches about Moscow stopped and filled with the multitude of people laden with gold, silver, jewels, chains, earrings, bracelets and treasure, that went for succour even to save their heads above water'.

The Kremlin itself was not too severely damaged, though the Tower of Ivan Velikii was partially destroyed. The Tartars finally withdrew, taking with them, besides treasure of all kinds, over a hundred thousand Russian girls and women to be sold in the slave marts.

Twenty-five years previously, after the great fire of 1547, Ivan was contrite and humble, promising the people of Moscow and Russia that he would rule well and wisely. Now, however, Ivan was not so affected by another equally great, if not greater, calamity. He promised the people nothing to compensate them for their loss of property and, even worse, their wives and daughters now in slavery. Concerning the calamity that had befallen Moscow, Ivan remarked, 'It was the hand of God punishing me for my sins. The Khan was only an instrument of God's anger!' He then returned from his sanctuary three hundred and fifty miles away from Moscow, and gave orders that Moscow should be rebuilt.

XI

Ivan the Terrible: Last Years

DURING this dreary period Ivan frequently felt that the Kremlin was not a suitable place for him to reside, and time after time he deserted it to live elsewhere. The Kremlin with its formal court life, its ceremonies that had been instituted by his grandfather and carried out so faithfully by his father, represented to Ivan too much of the very past he was striving to break Russia away from. He preferred, instead, the fortified lodges which he had had built in the *Oprichnina* quarter of the city and, later, the new palace at Alexandrov, which Ivan had ordered to be built for him and his *Oprichnina* henchmen.

From the time he moved into Alexandrov, he visited the Kremlin sporadically, and then only for brief periods. Alexandrov soon became the actual headquarters of Ivan's government, and eventually there grew up in the dense forests that surrounded it quite a large collection of houses that included his palace and the headquarters of the *Oprichnina*. Fearful as ever of being attacked by traitors, he had this secluded lair surrounded by a rampart and a moat, fortified still further by barricades that barred every possible approach to it. During the time that Alexandrov became the 'second capital', the Kremlin was for all intents and purposes not the seat of the government, for with power firmly in his hands, decisions were made at Alexandrov and not in Moscow.

The long succession of wives, some legal, some extra-legal, that followed after Anastasia's death, were often left behind in the *terem* quarters of the Kremlin. There, in the manner of the times, they were secluded from the gaze of men and idled away their time.

Ivan had little love or regard for any of his wives, except of course, his first—Anastasia. Shortly after the first Czarina's death, Ivan asked for the hand of the daughter of the King of Poland. The Polish king refused, sending Ivan instead a white mare which he averred was the only suitable female for the Czar. After the customary year's mourning for the late Czarina, Ivan finally married Maria, the daughter of a Moslem Circassian prince. She died shortly thereafter, and Ivan married again and again in rapid succession until he had accumulated the total of seven.

With regard to his many wives, Ivan, interestingly enough, was quite gallant. He did not kill them when he tired of them; he sent them away to convents where, generously supported by Ivan's gifts of money, they lived out their lives. Ivan never again after Anastasia's death seems to have been in love or even enamoured of a woman. His last six marriages had little meaning for him. Even his regular, organized harem of sixty young girls, and the hundreds of virgins that flitted through his bedroom in the Kremlin and other dwelling places, such as Alexandrov, were of no real consequence, and there is reason to believe that the harem was maintained so that he could appear as a powerful Eastern potentate, rather than for the gratification of his sexual desires.

One of the most interesting events in Ivan's personal life, for Westerners at least, was his profound yearning to marry a member of British royalty. Ever since Richard Chancellor's visit to Moscow in 1553, Ivan had been an Anglophile, and over the years had granted the British many trade privileges in Russia. Ivan felt so strongly in favour of the British and things British that near the end of his life, believing that his enemies were plotting his life, he asked Queen Elizabeth if she would grant him sanctuary in England should the occasion arise that he would have to flee Russia. The Queen agreed, even promising him the right to exercise his own worship in England.

Ivan at first wished to marry Queen Elizabeth herself, and by so doing unite the two powerful countries in an alliance. However, when Ivan realized that the Virgin Queen had no intention or desire to marry him, he asked for the hand of Lady Mary Hastings, who was described by a contemporary as a 'swarthy, pock-marked' young lady. Elizabeth, having heard of Ivan's 'terribleness', was loath to allow her to marry the Czar and tried to dissuade Ivan from his project. After Ivan had requested a picture of Lady Mary, the Queen sent one with the following letter:

'I do not find her [Lady Mary Hastings] beautiful, and I cannot imagine that she would be found so by such a connoisseur of beauty as my brother Ivan. She has but lately had the small pox and our painter has been obliged to depict her with a red face, deeply pitted.'

The Kremlin in the early twentieth century

Construction of the early walls

The Arsenal Tower

The Beklemishev Tower

The Secret Tower

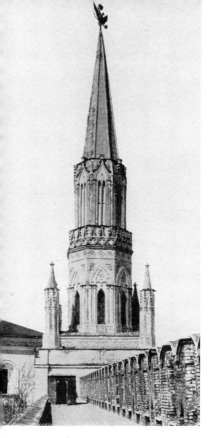

The southern wall of the Kremlin

The Nicholas Tower

The Trinity Tower

The Saviour Tower

The Cathedrals of the Archangel Michael (*left*) and the Annunciation (*right*)

The Church of the Saviour in the Wood

Top: The Cathedral of
the Assumption

Right: A doorway of
the Terem Palace

The interior
of the
Cathedral of
the Assumption

The Tower of Ivan the G

The Seat of the Patriarch
in the Cathedral of the Assumption

The Cathedral of St. Basil the Blessed

A staircase in the Cathedral of St. Basil the Blessed

Above: The Red Stairway and the Palace of Facets

Below: The Great Hall of the Palace of Facets

The City of Moscow in 1610

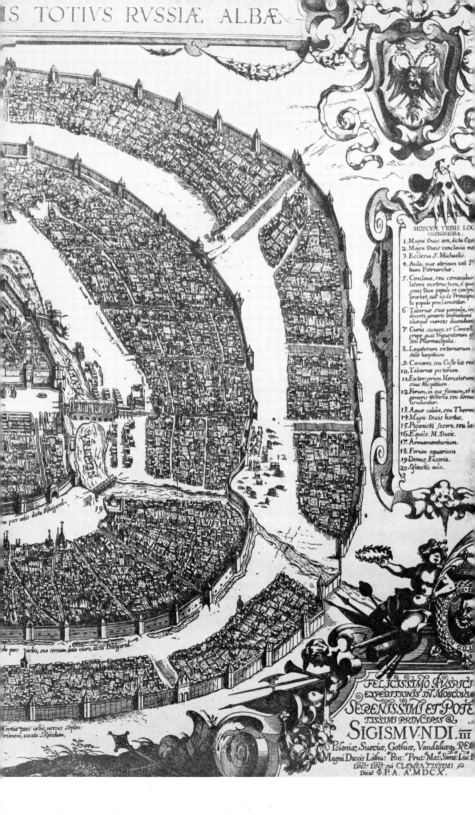

Above: A wedding feast in the Palace of Facets. *Below:* The reception of an ambassador in the seventeenth-century Kremlin

The Cathedral Square in the seventeenth century

The Terem Palace

A bedroom in the Terem Palace

A window in the Terem Palace

A staircase in the Terem Palace

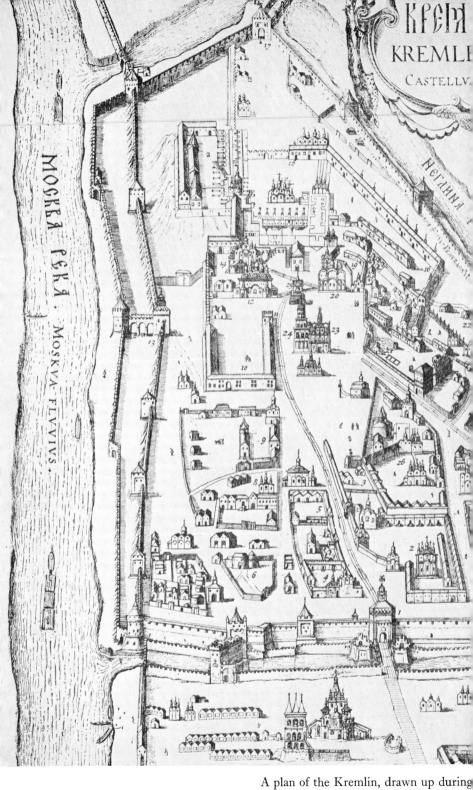

КРЕМЛ

KREMLE

CASTELLV

Неглина

МОСКВА РЕКА ·

MOSKVA FLVVIVS ·

A plan of the Kremlin, drawn up during

he reign of Boris Godunov (1598–1605)

The corridor between the
Konstantin Tower and
the Alarm Tower

A secret passage
near the
Nicholas Tower

A seventeenth-century model of the Kremlin

A seventeenth-century Easter procession in the Red Square

A view of the Kremlin from the Red Square in 1661

A view of the Kremlin from the Moscow River side in 1661

The Kremlin in the eighteenth century

The Grand Kremlin Palace

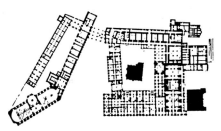

The lower floor of the Grand Kremlin Palace, with the *Oruzheinaia Palata* at the left

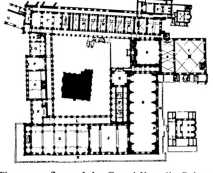

The upper floor of the Grand Kremlin Palace

A—*Red Stairway*
B—*Holy Vestibule*
C—*Palace of Facets*
D—*St. Vladimir's Hall*
E—*Antechamber*
F—*Grand Stairway*
G—*St. George's Hall*
J—*Alexander Hall*
K—*St. Andrew's Hall*
N—*Guard Room*

O—*St. Catherine's Hall*
P—*State Drawing Room*
Q—*State Bedroom*
T—*Chapel of the Holy Virgin's Nativity*
U—*Winter Garden*
A'—*Golden Czaritsa Chamber*
B'—*Church of St. Catherine the Martyr*
C'—*Church of Investiture*
D'—*Old Terem Chambers*
E'—*Church of the Saviour in the Wood*

St. George's Hall in the Grand Kremlin Palace

St. Andrew's Hall in the Grand Kremlin Palace

St. Vladimir's Hall in the Grand Kremlin Palace

The Seal of
the City of
Moscow

The crown of Grand Prince Vladimir Monomakh

The armament of a foot soldier

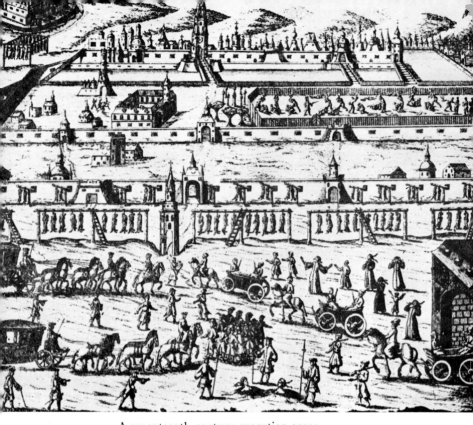

A seventeenth-century execution scene

The knout

Above: The Czar Cannon

Left: The Czar Bell

The double throne of Peter and Ivan

A parade carriage from the reign of Catherine the Great

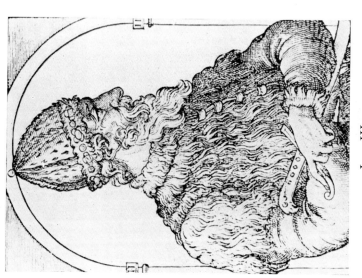

Ivan III

Ivan IV (the Terrible)

Above: Ivan III defies the Khan's emissaries

Below: Ivan the Terrible with the dying Czarevich

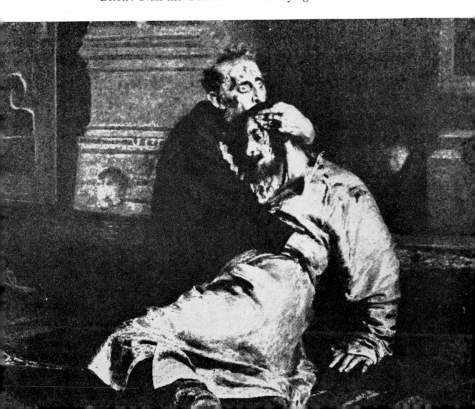

The False Dmitri

The Empress Marina

Peter the Great

Catherine I

Elizabeth I

Catherine the Great

Nicholas I   Peter the Great   Alexander I
Alexander III   Catherine the Great Nicholas II
Catherine I   Alexander II   Peter II

Napoleon fleeing the Kremlin during the burning of Moscow

The Red Square in 1820

The Coronation of Nicholas I in the Kremlin

A physical culture parade in the Red Square

The Lenin Mausoleum

The Red Square today

Lenin and Stalin in the Red Square Mausoleum

Pissemsky, Ivan's Ambassador to England, however, thought differently about the charms of Lady Mary, and described her as 'tall, well-built, and slender, possessing a pale face, grey eyes, and flaxen hair, and long and tapered fingers'.

To further discourage Ivan, the Queen gave secret instructions to Jerome Bowes, her envoy to Russia, not to anger the Czar but to gently dissuade him from his intentions. Bowes brought the matter to the Czar, carefully pointing out that Lady Mary was in poor health, that the life in Russia would be alien to her, and that she would be unhappy leaving her friends and family in England. Finally, Bowes told the Czar that the Queen had instructed him to say that unless the consent of the lady herself 'might be procured, which is a matter very doubtful, the match could not in any sort be brought to pass; considering that in those cases, as over the rest of our subjects, we have not authority other than by way of persuasion to make them like such matches as by good apparent reasons, may tend to their advancement'.

Incredulously, Ivan asked the Ambassador if it was indeed true that a subject in England could defy the Queen by not marrying one whom the Queen had designated, and that the Queen had no more power over her subjects than 'persuasion'. The Ambassador replied that such was the case. Infuriated, Ivan wrote the Queen the following sharp letter:

'We had supposed that thou wast a sovereign in thy State and in possession of the supreme power in the State, that thou hadst regard for the honour of thy rank and wast heedful of the advantage of thy realm. But now we see that in thy State other people rule, independently of thee—and what sort of people, at that? Common tradesmen, and thou art nothing but a common wench.'

Ivan's lack of respect for the Queen and his abuse of her was not only a result of his being turned down in marriage by Elizabeth, and later by Lady Mary, but was also rooted in the general attitude that the Russians of the time had towards women. The Western romantic attitude towards women was completely alien to the Russian, who regarded the relationship between the sexes in one of two ways—marriage in the patriarchal manner or carnal intercourse.

Among the upper classes women were confined to the *terem*, and mixed company was a rarity. The practice of isolating women was particularly severe in the Kremlin, where the system of secluding

4—TK

the distaff side of the royal family was not only a result of the established etiquette of the court but was a consequence of a deep-seated
fear that criminal attempts might be made upon them. The royal
consorts and daughters were so isolated that one foreigner at the
Kremlin wrote that 'barely one courtier in a hundred can boast of
having seen the Tsaritsa or the Princesses'.

Though the women of the royal family lived in seclusion, the
living quarters themselves were extremely elaborate. The apartment
of the Czaritsa in the Irene Palace, for instance, was a magnificent
place and contained some of the most exquisite art works and
decorative pieces in the Kremlin. Archbishop Arsenius, who visited
the Czaritsa Irina, Ivan's daughter-in-law, described it in detail.

'The apartment of the Czaritsa', he wrote, 'which was spherical
in shape, shone with the purest gold; and by the ingenious design
of the master builder, even words spoken in a whisper were dis-
tinctly audible. The vault was covered with gold and decorated with
wonderful paintings. The walls were adorned with the costliest
mosaics, which portrayed the acts of the saints, hosts of angels,
martyrs and elders of the church; while above the magnificent
throne, adorned with a blaze of jewels, a large icon of the Most Holy
Immaculate Virgin, with the Eternal Child in her arms, surrounded
by saints in golden crowns adorned with pearls, rubies, and
sapphires. The floor was covered with cunningly wrought carpets,
on which the sports of hunting and hawking were represented life-
like; other figures of birds and beasts, carved in precious metals,
glittered on all sides of the apartment. In the centre of the vaulted
ceiling, an exquisitely sculptured lion held in his mouth a serpent
twisted into a ring, from which a golden chandelier was suspended.'

The *terem* existed not only in the Kremlin; it was a common
feature in every nobleman's house. Except for the fact that they had
not the polygamous feature, the *terems* resembled to a marked degree
the harems of the Mohammedan countries. In the *terem*, which was
usually the uppermost storey of the house, the wife, daughters and
unmarried female relations who had not joined nunneries spent
their hours sewing, knitting, weaving, gossiping, or just plain idling.
None of them was allowed to be seen by men, except by the closest
male relations. Only on rare occasions did they leave their homes,
and then usually to attend church services. On still rarer occasions
wandering minstrels, usually blind, were allowed to enter the *terem*

to entertain the ladies with songs, accompanying themselves on *goussli*, or ancient zithers.

Except for a few who were 'liberated', almost all the women of the nobility were illiterate and completely ignorant of affairs in general. Even the upbringing of children was usually denied them the youngsters being entrusted to ignorant and superstitious nurses who filled the children's heads with all kinds of nonsense.

Women of the upper class were regarded as immature, helpless creatures who had to be kept under constant tutelage. The wife was considered to be inferior to her husband who regarded her and treated her as a child. He was her teacher; she was his pupil.

From the time she was born until she died, the noblewoman was always under the guardianship of some man—a father, a husband, her husband's father, an elder brother, grandfather, uncle. She was constantly being admonished 'to obey her husband as the slave obeys his master' and to look upon herself as a person who had no rights. She was the property of the man and looked upon him as her lord. And as a slave or as a pupil, or both, she dared not object when her master and teacher punished her. In fact, the husband was urged to chastise his wife, and the priest Sylvester in his book on conduct, *Domostroy*, urged the husband not to neglect the chastisement of his wife, advising him not to employ too thick a stick, however, or staffs tipped with iron, or whip her before other men, but to correct her without anger or violence in private. It was not an uncommon sight, even among the nobility, to see an old, feeble husband beating a fat, robust wife with a cudgel, the woman not daring to defend herself or even to make the slightest sign of protest.

The standards of beauty at the time, especially among the nobility, as stated in a book on beauty which appeared somewhat later but which applies just as well to Ivan's time, were that a woman should have 'a face as white as snow, poppy-red cheeks, black eyebrows, round as a cartwheel; eyes like a hawk, the face of a white hare, and the gait of a swan, and a well-rounded figure'. In order to achieve the 'well-rounded figure', women often stayed in bed for weeks on end, gorging themselves with food and drinking vodka.

By present standards of feminine toilet, the colouring of their faces was very complicated and unaesthetic. One visitor to Moscow wrote that the women 'paint themselves all colours—not only their faces, but their eyes, neck and hands. They lay on white, red, blue and black. Black eyelashes they tint white, and white ones black, or some dark colour, but they put on the paint so badly that it is visible to everyone'. Moscow women considered white teeth suitable 'only for blackamoors and monkeys', and therefore painted theirs black. Together with their heavily painted faces, their black teeth, and their enormous 'well-rounded figures', the noblewomen of the period seemed to a visiting Italian nobleman as 'no longer retaining any refined vestige of their sex'.

Though women played an important part in court life in most of Europe, they had, except on a few rare occasions, no influence in the Kremlin until long after Ivan's time. It was a male society, and women had no place in it except as breeders and housekeepers.

As time went on, however, women finally did manage to escape from the stultifying influences of the *terem*, and by the time of Catherine the Great, and for some years before, were participating to an extent in the life about them. Nevertheless, even as late as Catherine's time, the Russian noblewoman had little of the refinement of her Western counterparts, matching her only in the number of bedroom intrigues, which was standard behaviour in the history of all European courts. As for the Russian noblewoman and her love life as she became liberated from the *terem*, Masson, the French courtier, wrote the following informative bit about the court of Catherine:

'Nowhere did so many women arrogate to themselves the right of making the first advances, and being the active party, in affairs of love. The example of Catherine was but too well calculated to give them those bold and masculine tastes and manners.

'Almost all the ladies of the Court kept men, with the title and office of favourites. I do not say lovers, for that would imply sentiment; while theirs was merely gross desire, or, frequently, a wish to follow the fashion. This taste had become as common as eating and drinking, or dancing and music. Tender intrigues were unknown, and strong passions still more rare. Debauchery and ambition had banished love. Marriage was merely an association, in which convenience alone was considered; it was fortunate if friendship sometimes came, unsought, to lighten the chains which the interests of parents or vanity alone, had formed.'

In Ivan's time, however, what debaucheries there were, were almost always initiated by the man. Ivan himself, not satisfied with his harem of sixty women and the hundreds of virgins that graced his bed from time to time over the years, often ordered a girl brought to him that he happened to see on a hunting trip in the countryside or during a canter through the streets of Moscow. Except for condemnation by an intrepid clergyman now and then, the Czar was not criticized. Only Prince Kurbsky, from his self-imposed exile in Poland, dared to raise his voice against the actions of Ivan. In one of his letters he accused Ivan, among other things, of consorting with 'unworthy boyars, those who are now the companions of thy effeminacy and debauch, and who bring thee their children for thy lust'.

Kurbsky's condemnation of Ivan for his 'effeminacy' was caused by Ivan having as his constant companion for more than ten years a handsome, vigorous, and audacious man by the name of Basmanov. This companion was never away from the Czar's side, even sharing the same room with him in the Kremlin. Whether Kurbsky's criticism of Ivan for his friendship with Basmanov was just is open to question, since it was the custom for a Czar to have a companion. In fact, Ivan's father, Vasili III, had his particular boyar friend sleep in the same room with him and his wife, Helena Glinsky, which later cast suspicion on the true paternity of Ivan the Terrible himself.

As violent as Kurbsky's criticism of Ivan's personal life was, it was mild in comparison to Ivan's criticism of himself. By nature a brooding, reflective man, almost pathologically possessed with searching his own soul and actions, he constantly tortured himself with his own condemnations. This inward fire had a telling effect on his very person and eventually consumed him. As a young man he was described as being tall, well made, with high shoulders, muscular arms, and a broad chest. His eyes, though small and restless, sparkled; his nose was large and aquiline; and his hair, beard, and mustachios were of a beautiful texture and of imposing length. Later, after his false abdication, though still a man in his thirties, his brooding, his intellectual and religious fits, his very intensity of feeling, even more than his excessive drinking and sexual promiscuities, changed him considerably. At this time he was described as a man with 'a dark fierceness . . . his eyes were sunken . . . he was almost bald'.

And still much later, in 1581, when he was but a little over fifty years old, a tragedy occurred that not only turned him almost overnight into a decrepit old man in appearance but into a man who lost the will to live.

For some years, since the middle seventies of the sixteenth century, the Terror had tapered off, for Ivan, with his expanded empire, his boyar enemies partially beaten into submission, and his power consolidated, now felt secure; that is, as secure as so suspicious a monarch as Ivan could ever feel. By now he had become more reflective, more than ever taken up with his family, compensating himself for the loss of Anastasia—whom he never forgot or ceased to mourn ('Ah, had you only not separated me from the love of my youth, then the sacrifice of Kronos would not have taken place', he wrote fifteen years after Anastasia's death)—with his children and, to an extent, with his last wife, who because of her gentleness reminded him somewhat of his beloved Anastasia.

As with most monarchs approaching old age, Ivan's thoughts turned towards the continuation of his dynasty. The heir to Ivan's throne was his eldest son, the Czarevich Ivan, who was the offspring of his true love Anastasia, and, therefore, understandably his pride and joy. The Czarevich himself was a capable young man, just the opposite of his younger brother, Feodor, who was timid and monkish and, according to most accounts, feeble-minded. Ivan's third son, Dmitri, was still a young child.

But the Czarevich Ivan was destined not to reign. In 1581, as mentioned previously, a bitter tragedy, the result of Ivan's inordinate temper, took place. The Czarevich, a man of twenty-seven, was married by now and lived with his wife in the Kremlin, in quarters close to the Czar's. One evening Ivan entered his son's apartment and was greeted by his daughter-in-law, who was pregnant, in a dress that Ivan considered to be too revealing and coquettish for a woman in her condition. He upbraided her harshly for her immodesty. The Czarevich, resenting his father's condemnation of his wife, sprang to her defence. Angry words passed between them. Ivan became furious at what he considered to be his son's lack of respect, and suddenly struck the Czarevich with the iron-pointed staff he always carried with him. The Czarevich fell to the floor grievously wounded. A few days later he died.

Ivan's grief was unbounded. For days afterwards he gave himself up to wild lamentations, banging his head on the floor and tearing at his beard. He vowed that he would abdicate the throne and enter a monastery, though he never did. To all intents and purposes, his life was at an end; he never fully recovered from the shock of killing his own son and incessantly indulged himself in prayers and self-condemnation. He asked that Mass be said not only for his own son but for all the victims of the Terror, even furnishing long lists of names of those he had murdered, so that the people by their prayers could save the souls of his victims and thus his own as well.

Still, his greatest pity was for himself, and in his last days he constantly looked upon himself as a sinner, albeit a repentant one. No longer arrogant in his unlimited power, no more the inheritor of the mantle of the Caesars, he viewed himself as little more than a miserable human being, a victim of a life that was too demanding, too harsh, too full of problems and torments and tricks of fate. And near the end he cried out pitifully that he was, in spite of being one of the most powerful men in all the world, unloved, unwanted and alone in his misery. Revealingly—and pathetically—he wrote:

'The body is exhausted, the spirit is sick, the cords of my soul and my body have been stretched too tight, and there is no physician who can heal me. I waited for one capable of suffering and mourning with me; but nobody came to console me, they all returned evil for good and responded to all my love with hatred.'

Yet, in spite of his weariness with life and disgust with the people around him, he did not face his approaching death calmly. He prayed loudly, wildly that he should be delivered from his illnesses; he put his faith in doctors, then cursed them and called in sooth-sayers and astrologers, hoping to get from them a favourable sign. He insisted on painful mortifications of his flesh, indulged himself in hysterical pleas to God to be saved, and then, reversing his actions, spent many days in fervent, silent prayer.

On the day of his death he ordered that his priceless treasures be brought before him, asking those about him if it were possible that the glittering gems might have certain secret healing powers. Then, with his treasures about him, he sat down to play a game of chess with Boris Godunov, Czaritsa Irina's brother. As he set the king in place, he fell back in a swoon and shortly thereafter, on March 28, 1584, he died.

When his death was announced to the people of Muscovy, the entire nation went into mourning to an extent that had never before been seen in Russia. Even the wives and children of the thousands

XII

The Underground Kremlin

THOUGH it is the aboveground Kremlin that has always captured the imagination of Russians and non-Russians alike and has been the symbol of the Russian state and power for hundreds of years, there is another Kremlin, so to speak, one that is relatively unknown. It is the underground Kremlin—a vast network of passageways, crypts, waterways, hidden doors, and all manner of mysterious phenomena that would make the trappings of a Gothic novel seem pale, indeed.

Like most ancient cities, the Kremlin—which is, in fact, a miniature city—was constructed with an elaborate underground structure; the numerous crypts were used as burial places for the dead or to store treasures, and the various passageways, many of them tunnelling under the Kremlin walls and leading to houses outside the Kremlin area, were used for secret ingress and egress to and from the Kremlin. In addition, there were passageways that led to underground water supplies.

The Italian Aristotele, for instance, in building the Cathedrals of the Assumption and the Annunciation, honeycombed their subterranean areas with all manner of crypts and passageways. Solario constructed *tainiks*, secret passages, in several of the towers he built, a couple of them leading to the Moscow River. Only thirty years or so ago, during the construction of the Lenin Mausoleum, a shaft of unknown depth was discovered in the Senate Tower, which some experts believe might well be the main trap door leading from the Kremlin to subterranean Moscow itself.

Many of these *tainiks* have never been seen, for they have been sealed off by later construction work, and their existence is known not by actual sight but by accounts of them written down in one place or another. For instance, one account, the so-called Krekshin chronicle, contains the following passage: 'Peter the foreigner, that is Solario, built two towers with *tainiks* and many chambers with underground passages divided off by heavy doors; also walled waterways like rivers flowing underground across the whole of the Kremlin, as protection in the event of a siege'.

Many of the underground passages extended from the Kremlin to various points in Moscow; they were divided into sections, and some of them it seems were the private property of individuals, who had heavy iron doors with heavy padlocks erected to bar entrance to them by others besides themselves. The sealing off of passages by means of heavy doors and padlocks was not done out of spite or an inordinate desire to keep strangers out, but was a necessity, for it was here that the wealthy kept their prized possessions.

A Prince Shcherbatov, who undertook an investigation of certain phases of the underground Kremlin in 1894, discovered a passage near the Nicholas Tower that reached to a depth of thirty-five feet. This one passage alone, he concluded, began at the Secret Tower, ran across the entire Kremlin, went under the Kremlin wall in the vicinity of the Nicholas Tower, continued on under the moat, where it became for a while a vast chamber, and then continued on into Nicholas Street, in the Kitaigorod section of Moscow. Other passageways of this nature have also been discovered; one of them, for instance, going underground from the Secret Gate, passing under St. Basil's Cathedral, and terminating in a section of Moscow called Varvarka.

The Kremlin, it must be remembered, in addition to being a miniature city was a fortress, and as such the possibility of its being able to sustain itself during a long siege was kept in mind by the designers. Thus the Italians who built it provided for, among other things, a water supply within the Kremlin area that could be relied upon. The focal point for the water system was the corner Arsenal Tower, for under it was a spring. Solario built a cistern around it, and from it had pipes placed so that they led into various underground galleries. Over the years the pipes decayed, and the water disappeared into the ground, causing at one time serious deterioration to the tower itself.

From time to time, other waterways have been discovered. One of them that was found, for instance, had been blocked off by the building of the Arsenal in the early eighteenth century. Numerous waterways and other passageways connected the Kremlin with Kitaigorod, many of these passages being designed for emergency entrance to, and exit from, the Kremlin, especially after the Kremlin was turned into an island by the construction of the moat around it.

Certain extremely powerful people in the Kremlin had passageways that led from the citadel directly to houses that they occupied in other parts of Moscow. On occasion, these passageways were instrumental in saving a person's life. For instance, a certain boyar named Morozov, who during the reign of Czar Alexi was an extremely influential figure, abused his power and a rebellion flared up in Moscow. A mob broke into the Kremlin and burned Morozov's house, including his carriage made of silver, a wedding present from the Czar himself. The mob demanded Morozov's life as well as the lives of two of his supporters. The Czar, frightened, handed over one of the men to the crowd, who killed him on the spot. Morozov, however, together with the other aide, escaped from the Kremlin by means of an underground passage that led out of the Kremlin to an area in Moscow called Dmitrovka. His companion then escaped to a monastery outside Moscow, but Morozov was recognized by wagoners, who raised a hue and cry, and, together with other Moscow citizens, pursued him. Morozov, with the enraged mob at his heels, was fleeing in the direction of the Kremlin when suddenly he disappeared. Unknown to his pursuers he had entered the underground maze by means of a secret entrance, and had made his way back to the Kremlin. There he was given refuge by the Czar, and after a few days, when the temper of the people had cooled, the Czar led Morozov before the townspeople and begged them to forgive him. They did.

Though the underground system of passageways was used on occasion to go in and out of the Kremlin and for waterways, its most important function, in time, was as a storage place for the vast wealth accumulated by the royal family and rich boyars. Ivan the Terrible made a practice of demanding to be shown presents that any of his court had received from foreigners, and when he liked a particular object, he expropriated it. After military compaigns, he came back to the Kremlin with his carts filled with booty. From Novgorod alone, for example, he took away over three hundred carts loaded with gold, silver, precious stones, and other valuables.

Over the years, as the Kremlin buildings, because of fire and invasion and the need for expansion and improvement, were reconstructed or torn down to make way for new structures, many of these passageways were sealed up. Therefore, in more modern times, it has been almost impossible to trace thoroughly the underground Kremlin, without literally destroying the foundations of many present buildings or, at best, digging deeply under the present buildings, with the constant danger of doing permanent damage to them. No government, Czarist or Communist, has been willing to undertake such elaborate and dangerous operations, with the result that what is known about the Kremlin that lies underground is of a fragmentary nature, most of it the result of sporadic efforts undertaken during the past three hundred years to find what several archaeologists believe would be one of the greatest discoveries of contemporary archaeology—the so-called lost library of Ivan the Terrible.

Ivan, in addition to being a self-appointed scourge of God, and as such one of the greatest tyrants in history, was also for his time a man of great learning and culture. Even as a young boy, Ivan was deeply interested in antiquity, and throughout his life was an avid collector of ancient manuscripts, both Russian and foreign.

The core of his library were Greek manuscripts that Sophia Paleologus brought with her, in 1472, as a dowry for Ivan III. What these manuscripts were, no one knows, but there is little doubt that they existed, for they are mentioned in several chronicles of the time. Some antiquarians, such as Dr Edward Tremer, who was a lecturer-philologist at Strassburg University in the late nineteenth century, believed that they may well have contained, among other priceless ancient Greek works, the manuscripts of Homer.

Vasili III, Ivan's father, was also a collector of manuscripts on a small scale, and the Kremlin collection, especially of Russian manuscripts, grew during his reign. However, it was Ivan himself who relentlessly pursued the gathering together of manuscripts from all over Russia as well as a good part of Europe and the Near East. Though known as a skinflint, Ivan spared no expense in tracking down valuable works, and dispatched agents to all parts of Europe, the then-hostile Ukraine, and Turkish Byzantium, with strict orders to bring back, at whatever cost, manuscripts in which he was interested. His agents were singularly successful, and soon Ivan's collection grew into, considering the times, an extensive library, reputed to contain over eight hundred rare books and manuscripts. In 1554, from the Ukraine, and especially from Kiev, the seat of ancient Russian scholarship, Ivan's agents obtained almost the entire extant collection of Yaroslav the Wise who, prior to Ivan, had been the most cultured prince in Russia. In addition, the agents not only brought back a large number of books and manuscripts but Kievan scholars as well.

Ivan understood full well the great value of his library, and in order to safeguard the works from possible damage by fire, theft, or destruction by invaders, he had them secreted in underground vaults. The Czar's envoys scoured Russia for scholars who could translate some of the works, but Russian scholarship in the sixteenth century was not very advanced, and he was forced to turn to foreigners, mainly Germans, for assistance. A learned German, the Dorpat pastor Vetterman, was persuaded to undertake the task. Six persons —three Russians, presumably security guards rather than scholars, and three German scholars—were assigned to Vetterman, to assist him. The vaults were then opened to Vetterman and his staff. However, the translations never took place. The exact reason is unknown, though two guesses have been ventured. One is that the Germans refused to work in the gloomy underground vaults under constant supervision by the security forces of the Czar. The other possible explanation that has been given is that the Russians themselves refused to be, for all intents and purposes, incarcerated in underground dungeons, cultural considerations notwithstanding.

Whatever the reason, the fact is that the project was abandoned, Vetterman and the other Germans were dismissed, and in a rage at being thwarted by such human frailty, Ivan ordered the vaults to be sealed. To this very day the vaults containing the priceless manuscripts have never been found.

Throughout the following centuries attempts were made to unearth the lost library. The Poles, when they captured the Kremlin during the Time of Troubles, looked for it. They did not find the lost library, though they did discover one manuscript, not part of the library, that had to do with certain Constantinian privileges. Later this document was presented by the Roman Catholic Poles to the Vatican as a gift.

The next serious attempt to find the lost library was undertaken during the regency of Princess Sophia, during the early reign of Peter the Great. She entrusted the task to one Makaryev, who was sworn to secrecy concerning his efforts, as well as any information about the library that was given him. He penetrated the maze of underground passageways, to some extent at least, and there are records that attest to the fact that he managed to make his way underground from the Secret Tower as far as the Arsenal Tower. It is not clear at what place in his underground journey he saw certain arched chambers that contained chests piled to the very top of the chamber, but he did see the chambers and the chests, or so at least he reported to Princess Sophia. The Princess told Makaryev to keep the information secret, under pain of death, and that when times were more propitious further action would be taken. However, Sophia soon lost her power, and Makaryev shortly thereafter died not without fortunately revealing his secret to the sexton Konon Osipov, the bellringer of the Moscow Church of St. John the Baptist.

Osipov, it appears, was so fired by the magnitude of the secret that had been entrusted to him by Makaryev that he devoted the next thirty years of his life, until his death, to the task of discovering the treasure. The Moscow archives during this period briefly mention his searches, and from these tiny bits of information it would seem that the following occurred.

In 1724, Osipov, after numerous attempts, finally convinced Peter the Great to order the Senate to furnish the necessary means for exploring and excavating the underground Kremlin. Osipov, having Makaryev's experience to go on, proceeded in the same way that his predecessor had done, by starting at the Secret Tower and proceeding to the Arsenal Tower. Somewhere along the way, by a stroke of luck, he discovered an opening with steps that led to— where? He did not know, and could not find out at the time, because the passageway was blocked by a fallen arch that had to be cleared away if he wished to proceed farther. However, the immediate section was in a deteriorated condition and to dig there might have caused a general collapse of the area. He was forbidden to do so, and orders were given to fill up the passageway.

Almost distraught at this bad luck, Osipov tried to beat the problem by digging deep under the Kremlin so that he could cross below the blocked path. In the opinion of an early twentieth-century archaeologist, this was an extremely rash thing to do, since Osipov by necessity would have to excavate to a depth of twenty *arshin*, or about forty-seven feet. His plan failed and subsequently all excavations stopped.

Soon afterwards Peter died and Osipov found it impossible to interest Peter's successor in what had by now become an obsession with him. He made repeated requests to Peter II, and to his successor, Anna I, and finally in about 1735, after ten years of fruitless entreaty, Osipov got Anna and her minister-lover Biron to agree to allow him to take certain actions. What these actions were the documents in the archives do not state, but the conclusion may possibly be drawn that because of the lack of mention the results were not important enough to be recorded, or that Osipov, an extremely old man by now, died soon after the 'actions' began, and there was nothing to report.

For the next hundred and fifty years or so, little or nothing was done to uncover the lost library, though the story about it had become a matter of some archaeological interest, and in Russia itself almost a legend.

The Germans, who had always been most active in scholarly work on Russia and, in the main, most responsible for uncovering and translating ancient manuscripts and archives, now took an active interest. The previously mentioned Dr Tremer arrived in Moscow in 1891 with the avowed purpose of trying to find the Homeric manuscripts, which he believed were possibly part of Ivan's library. The Russian scholars of the time viewed him with 'deadly scepticism', as Tremer complained in an article he wrote later about his experiences in Russia.

Tremer was unsuccessful in gaining permission to make a search for the lost library and returned to Strassburg University, more convinced than ever, because of what information he had been able to uncover in Russia, that the library of Ivan actually did exist, and that its treasures were as great as he suspected they were and much greater than most other authorities believed them to be. In his article Tremer expressed the fervid hope that though he had failed other archaeologists 'would not rest until it would be completely proven that the aforementioned library was actually destroyed'.

Tremer's article caused a sensation, and after a while the Czarist government made some half-hearted attempts to excavate again for the library, with no results. Then, for the next twenty years, nothing at all was done. Just before the outbreak of the First World War, however, a commission presented to the Czarist government a project that called for varied activities to uncover various treasures, among them the lost library. An archaeological mission was set up, and at the same time access was given scholars to Russian archives.

What was most important was that the government agreed to allow the underground Kremlin to be explored. Excavations actually began, especially around the Arsenal Tower, and resulted in some valuable clues, but the outbreak of the war halted activities.

For the past forty years or so if there has been any activity under the Communists to uncover the library, the efforts have been secret. Except for a plea by I. Stelletsky, a Russian archaeologist, in 1924, that the Bolshevik government should aid the search for the lost library now that there was a new régime that had 'a passionate enthusiasm for the building of a new life [that] will melt, at last, the frozen crust of inveterate Russian scepticism in this process', nothing seems to have been forthcoming from the Soviets on this hidden treasure—a treasure that Tremer fully believed was not only the concern of scientists and specialists, 'but the loss of which should grieve the whole educated world, and the discovery of which would enrich Russia with new glory'.

Obviously Stelletsky agreed with his German colleague, for he, too, firmly believed that if the lost library were found 'Russia would renew for Europe the times of the Medici, Petrarch, and Boccaccio, when from the dust of libraries was extracted the unknown treasures of antiquity'.

XIII

The Time of Troubles

FEODOR I (1584–98), who succeeded his father Ivan IV to the throne, has the distinction of being the only ruler of Russia about whom most historians agree—that he was a feeble-minded, almost idiotic, weakling whose main desire in life was to ring church bells.

Giles Fletcher described Feodor as an individual 'of a mean stature, somewhat lowe and grosse, of a sallowe complexion, and inclining to the Dropsie, Hawke nosed, unsteady in his pose by reason of some weaknesse of his limmes, heavy and unactive, yet commonly smiling almost to a laughter'. Sapiega, the Polish envoy to Russia at the time, described Feodor as 'short of stature, and meagre withal, and hath a gentle voice as of one who doth suffer, and likewise a simple countenance. Of mind hath he little or he hath none at all, inasmuch as, when seated upon the throne and receiving an ambassador, he refraineth not from smiling, nor from gazing first upon his sceptre, and then upon his orb'. The Swedish Ambassador, Petreius, wrote that Feodor 'was by nature practically an imbecile', that he took pleasure only in spiritual matters, and that it was his frequent custom to run from church to church, for the purpose of ringing the bells and having Mass celebrated.

The only kind words written about Feodor centred about his piety, for the Czar, as one writer commented, 'did all his life shun the baubles and vanities of this world, and think of things heavenly'. That he was extremely devout there is no doubt, and the historian Kluchevsky ventured the opinion that this extreme devoutness may have made him appear imbecilic, that he was actually cut out for a monk's cell and not a throne, and it was for that kind of life that he always yearned and for which his character fitted him.

Feodor inherited this weak physical nature from his mother, Anastasia, who was in failing health when she gave birth to him. Throughout his childhood he was surrounded on all sides by brutality and terror, and the horrible excesses of the *Oprichnina* and the hangmen, who led a busy life at the execution block on Red Square

just outside the Kremlin walls. As a child he was described as 'an un-
dersized, white-faced stripling who was disposed to dropsy and possessed of an unsteady, quasi-senile gait, due to a congenital affliction
of the lower limbs'. And in later life he was described thus:

'Though on his face there was a constant smile, it was a lifeless
one. It was the same smile with which, in his youth, he had had to
defend himself from the capricious anger of his father; until, in time
and more especially after the terrible death of his elder brother, that
smile became converted, through the force of habit, into an involuntary, automatic grimace. Often goaded to madness by his father, he
gradually lost all will-power, yet never quite dropped the look of
crushed abasement which he had learned so persistently to wear.'

There is little doubt that Ivan despised Feodor. The son was the
antithesis of the father in character, in intelligence, appearance and
ambition. Ivan made no secret of his loathing for Feodor, and even
on his deathbed kept his gaze on Boris Godunov, as though request-
ing him to protect the throne, while completely ignoring Feodor, his
son and heir. On more than one occasion, Ivan is supposed to have
said that all Feodor was capable of was to be a bellringer in a monastery—and a minor one at that. 'He is a sacristan, not a Czar's son',
Ivan once remarked bitterly.

In the circumstances, power passed now into the hands of the
boyars, who openly treated Feodor with contempt, even as Ivan
before them had done. Soon, a struggle took place between the
nobles for the regency, involving, among others, Nikita Romanov,
Feodor's uncle; Boris Godunov, Feodor's brother-in-law; Prince
Belsky; and Prince Shuisky. Dmitri, Czar Feodor's half brother and
the son of Ivan's seventh wife, was exiled from Moscow and sent to
Uglich, where he died under mysterious circumstances, an event
that was later the cause of one of the most fantastic chapters in
Russian history.

Though Feodor was Czar for fourteen years, it was in name only,
the reins of government passing from one group to another, though
Boris Godunov finally emerged as the real power behind the throne.
When Feodor died in 1598, leaving no heir behind him, the Moscow
branch of the house of Rurik, which had reached its apogee with
Ivan IV, came to a dismal, inglorious end, and ushered in a period
known as the Time of Troubles (1598–1613), which has been characterized as a 'school of violence, anarchy, political madness, treachery,

deceit, levity and petty egotism incapable of realizing the common needs'.

For the next fifteen years Russia was ruled first by Boris Godunov, until his death in 1605, and then, until the election of Michael Romanov as Czar in 1613, by a series of usurping boyars, the False Dmitri, and even, for a short period, by the Poles.

Boris Godunov, who was of Tartar ancestry, was a man of great ability and political shrewdness, though there is reason to believe that he was illiterate. Still, illiterate or not, he was a man of great bearing and dignity, who captured the popular imagination at times, and at other times forced the populace to adulate him. There is the story that when Boris, feigning a desire not to accept the throne, was approached by a delegation to accept the crown that the Sobor, the National Assembly, had offered him, a great cry went up for him to accept, the cry taking the form of a pathetic moan of entreaty by those present. However, there is reason to believe that the moan was not spontaneous, for there are accounts that say that those people who did not moan loudly enough were struck by Boris's supporters until they did.

Czar Boris's reign (1598–1605) was marked by intrigues, plots and counter-plots, and murder of real or supposed enemies who threatened his rule. From 1601 to 1603 there was a famine in which thousands of people died of starvation. Food was so scarce that cannibalism was resorted to, with parents eating their children, children their parents; and the flesh of human beings, peddled as beef, was offered for sale at exorbitant prices in the market places. Bandit gangs roamed the countryside and, on occasion, were bold enough to steal and murder at the very gates of Moscow itself. Though Boris seemed to have compassion for the poor, establishing public-works projects in an attempt to alleviate the suffering, he became more and more unpopular.

In this difficult situation his very right to the throne was challenged by a young man who claimed to be Prince Dmitri, the youngest son of Ivan the Terrible, who had supposedly been murdered in Uglich in 1591. The identity of the claimant is not clear, though he might have been one Yuri Otrepyev, the son of a gentleman retainer who had himself been a retainer in the household of the eldest Romanov. Later, he probably became a monk named Gregory, wandered from monastery to monastery, and then became a clerk in the offices of the Patriarch of Moscow. Throughout his wanderings, and during his position with the Patriarch, he said quite openly that someday he would become the Czar of Russia. Owing to these statements he was exiled by Boris to a monastery near the White Sea. In a short while he escaped, leaving a note in his cell that read: 'I am the Czarevich Dmitri, son of Ivan IV, I shall not forget your kindness when I am on my father's throne'.

He then journeyed south and joined the Zaporog Cossacks, where he learned how to ride and fight and also how to speak Polish. When he finally left the Cossacks, he entered the service of a Polish prince. While in the prince's service, he feigned a serious illness, had a Roman Catholic priest to attend him, and entrusted a document to him that read: 'I am the Czarevich Dmitri, son of Ivan IV. I was saved from my murderers and hidden. A priest's son died in my place'. The priest showed the document to the prince, who relayed the news to the King of Poland. Believing, or wishing to believe, that the young man was indeed the Czarevich Dmitri, so that he could utilize him to gain power in Russia, the King gave the adventurer, who became known in history as the False Dmitri, a palace, servants, money, and honoured him as the Czarevich, the rightful heir to the throne of Russia. In addition, the False Dmitri was affianced to Marina Mniszek, the daughter of the Voivode of Sandomir, though the nuptials were deferred until he should gain the throne.

The news that Ivan the Terrible's son was alive spread throughout Russia; it caused such a stir that Boris was forced to take cognizance of the movement, and he denounced the pretender as an impostor. The powerful Prince Shuisky and the Patriarch Job added their voices to the Czar's denunciation, but the False Dmitri's cause gained more and more adherents. Finally, in 1604, at the head of an army, the False Dmitri crossed the Polish-Russian frontier and headed towards Moscow. Malcontents and adventurers joined him by the thousand. After a series of Russian defeats, Boris chose Prince Shuisky to lead the Czarist forces against the pretender, and the False Dmitri was severely beaten. However, shortly thereafter, he was reinforced by forty thousand Cossacks, who rallied to his cause. The Russian army became demoralized not only because the pretender now had a formidable fighting force but, as it was said at the time, 'It is difficult to battle against a born Czarevich'.

In the midst of the crisis, Boris Godunov died, on April 13, 1605.

One of the most enigmatic figures of Russian history—mainly as a result of his own craftiness, which made it difficult to judge his true intentions—even his death was mysterious. At the time it was said that Boris Godunov, who 'lived like a lion, reigned like a fox, and died like a dog', had poisoned himself.

Two months later the False Dmitri entered Moscow in triumph, with the ostensible support not only of the Russian people but of many powerful Russian boyars. He was immediately crowned Czar. Almost from the outset of his reign, his right to the throne was challenged by various influential boyars, who not only wished to have power in their hands but also resented the Polish influences the False Dmitri and his Polish advisers were fostering upon the Russian court. In order to answer charges that he was not the real Dmitri, the Czar arranged for a meeting with his supposed mother, the Czaritsa Maria Nagoy, who had entered a convent and was now known as the nun Martha. At a dramatic meeting in a tent in a village near Moscow that was attended by many notables, Martha when confronted by her 'son' embraced him and swore that he was indeed her offspring.

Why Martha should have sworn that the Czar was her son is not clear, but the result of her strange action was not what the False Dmitri hoped it would be. The opposition was not silenced. Several months later, when the False Dmitri dropped the title of 'Czar' and assumed the title of 'Emperor', Russian sensibilities were further injured.

Ten months after he became ruler of Russia, he called Marina from Poland to join him in Moscow where, in an elaborate wedding ceremony in the Kremlin, she became Empress. When news spread that Marina had refused to give up her Roman Catholicism for Russian Orthodoxy, the opposition, led by Prince Shuisky, became strengthened. Less than two weeks after the wedding a mob broke into the Kremlin with the avowed intention of killing the Emperor. When the mob entered his bedroom, the False Dmitri jumped out of a window to escape them, and as he lay injured in the courtyard, he was murdered. His naked body was exposed for a while to public view on the Red Square, and then his remains were put into a cannon and shot in the direction of Poland, from where he had started his triumphal march into Russia. The Empress Marina escaped.

The tragi-comedy continued. A second False Dmitri claimed

power. Marina made her way to his camp and joined forces with him, claiming that the second False Dmitri was really the first one, that he had not been killed in the Kremlin but had escaped. Martha again was called on to verify that the second False Dmitri was her son. Once again there was a publicly staged reunion; Martha and the second False Dmitri embraced and shed tears, with Martha vowing as strongly the second time as she had the first time that the pretender was her son. The second False Dmitri at the head of an army marched towards Moscow, rallying people around him for his cause. A third and a fourth and fifth False Dmitri arose in various parts of Russia, all claiming to be the youngest son of Ivan the Terrible.

Though this was the most flagrant case of impostors in Russian history, it was by no means a rare thing. The archives of seventeenth- and eighteenth-century Russia contain many accounts of other impostors beside False Dmitris; there were False Alexis, False Peter IIs, False Peter IIIs. In such an immense country, with the most primitive means of communication, it was difficult for the authorities in Moscow to suppress quickly would-be usurpers, especially if they were in faraway provinces. Besides, there is reason to believe that the ignorant and highly superstitious masses of the people, who often supported these claimants to the Russian throne, revelled in the excitement of being deceived.

Ever since Boris had become Czar, the situation in Russia had been a difficult one—now it became chaotic. Shortly after the first False Dmitri's death, Prince Shuisky became Czar but was soon forced to abdicate. The forces of the second False Dmitri were on the march, but most of the boyars, many of whom had welcomed the first False Dmitri, refused to support him. The Cossacks were in revolt. Serfs burned the houses of their masters. Huge bandit gangs roamed the countryside. Polish troops crossed the Polish-Russian frontier.

It was during this period that the Kremlin for the first time in Russian history was occupied by a European power. The Poles, who had sponsored and supported the first and, after his death, the second False Dmitri, now were invited by a disorganized Russian ruling class to put the son of the Polish King upon the Russian throne. King Sigismond of Poland refused, hoping to get the throne for himself. During the confusion Polish troops entered Moscow, fired the city, and occupied the Kremlin. The Russians immediately besieged the fortress. The ludicrous—and tragic—situation now developed in which the Kremlin, which had been strengthened over the centuries to house Russian defenders against invaders, now housed the invader, with the Russians besieging the fortress.

The Polish occupancy of the Kremlin lasted for almost two years, until finally under the leadership of Minin, a butcher from Novgorod, and Prince Posharsky, a nobleman, the Russian people rallied together, gave up their possessions to finance the raising of an army, marched to Moscow, and delivered the city from the Poles.

The two-year period in which the Poles occupied the Kremlin were years, especially near the end, of the greatest privation for the Polish occupants. An Englishman with the Polish troops in the Kremlin wrote the following account of its occupation:

'During the time of this cruel siege, wherein I continued 22 months, being lodged in the Imperial Palace, several objects of misery presented themselves to my sight and observation, from the besieged; as the eating of the flesh of horses, dogs, cats, and all sorts of leather, boyled in ditch-water; which served in stead of Tripes....

'But after the famine grew very great, and all women, children, and aged persons turned out of the City, to the Russians (who received them very courteously, very much condoling their miserable conditions), there followed a very great judgment of God upon the Polonians (obstinacie and hardness of heart), who all bound themselves by Oath, and receiving the Sacrament upon it, not to yield up the City to the Russians, so long as there was a man of them alive: which brought them to that extremity, that they by casting lots (who should die next, to maintain the rest alive) did devour one another, from 3,000 to 4,000 persons. And at the surrender of the City, divers Commanders of the Russian Army seizing upon sundry large chests, conceiving them to be full of treasure, having them broken up, found in them nothing but the bodies of men slain for food to the living.'

Other accounts spoke of the pestilence that broke out among the starved Poles within the Kremlin. There is little doubt that the horrors of the beseiged were probably greater than the horrors of the besiegers, though the Russians themselves were also starving, because of the lack of food deliveries and the general disorganization of the countryside.

During the occupation of the Kremlin by the Poles the fortress was damaged by Russian shelling and Polish vandalism. The Tower of Ivan Velikii was partially destroyed; almost all the palaces were damaged to some extent, most of them having gaping holes in their roofs and shattered glass in their windows; and a large number of art works within the palaces and cathedrals were either destroyed or mutilated. Much of the destruction of the precious art pieces was a result of the Poles' anti-Orthodox feeling towards the sacred objects of the Russian Church, and partly the result of the spirit of vandalism, frustration and misery that seized the forlorn Poles as their situation within the fortress became hopeless. Shuisky had melted down the gold statues of the twelve apostles that were reputed to be worth three hundred thousand pounds sterling, in order to raise money to pay his troops, and the Poles likewise resorted to similar activities for similar reasons. Some of the destruction was also due to the desire of the mercenary troops in the Kremlin to loot it of precious jewels and other treasures, for they hoped that when the time came for their escape they would have booty to compensate them for their two years of misery. A number of soldiers were successful in getting away with valuables, and the very crown jewels of Russia were supposed to have been taken by one band of Poles who made their way together with the gems to Lithuania.

Finally, with the Poles expelled from Russia and a Russian army, under Minin and Posharsky, firmly in control of the country, a National Assembly, the Zemsky Sobor, was called. In a wave of patriotic fervour, and a unity of purpose that Russia had not seen for a long time, the sixteen-year-old Michael Romanov was nominated by the Sobor to rule the country. He was a logical candidate for the throne, since he was the grandnephew of Anastasia, Ivan IV's wife; a member of the Romanov family, which had gone through the Time of Troubles with a relatively good record of patriotic actions; and was too young to have been personally involved in the miserable politics of the period. Michael's election by the Sobor was unanimous, and on July 11, 1613, at the Cathedral of the Assumption in the Kremlin, he was crowned Czar of All Russia.

The Kremlin once again became, as it had since the time of Ivan Kalita, the centre of Russian state power and, except for a brief tenancy by Napoleon two hundred years later, was never again occupied by a foreign power.

XIV

The First Three Romanov Czars

MICHAEL I (1613–45) did not immediately move into the Kremlin after his coronation as Czar. The fortress was in such a deplorable condition that the boyars who were entrusted with making suitable arrangements for the new Czar's living quarters were unable to do so in the Kremlin area. Furthermore, the treasury was so depleted that there was no money available to pay carpenters, masons, and other artisans necessary to restore the sorry-looking citadel. For a short while Michael found quarters elsewhere, until money could be raised to pay the workmen and the Kremlin once more be made fit for a king. Conditions were so bad at the beginning of Michael's reign that the Czar himself is supposed to have begged the wealthy boyars, especially the extremely rich Stroganovs, to supply him with money, food, cloth and other wares so that he could pay, feed and clothe his soldiers.

The miserable condition of the Kremlin mirrored the miserable condition of Russia itself, which was practically prostrate after so many years of internal disorder and foreign intervention. The Time of Troubles had taught the ruling class little, except to make them more determined than ever to hold and consolidate their power by the most oppressive methods. Whatever semblances of popular government had briefly come to the surface during the calling together of the Zemsky Sobor and the crossing of rigid class lines that the campaign of Minin and Posharsky had called forth were soon forgotten, and Russia sank once again into bitter reaction, more severe in many respects than during the time of Ivan the Terrible. The government was little more than an instrument of oppression, the structure of the state being organized to perpetuate the autocratic power of the Czar, the special privileges of the boyar class, and the protection of the merchants. At the same time, the mass of Russians were kept in such poverty and ignorance and fear that for all intents and purposes they were not solid citizenry of a nation but an abject, voiceless, and supine glob of protoplasm, living in conditions close to the animal state, without dignity and without hope.

The first three Romanov rulers—Michael, Alexi I (1645–76), and
Feodor II (1672–82)—were not, per se, violent and vicious men, as
say Ivan IV had been. In a sense they were worse. They were medi-
ocre. And their mediocrity allowed the stronger forces within Russia,
the powerful boyar class for instance, to lead Russia farther into
the abyss of reaction and serfdom that was to be her lot long after
the rest of Europe had made giant strides towards emancipation
from feudalism.

From most accounts of the first three Romanovs, they were, for
Russian rulers, gentle individuals. In fact, Alexi, the son of Michael,
was called 'the gentle Czar', and was described by Meirberg, the
Austrian Ambassador to Russia, as a ruler who had a 'combination
of goodness and kindliness of character with respect for the human
dignity that attracted both friend and foe . . . nor could foreigners
ever sufficiently admire the fact that, despite the Sovereign's unlimited power over a people which was fully inured to slavery, he
made no attempt against the property, the life, or the honour of a
single individual. The evil acts of others affected him the more in
that they imposed upon him the distasteful duty of meting out
punishment. Yet his wrath was transient—it passed in a momentary
flash, and never advanced beyond threats and kicks'.

During the reign of Michael, and especially during the reign of
Alexi, the stilted court etiquette, which most foreigners attached to
the Russian court had found so strained and bothersome, was molli-
fied somewhat. For the first time, during Alexi's day, there was a
relaxed feeling in the court; the Czar jested with the courtiers,
visited them at their homes as an ordinary guest, and, in turn, invited
dignitaries to intimate evening suppers in his private quarters where
without court fanfare he talked to them about a diverse number of
subjects, even entering into discussions about domestic affairs.

Though Alexi initiated a somewhat more relaxed personal atmosphere in the court, the formal ceremonies and traditions of the
Kremlin were not in the least altered. Like Ivan III and Ivan IV
before him, he was eager to impress foreigners with the opulence of
his court and, like them, he was successful in doing so, for most
envoys returned to their respective countries with glowing accounts
of its magnificence. Guy Miège, for instance, a foreign diplomat,
wrote the following account of his audience with Alexi, in 1664:

'We came into a hall, through which we were to pass into that of the audience, and here it was we saw the guards of the Czar's body in a most splendid equipage, their vests of velvet being lined with sables, their caps richly adorned with pearls and precious stones, and their very partisans covered with gold and silver. . . . [Entering the audience hall] we were like those who, coming suddenly out of the dark, are dazzled with the brightness of the sun; the splendour of their jewels seeming to contend for priority with that of the day, so that we were lost, as it were, in this confusion of glory. The Czar, like a sparkling sun (to speak in the Russian dialect), darted forth most sumptuous rays, being most magnificently placed upon his throne, with his sceptre in his hand, and having his crown upon his head. His throne was of massy silver gilt, wrought curiously on the top with several works and pyramids, and being seven or eight steps higher than the floor it rendered the person of the Prince transcendently majestic. His crown (which he wore upon a cap lined with black sables) was covered quite over with precious stones; it terminated towards the top in the form of a pyramid, with a golden cross on the spire. The sceptre glistened also all over with jewels. . . . By his side he had four of the tallest of his lords standing below his throne, each of them with his battle-axe upon his shoulder, and with a profound gravity casting their eyes now and then upon the Czar inviting us to an admiration of his grandeur. Their habits were no less remarkable than their countenances, being all four of them, from the top of their head to the sole of their foot, clothed in white vests of ermine, and having great chains of gold, and their caps of that large sort which they use in the ceremonies, but whereas others were of black fox, these were of ermine, as well as their vests; their very boots also were covered with the same. But that which was further admirable was the glorious equipage of the Boyars present at this audience, who were as so many beams of the sun . . . and seemed to have no lustre but to do homage withal to their great monarch. They were about two hundred, clothed all with vests of cloth of gold, cloth of silver set with jewels, all placed in order upon benches covered with tapestry about the wall . . . . At the entrance to the hall there was a great number also of his *goses*, which are his merchants or factors, whom he furnishes with rich robes to appear at such ceremonies. This was the splendour we found this great prince in, with a countenance perfectly majestic, as having not only the advantage of a handsome proportion, but of a lively and vigorous age, for this was but his four and thirtieth year.'

That the Czar cut a good figure is attested to by most people who described him at the time. Dr Collins, an Englishman who was court physician at the time, described Alexi as 'a goodly person, of a sanguine complexion, light-brown hair, his beard uncut. He is tall and fat, of majestical department. . . . The Czar is about six foot high, has a somewhat low forehead and a stern countenance'. The doctor thought it noteworthy too, in describing Alexi, to mention a fact that had been noticeably lacking in many previous Czars: Alexi was, he wrote, 'chastely uxorious'.

Alexi fancied himself somewhat of a writer and, next to Ivan the Terrible and Catherine the Great, wrote more than any other Russian monarch. He tried his hand at writing a history of his military campaigns, and even wrote some lines of verse, which he at least thought were poetry. He was very proud of recounting the fact that by the time he was twelve years of age he had accumulated a library, mostly gifts from his father and tutors. The library consisted of thirteen books.

Like the Czars before him—and after him with one or two exceptions—Alexi was extremely pious and in the observance of his religion was called 'the strictest man in the world'. It was said that he never missed a church service, that if he was ill he would have the service performed in his bedroom, that he would often stand for four or five hours at a time while attending some special service, and that he was especially diligent in keeping fasts, which totalled about eight months of abstinence through the year.

The devout Romanovs had several new churches erected in the Kremlin during their reigns, though none of them was of the magnificence of the earlier cathedrals built under the two Ivans by the Italians. The Cathedral of the Twelve Apostles was built during Alexi's reign, on the north side of Cathedral Square in 1655, and the Church of the Resurrection was erected in 1681, under Feodor II's rule. In addition to churches, the Palace of the Patriarchs (*Patriarshaia Palata*), on the north side of Cathedral Square, was built in 1650, to house the patriarchate. For years it contained the finest collection of ecclesiastical art in Russia, including, among other things, gem-studded sacredotal robes and vestments, crowns, mitres, panagias, pectoral crosses, pastoral staffs, censers, and chalices, as well as elaborately bound and illuminated service books.

One of the results of the somewhat more relaxed atmosphere in the court during Alexi's time was the decision to build a theatre and place of entertainment. The Czar ordered that a large house within the Kremlin area, which had belonged to the recently deceased powerful boyar Miloslavsky, be remodelled for this purpose. The project was undertaken in 1650, and the next year it was ready to receive dancers, singers and theatrical groups.

The *Granovitaia Palata*, the living quarters of the Czars and their families, was a distinctive place, with huge gilt girders, deeply splayed mica windows, ceilings of polychrome arabesques on a gold ground, and walls that were lavishly frescoed. Even so, it was constantly being remodelled and redecorated. During Alexi's reign the interior of the palace was reworked, and during the time of Feodor decorations, furniture and accessories of all kinds were given special attention. The furnishings of the palace remained more or less in the same style for the next hundred and fifty years, until its restoration in 1830.

Just prior to, during, and shortly after the seventeenth century, there were several curiosities added to the Kremlin that over the years often attracted more attention, especially from sightseers, than the elaborate palaces and cathedrals. The first was the Czar Cannon (*Czar Pushka*), a huge cannon that was cast in 1586 by the master craftsman Chekhov of Moscow. The cannon, supposedly the world's largest, is sixteen feet long, three feet in diameter, and weighs about eighty-five thousand pounds. It is one of the sights that is proudly shown by the guides to every visitor to the Kremlin—that is when visitors have been allowed. The cannon is highly ornamented, and from the time it was cast was never looked upon as a war weapon but as a work of art.

The companion piece of the Czar Cannon is the Czar Bell (*Czar Kolokol*), also reputed to be the largest in the world. It was originally cast during the time of Boris Godunov and weighed 286,000 pounds. In 1735 it was recast by the Moscow bell founder Motorin, and its weight increased to 432,000 pounds. Why a bell of such immense weight should have been made, first at the direction of Boris Godunov, and then melted down and its size increased by order of the Czarina Anna, so that it became 'a mountain of metal', as one observer called it, is perhaps explained by the attempt of Russian rulers to prove their profound piety. Just as the building of a church showed a meritorious religious act, so did the presentation of bells to a church. The size of the church or the bells was important, for the piety of the donor was measured by the magnitude of the gift. By giving the Church the largest bell ever made, Boris Godunov hoped to show that he was the most pious of all Russian rulers, and later the Czarina Anna, who certainly wasn't the most devout, tried to be so considered by donating to the Church a bell that surpassed Czar Boris's. Over the years, the gigantic half-million-pound bell has been the source of many anti-Russian remarks, the most popular one being that the casting of so large a bell demonstrated the folly of the Russians in their desire to have the biggest of objects, for when the bell was finally made it was so heavy that it could not be suspended, and remained, useless, on the ground. For years the sight of the unsuspended mammoth of bells and the gigantic, non-utilitarian Czar Cannon, which was close by, caused cynical people to remark that 'the Kremlin is famous for its cannon that was never fired and its bell that never rang'. The Russians claim, however, that the bell was really raised to the belltower, but that a fire in 1737 burned the belltower, causing the bell to fall to the ground where, in a damaged condition, it remained deeply imbedded until 1836 when the architect Monferrand succeeded in raising the bell from its pit and placing it on its present base.

Another main attraction in the Kremlin is the Tower of Ivan the Great (*Ivan Velikii*), that 'goodly stepill of hewen stoen in the inner Castell of Musco, with . . . great, sweet-sounding bells in it', which was one of the public-works projects that Boris Godunov initiated during the famine of 1601–3. It stands opposite the Cathedral of the Assumption, and is the tallest structure in the Kremlin. It is the dominant tower of a series of three. The other two are the Bono Tower, built between 1532–43, which contains the chief, or signal, bell of Moscow, and the Tower of Patriarch Philaret, built in 1624, which formerly housed the valuable collection of ancient ecclesiastical art of the Patriarchal Sacristy.

The Belltower of Ivan Velikii, because of its height (270 feet), dominates not only the Kremlin but is a landmark for all of Moscow since it is visible from almost every part of the capital, and travellers to Moscow, particularly from the east, south, and west, are able to take their bearings from it. For many years the bells, thirty-three in number and including, supposedly, the famous bell of Novgorod, were tolled only upon great festivals or to honour important foreign dignitaries when they first arrived in Moscow. The bells are immense, weighing from seven thousand to a hundred and twenty-four thousand pounds each, and twenty-four men are required to set the bells ringing. In the past, Muscovites eagerly volunteered for the job, considering it a great honour and a pious service to be permitted to ring them.

The ringing of bells in Russia, especially in the late Middle Ages, and even to an extent in more recent times, was regarded with genuine fondness by the Russians for the varied sounds they made. The bells were capable of creating many effects—sadness, joy, alarm. On certain days, commemorating a particular event, all the bells of Moscow often tolled at once—beginning with the chief bell in the Bono Belfry, then those in the Belltower of Ivan Velikii, and finally all the bells in the Kremlin, as well as in the churches of Moscow—making rolling waves of sound, sometimes mellifluous, sometimes strident, depending upon the nature of the event to be celebrated.

Russian life was inextricably tied to the Church, and probably no one in Russia, with the exception of the members of certain church orders themselves, devoted as much time and energy to religious matters as the pious Czars. In fact, so much time was spent in prayer and attending services that one wonders how the rulers found time to attend to state matters. The average day in the life of most Czars, at least until the time of the iconoclastic Peter, was quite similar to a typical day in the life of Czar Feodor I, described by Giles Fletcher.

The Czar arose at four in the morning and, after dressing and washing, was blessed by the priest of the chamber, who put the cross first on his forehead, next upon his cheeks, and finally offered the end of the cross for him to kiss. A painted image, the saint of the day, was brought into the chamber and the Czar prayed before it, first crossing himself in the Russian manner—on the forehead, then on both sides of his breast—and then saying, '*Aspody Pomeluy, Pomeluy mena hospoduy, sacroy mena gresnick Syhodestua* . . . (Help me O Lord my God, Lord comfort me, defend and keep me a sinner from doing evil, etc.)'. The Czar then prostrated himself on the ground and for about fifteen minutes knocked his head against the floor.

Then, together with his wife, he went to private chapel for morning services.

Upon returning from chapel the Czar sat in his great chamber and held court. At nine o'clock he again went to church, this time for high services, which lasted for about two hours. After a short stay in his quarters he went to the midday dinner, which usually consisted of about twenty courses. To forestall an attempt on the Czar's life by poison, each dish was tasted first by the cook himself and then by the official court taster. The dining hall was usually crowded with members of the nobility, for the Czar rarely dined alone. During the course of the meal, the ruler would honour various noblemen by ordering one of the lackeys to bring them food from his own table.

After dinner the Czar rested, usually for as long as three hours. When he arose, he went to vespers. After attending evensong, he was entertained by tumblers and singers. Often, the entertainment consisted of a man fighting a bear. A man armed with a pike was locked in a circular walled area, the bear was then turned loose in the area, and the man, unable to escape, had to fight until either he or the bear was killed. After the 'entertainment' was over, the Czar went to supper. Before bedtime the priest again came into the Czar's chamber. Prayers were said, the Czar was blessed, and, in general, the ritual of the morning was repeated, including the fifteen minutes of head-pounding on the floor. The priest then left the chamber, and the Czar went to bed.

In other respects besides religion, the life of the Czars was quite circumscribed. Russian rulers almost never crossed the borders of Russia, many of them, in fact, never travelling very extensively in their own country. They had relatively little contact with the outside world, and except for occasional audiences with foreign ambassadors or other diplomatic representatives, the Czars were quite ignorant of the peoples and manners of other countries, and even of their own. They were quite content, it seems, to spend most of their lives within the narrow confines and atmosphere of the Kremlin.

These particular characteristics of the Czars, as well as many others, came to an abrupt end with Peter I. For the first time in Russian history, a Czar broke away from Russian isolationism, which, like the high, protective, crenellated walls of the Kremlin itself, was a defence barrier against the outside world. The era of the early Romanovs, as with the Ruriks before them, was an era in which few

Western ideas were allowed past the frontiers. Now things were to change. The not so splendid isolation was coming to an end. And with the changes that were to take place in Russia itself during the rule of Peter the Great, the Kremlin and all it represented would be an anachronism. Its days as the administrative centre and symbol of Russian power were numbered.

XV

Sophia's Regency and the Young Peter

IN 1682 when Czar Feodor II, the eldest son of Czar Alexi, died, he was childless. A struggle for power immediately ensued between the Miloslavskys, Alexi's first wife's family, and his second wife's family, the Naryshkins. There were two main candidates for the vacated throne—Ivan, 'sickly, three parts blind, and more than half an idiot', who was Feodor's full brother, and Feodor's half brother, Peter, a strong, healthy boy, who was then ten years of age. Through the influential boyars who had appealed to a hastily assembled crowd in Red Square, Peter was named Czar and Natalia Naryshkin, his mother, was proclaimed regent.

Natalia and Peter, who during the reign of Feodor had spent most of their time away from the Kremlin in a villa in the country, now took up residence in the fortress. However, Sophia, the most energetic of Alexi's daughters, realizing that she and her sisters, daughters of the defeated Miloslavskys, would be forced to spend the rest of their lives in a nunnery, owing to the demands of Russian court etiquette, decided to make a bid for power. Sophia incited the *streltsy*, the palace guard, to riot, claiming that Natalia was treating Ivan unjustly. Natalia took Ivan and Peter to the Red Stairway in the Kremlin and showed the mob that all was well with the children. However, under further incitation, the mob went wild and for three days looted and murdered. One of those murdered was Peter's uncle, another was his best friend, Artamon Matvyeev, who was hacked to pieces right before the young Czar's eyes. The rioting was finally brought under control, and a decision was made that Peter and Ivan should reign jointly, with Sophia as regent. A double silver-gilt throne for the two boy Czars was made which contained two small seats, as well as a silken curtain, from behind which Sophia could act as prompter. Russia now had two visible Czars and one invisible ruler.

The coming to power of Sophia as the real ruler of Russia was the beginning of a gynocracy which later held sway for seventy years, from the time of Catherine I to Catherine II. That Sophia could have emerged from the seclusion of the Kremlin *terem* to seize control of the government was in itself a remarkable thing, since the Kremlin *terem* was in most respects even more confining than the *terems* of other noble families. The girls and women there had a regimen of the most exacting solitude, the strictest acts of devotion and rigidly enforced fastings. Only the Patriarch and the closest relatives were allowed as visitors. Even when one of the women became ill, the court physician often was not called in. In cases of very serious ailment, the doctor was permitted to enter the *terem*, but when he did the shutters were closed and he was not allowed to look at the patient, and had to take her pulse by putting his hand under the curtains of the bed. The women had no position in the life of the court and were forbidden to appear at any functions whatsoever except funerals, when heavily veiled they followed the bier. Except for their names which were included in the daily prayers of the official liturgy, they were unknown by the nation at large. The women knew next to nothing of life itself, their entire lives spent in the narrow confines of their own circle of women inmates. The fate of most of these women, who because of their rank were unable to marry just any man at all, was spinsterhood, and usually later in life a nunnery.

Somehow or other Sophia must have managed to violate the laws and customs of the Kremlin *terem* and to have had contacts with the outside, for when she emerged from the *terem* to take over the regency she was certainly no ignorant, backward woman. De Neuville, a diplomatic agent sent to Moscow by Marquis de Bethune, the French Ambassador to Poland, described her in 1689 as follows:

'Her mind and her great ability bear no relation to the deformity of her person, as she is immensibly fat, with a head as large as a bushel, hairs on her face and tumors on her legs, and at least forty years old [she was actually thirty-two at the time]. . . . She is as acute, subtle, and shrewd in mind, as she is broad, short, and coarse in person. And though she had never read Machiavelli, nor learnt anything about him, all his maxims come naturally to her.'

Sophia, like the women monarchs of Russia who ruled in the eighteenth century, had many lovers. Her chief lover, and in many ways chief of state, was Vasili Galitzin, for whom Sophia had an overwhelming passion. In a most un-*terem*like letter she sent to

him when he was leading a campaign in the Crimea, she wrote:
'My joy, my love, the delight of my eyes! Dare I really believe, oh my
heart, that soon I shall see you again, who art all the world to me? . . .
I do pray, and God, who hears me, knows how I long to see thee,
oh my world, oh my soul! I trust in His mercy, which will grant me
to see thee soon, oh all my hope!' It is little wonder that she urged
Galitzin to send his wife to a nunnery so that she could have him all
to herself. Though he was not anxious to do so, for he was in his
fashion devoted to his wife and children, he finally acceded to
Sophia's request.

Sophia has been characterized by historians as a 'second Lucrezia
Borgia' (Voltaire), on the one hand, and 'one of the greatest women
the world has ever seen' (Karamzin), on the other. Certainly in
the Kremlin itself, during her reign, there was a faint glimmer of day-
light after so many centuries of gloom. Following the example of
Alexi, she allowed plays to be presented in the Kremlin and is said
to have written some herself, even acting in a couple of them. The very
fact that a woman was now in the limelight, for the first time, was a
sharp departure from *terem* ways. However, Sophia did not break
radically from Kremlin tradition; the breakdown of the old and the
introduction of new ways had to wait for the coming to actual power
of Peter, the supreme iconoclast. By and large the Byzantine character of the Kremlin was still in evidence under the regency of Sophia.
The old, old liturgical arguments continued as to how many fingers
should be used when crossing oneself in prayer, how many times
'hallelujah' should be said, whether the Trinity shouldn't consist of
four persons, with the Saviour occupying a separate throne, and so
on. No real break was made in Kremlin court customs, though a
certain relaxation did set in. The Church was as powerful as ever,
and Sophia ran to its protective arms whenever she was in danger.

One such occasion was in the beginning of her reign, when she
was threatened by the very group that she had appealed to for
assistance to gain power, the *streltsy*. In October, 1682, she and her
lover Galitzin left the Kremlin to seek sanctuary in the traditional
place of refuge for royalty in time of danger—the Novodevichi
Convent, then on the outskirts of Moscow. Boris Godunov had
sought shelter there a century earlier and, later, Peter himself was
to go there for refuge and protection.

The Novodevichi Convent and five other convents that ringed

Moscow may well be considered to have been Moscow's other Kremlins, for they, too, were huge citadels, often self-sufficient, housing hundreds and even thousands of persons, and were designed and used for defensive purposes as well as religious ones.

The Novodevichi Convent on the western approaches to Moscow was strategically of great importance, lying as it did on the loop of the Moscow River. Probably the most beautiful of Moscow's convents, it was next to the Kremlin itself the most formidable fortress in the area, having high, strong walls. It was founded in 1524 by Vasili III in memory of his conquest of Smolensk, and in its cemeteries are the graves of a host of famous people, including the writer Chekhov, the composer Scriabin, the historian Soloviev, as well as, in its vaults, the tombs of Sophia herself and Eudoxia, Peter the Great's first wife. Its courtyard is one of the scenes of Moussorgsky's opera *Boris Godunov*, for it was here that Boris retired prior to becoming Czar in 1598. Like the Kremlin itself, it has been the scene of numerous bloody battles and executions; three hundred *streltsy* soldiers, for instance, were put to death there, and in 1812 the convent was sacked by Napoleon. Under the Soviet government, one of its two cathedrals was turned into a museum, another is open for worship, and the convent buildings house the Theological Institute and the Seminary which train priests for the Russian Orthodox Church.

Another famous 'Kremlin' is the Donskoi Monastery, built by Czar Feodor in 1592 after his victory over the Khan Kazy-Ghirey and the Crimean Tartars. Its walls, too, are massive, red in colour, and have loopholes and huge round turrets at the corners. As a defence structure it was of great importance since it is situated in the defile leading to the Kremlin itself, at the two bends of the Moscow River.

The Novospassky Convent, built in 1462, had a beautiful cathedral added in 1645 and a belfry in 1785. At one time it was used as a burial ground for high-placed boyars, as well as certain influential members of the Romanov family. Under the Soviets it was turned into residential quarters.

The other 'Kremlins' include the Simonov, built in 1317, destroyed in the Time of Troubles and then rebuilt, and now the site of what until recently was called the Stalin Automobile Works; the Andrionov, founded in 1360 on the high bank of the Yanza River, and now used as living quarters; and the Danilov, founded in 1272 by Prince Daniel, and containing his tomb as well as those of many famous Russian writers, including Gogol, and today used, too, as a dwelling place.

Over the centuries these six 'Kremlins' were the keystone of Moscow's defences, barring the way to the Poles, Lithuanians and other Europeans from the west and the Tartars from the south. The northern and eastern frontiers, as a rule, were peaceful. In the olden days these fortresses had the characteristics of the Russian *obitiels*, small fortified towns that had a population consisting of monks, novices and serving brothers, numbering in many cases thousands of people. Within the monastery-fortresses, there were often a half dozen or more churches, as well as workshops of all kinds.

Of particular interest at the time that Sophia and her lover Galitzin took refuge in the Novodevichi Convent was the fact that the *streltsy*, usually so arrogant and insolent, came as suppliants. Expecting to be put to death for their attempted insurrection, they marched to the convent with ropes that they had placed around their necks and carried axes and blocks for their own execution. The Patriarch interceded on behalf of the *streltsy* and, magnanimously, Sophia spared most of them, contenting herself with having only a few of the ringleaders put to death.

The seven years of Sophia's regency were, for Russia of that time, quite enlightened, with Galitzin even raising the question—but doing nothing about it—of emancipating the serfs.

During this period, Peter lived with his mother under constant surveillance at Preobrazhenskoe, a village near Moscow. Only when his presence was required for some state occasion or other did he return to the Kremlin to take his place beside his half brother Ivan. There is little doubt that Peter hated to return to the fortress even on these occasions. His memories of the Kremlin were far from pleasant, consisting as they did of such horrors as the murder before his very eyes of his uncle and tutor, through whose blood, it was said, the *streltsy* had made Peter walk. From childhood on he suffered from convulsions, and this experience is supposed to have been a contributing factor because of the nervous shock it gave him at the time. At Kolomna, the summer palace of the Czars, where Peter also spent much of his early childhood, he seemed to have been happier. There, at least, he could escape from the rigid and gloomy atmosphere of the Kremlin; he could look upon the pleasant green hills and the flow of the Moscow River from one of the three thousand windows that the palace contained; and there, too, he could be driven in a small gilded carriage drawn by ponies, with four dwarfs accompanying him on foot and a fifth riding upon a miniature horse.

Peter was not a precocious child; in fact, in many ways he was quite backward. He was almost three years old before he stopped using a wet nurse, and at eleven he still could not read or write. Like Ivan the Terrible, who also had a difficult and precarious childhood because of court intrigues, Peter was interested in all manner of things, though, unlike Ivan, books at this time were of no interest to him. Peter's interests centred around guns and boats, and in these and other things that interested him he showed unmistakable signs of being an alert and inquisitive child.

Separated as he was from the stultifying influence of the Kremlin with its gloomy ritual and brooding Byzantine atmosphere, Peter grew up in surroundings that were not typical for a Russian prince and Czar. Early in his adolescence he was attracted by the *sloboda*, the suburbs, where most of Moscow's non-Russian population lived at this time. Here were the foreign merchants, teachers, physicians, apothecaries, artists, and here, too, was the centre of whatever culture, education and sophistication existed in Russia at the time. English ladies had novels sent to them from England; German residents danced the *Grossvatertanz*, considered at the time to be a wild form of entertainment; the Dutch worshipped under the tutelege of a Calvinist minister; the foreign ambassadors, English, Danish, Swedish, Dutch, and others, brought with them their own indigenous customs and culture. Even the buildings of the *sloboda* were more comfortable and pleasant-looking than the typical Russian ones. They were mostly of brick, with flowery gardens, tree-lined pathways, and fountains. The pleasant strangeness of the foreigners intrigued the young Czar, and as he grew older he spent as much time in the *sloboda* as he could, making friends with many of the residents there, friendships that lasted in many cases till the end of his life. It was here in the foreign quarter that Peter got his first ideas for the Westernization of Russia.

In 1689, when Peter was seventeen, he married Eudoxia Lapouhin, the daughter of a prominent boyar. There is reason to believe that he did not wish to marry but did so at the urging of his mother.

He did not love Eudoxia, and after about three months of marriage he practically deserted her, spending most of his time in the *sloboda* with his foreign friends and with women, unlike the devout and prim Eudoxia, who catered for the carousing tastes of the young Czar.

In that same year Sophia's highhanded ways aroused Peter's suspicions—he even believed that his half sister was plotting to kill him—and, though he was barely eighteen, he decided to make a bid for complete power. After a brief struggle, in which the troops of her erstwhile loyal *streltsy* rallied to Peter's cause, Sophia found herself completely isolated. Meekly, she capitulated. Her lover Galitzin was exiled to the icy north of Russia, with a daily allowance of one rouble to support himself and his family of five. Sophia—as she had always feared would happen—was sent to a convent.

With power now in his hands, Peter refused to assume the responsibilities of governing. He entrusted the government to his supporters so that he could be free to follow his own amusements, and now more than ever he surrounded himself with foreign companions, such as the Scot Patrick Gordon and the Swiss Francis Lefort. As for his feeble-minded half-brother Ivan, Peter made no move to depose him from the dual throne they shared together. He treated him indulgently, even kindly, until the very end of Ivan's life in 1696.

The years between his *coup d'état* of 1689 and his now famous trip through Europe, which began in 1697, were but a continuation of his foot-loose existence. Hating the Kremlin and what it represented, he spent little or no time there. Sometimes he was at Preobrazhenskoe; at other times he was at the lake of Pereaslavl, sailing boats; and at still other times he was at Archangel, which, like the *sloboda*, was the one other place in Russia where he could be in the company of foreigners, as well as be near boats and water for which he had taken such a fancy.

Except for an occasional military exploit, such as the campaign he participated in against the Turkish fortress of Azov in 1695, Peter's life centred around the pursuit of his own amusements. And these amusements, like everything he was to do, were on a colossal scale. His parties, at this time and later, were orgies, where Peter insisted that everyone present consume huge quantities of liquor until each and every person, including the women, was stupefyingly drunk. Sometimes the parties were of an intimate nature, and at other times

hundreds of people attended. Peter's own residence at Preobrazhenskoe was shabby, for he hated to live in a large, sumptuously
furnished house, probably because of his strong feeling against any
kind of establishment that reminded him of the opulence and
immensity of the hated Kremlin. However, he insisted that his
friends have fine houses. Lefort, for instance, at Peter's insistence,
and possibly at Peter's expense (though this is doubtful, for Peter,
like most Czars, was an inveterate penny pincher), had an immense
palace, with a ballroom that accommodated more than fifteen hundred persons, a dining-room that was hung with Spanish leather,
and a yellow and bright red damask bedroom that was so large it
boasted a bed eleven feet wide.

When Peter, at Lefort's suggestions, decided to tour Europe, it
was a most unusual step for a Russian Czar, none of whom for hundreds of years had ever left Russia. Before Peter, the last ruler to
take any trip of consequence outside Russia's borders was the Grand
Duke of Kiev, Izaslav, who paid a visit to the Emperor Henry IV
at Mayence in 1075. From the time of Ivan the Terrible, foreign
travel was not only frowned upon but during certain periods the
very desire to travel abroad was considered to be high treason, not
only on the part of important government officials but ordinary subjects as well. During Czar Alexi's reign, for instance, a certain Prince
Hvorostinin was severely punished for having said to some friends
that he wished to visit Poland and Rome so that he could 'find some-
body to talk with'. Though a trickle of foreigners was permitted into
Russia, where they were tolerated and at times treated with consideration and respect, for the Russians needed their talents, the
Russian himself was forbidden to cross the frontiers. Except for
Russian diplomatic staffs stationed in foreign countries and the few
instances when a handful of Russian students was permitted to study
abroad—under constant surveillance by representatives of the
Russian embassy, lest they refuse to return—few Russians legally
left Russia.

It is little wonder, therefore, that Peter's trip through Europe
caused such a stir of interest and curiosity. Word of his boorishness
preceded him ('He is puzzled with his napkin, which he does not
know how to use, and eats in dirty and slovenly fashion. He forces
the whole company to remain at table for four hours, drinking endless toasts to his health and standing each time', one biographer of

Peter wrote), but the nobility couldn't resist having him at their palaces. One of them, for example, Sophia Charlotte, the Electress of Brandenburg, who later became Queen of Prussia, was so anxious to see him—and be seen by him—that, as she wrote at the time, she 'would willingly keep the money generally spent on rare animals for use on this occasion'. And later, writing to her state minister, Fuchs, she again says how anxious she is to meet Peter. 'Though I am a great enemy of dirt', she wrote, 'my curiosity, this time, is too strong for me.'

Among the common people with whom he came into contact, he was truly Peter Mikhailov, the name he assumed as a disguise, but his time was spent not only among the boatbuilders at Zaandam, in Holland, and Deptford, in England, and carousing with Dutch maidens in working-class taverns; for there were occasions, too, when he was with the nobility, and at such times he insisted on being known as Peter I, Czar of All Russia. In the palaces of his foreign hosts he shocked the nobility with his extravagant behaviour, as he had done at Deptford, when he and his companions, roaring drunk, had torn up the town to the amazement of the staid British towns-people. One noblewoman was stunned at the precipitant manner in which Peter had ordered one of her maids to come to his room and later expressed her incredulity when she heard that Peter had given the maid only a pittance for her very personal services. Still, as stingy as Peter was, his predilection for the bizarre often got the better of him. One night at Koenigsberg, for instance, as he was sitting at the table with the Electress he was intrigued by her breasts which were provocatively exposed by her low-cut gown and, impetuously, he took a huge ruby out of his pocket and threw it into her bosom.

Though there are innumerable references to Peter's carousing ('The Czar has happened on a peasant girl of Saardam', one un-signed letter in the Leibnitz collection states, 'who pleases his fancy, and on holidays, he betakes himself there alone in his boat, to take his pleasure with her, after the manner of Hercules'), he was busy, too, investigating the arts, crafts and sciences that Europe had to offer at the time. He personally measured the width of a bridge; nearly got cut in two trying to stop a sawmill; clung to the driving wheel of a machine in a silk factory, and almost was carried into one of the other wheels; studied architecture at Leyden with Simon Schynvoet, mechanics with Van der Heyden, fortifications under

Coehorn, printing with Tessing, anatomy with Ruysch, and natural history with Leuwenhoek. At Boerhaave in the anatomical theatre, when his companions expressed disgust during a dissection, he forced them to bite the corpse as a punishment for their lack of respect for science. Nothing seemed to escape his curiosity. He learned to use a compass, pull teeth (which 'art' he continued to practise for the rest of his life, insisting on occasion that some man or woman in his company submit to tooth-pulling whether he or she needed it or not), took drawing lessons, learned to engrave on copper, and, of course, spent a good deal of time learning boat-building.

Peter's interests and activities were so numerous that it appears as though it would be impossible for one man to be so active. But he was, and nature had equipped him admirably for such far-flung and strenuous activities. He was a giant of a man, six feet eight inches tall, powerfully built, and with magnificent proportions. He was quick in movement and took long steps and swung his arms unrestrainedly when he walked, though he rounded his shoulders somewhat, an affectation he apparently picked up from Dutch sailors. He was dark-complexioned, 'as if he had been born in Africa', according to one contemporary; had thick hair and dark, full eyebrows; full, round cheeks; large eyes, which at times were somewhat wild-looking; and a well-shaped nose and mouth.

From early childhood, as has been mentioned previously, Peter was subject to convulsions which often distorted his appearance. They were sometimes of short duration but on occasion they lasted for hours, during which time he was in such a pitiable condition that he would allow no one near him except his closest attendant and, later, Catherine, his second wife. The paroxysm was preceded, according to one eyewitness, 'by a strong contortion of the neck towards the left side, and by a violent contraction of the muscles of the face'. At such times he would often grab hold of the person nearest to him. On one such occasion, in 1718, he was dining with the Queen of Prussia and grabbed the arm of the Queen. She cried out in pain. 'Catherine's bones are not so tender', he muttered angrily.

Because of these convulsions, Peter slept holding on to the shoulders of an orderly when he was not in the same bed with his wife. His insistence on having the orderly with him at bedtimes has raised questions as to whether Peter, like other Russian Czars who also insisted on having a male companion with them at night, was not homosexually inclined. Alexander Gordon, however, who knew Peter well, insisted in his account of the Czar that the reason Peter went to bed with an orderly was 'to prevent a surprise or any attempt on his life'.

In 1698, while in Vienna, news reached Peter that the *streltsy*, the Moscow guards that had caused him so much trouble in the past, had revolted and intended to restore Sophia to power. Peter decided to return to Moscow, but before he arrived his lieutenants had successfully put down the uprising. Upon hearing this news, Peter delayed his immediate return, travelled a while longer, and then, with his mind made up to severely punish the *streltsy*, he finally returned to Moscow near the end of July, 1698.

And with Peter's return, a reign of terror began that rivalled the terror unleashed by Ivan the Terrible—and in many ways surpassed it.

XVI

Peter the Great

JUST outside the Kremlin walls on Red Square, south of the present-day Lenin and Stalin Mausoleum, is the *Lebnoye Meso*, or Place of Skulls, which in former days was used for executions. It was a gruesome spot, for all around the *Lebnoye Meso*, which consisted of a platform built of brick and surrounded by a wooden palisade, there were pikes crowned with human heads and gallows trees with human fruit hanging from them.

This Russian version of the Place de la Gréve had been for many decades before Peter's time the scene of executions and terror, as well as—strangely enough—a holy place. Here, early in his reign, Ivan the Terrible came to confess publicly his crimes and, later, on the same spot had hundreds of people publicly executed. Here, too, where according to legend the head of Adam lies buried, the False Dmitri proclaimed his accession; later, his corpse, a mask on its face and a musical instrument in its hand, was exposed to public view in the *Lebnoye Meso*. In 1671, Stenka Razin, the leader of a Cossack rebellion, and his followers were put to death at this place. But here, too, holy images and relics were first deposited upon being brought into Moscow, and on solemn occasions various religious ceremonies were performed. Surrounded by the skulls and corpses that decorated the *Lebnoye Meso*, the Patriarch blessed the faithful here, and the Czars had important ukases read to the people. And it was at the Place of Skulls that a change of rulers was announced to the inhabitants of Moscow.

It was at this infamous Place of Skulls that Peter carried out the bulk of the executions of the *streltsy*. Immediately upon his return from his trip through Europe, Peter summarily condemned thousands of his enemies. On the road in front of his house in Preobraz-henskoe, Peter himself chopped off the heads of five *streltsy*, and a few days later at the *Lebnoye Meso* the Czar insisted that his example of personally bringing death to his enemies be emulated by his faithful boyars and ministers. Korb, the Austrian consular official who was in Moscow at the time and who was an eyewitness of many of the assassinations, wrote that almost all of Peter's followers wielded the axe at one time or another. 'Some struck the blow unsteadily', Korb wrote, 'and with trembling hands assumed this new and unaccustomed task. The most unfortunate stroke among all the Boyars was given by him (probably Prince Galitzin), whose erring sword struck the back instead of the neck, and thus chopping the Strelitz almost in halves, would have roused him to desperation with pain, had not he reached the unhappy wretch a surer blow of an axe on the neck. . . . The Czar . . . looked on at the whole tragedy.'

All through the month of October the executions continued, a hundred to two hundred a day. Long lines of carts, two doomed men in each, daily filed through the streets to the execution spot. Behind the carts, in which the prisoners themselves were often half dead from the horrible tortures they had undergone on the rack or by the knout prior to their departure for the *Lebnoye Meso*, walked their wives and children, chanting dirges.

Altogether, thousands of *streltsy* were executed. The removal of their corpses was forbidden, and for five months in the main square of the city there were hundreds of rotting, stinking bodies which, because of lack of space in the Place of Skulls, hung from the battlements of the Kremlin itself. Executions took place elsewhere; one series of them being held right under Sophia's window in the convent where she had been exiled. When the executions at the convent were finally over, two hundred *streltsy* lay dead outside her window. Sophia herself escaped with her life; she was confined to an extremely narrow cell, whatever privileges she had had were taken away, even her royal identity, and until her death several years later she was known only as Nun Susanna.

Though Peter had always evidenced, even as a child, a streak of cruelty, until the execution of the *streltsy* it was mainly confined to practical jokes, extravagant clowning, and fun at the expense of other people's dignity. Now it became obvious that cruelty was the strongest personal characteristic of the Czar, and for the rest of his life was to be a dominant motivating factor for many of his actions. His buffoonery became vicious, his practical jokes degrading and depraved, and his 'fun' little more than satanic cruelty. At times he acted like a madman, and at other times like a power-crazed dictator, demonstrating his power over and over again in the most extreme and brutal manner possible in order to prove to everyone, including himself, that he was indeed omnipotent.

Peter not only demonstrated his power by means of terror but he also enjoyed terror for terror's sake. There was a macabre quality about him that fascinated people, in much the same way that the sight of a deadly cobra in a zoo is intriguing. One never knew when Peter would strike; and in the very striking he put on a show that left his audience dumbfounded. For instance, Peter condemned to death for the crime of infanticide a certain Mary Hamilton, descendant of a branch of the famous Scottish Hamilton family that had emigrated to Russia during Ivan the Terrible's time. Mary Hamilton herself was a maid of honour in the court and at one time had been the mistress of Peter. When the time came for her execution, Peter carried the white-gowned, black-ribboned woman in his arms to the scaffold, kissed her while her head was on the block, picked her head up after it had been severed from her body and exhibited it to the spectators, showing them the severed veins and vertebrae; and then, after kissing the lips, dropped the still-bleeding head on to the muddy ground, crossed himself, and departed.

The number of people Peter executed are legion. But even aside from the executions his savagery was unbounded, and it flared up at the slightest provocation. Korb stated that he 'superintended his household like a small shopkeeper, thrashed his wife like a peasant, and sought his pleasures like a brawler'. Even Gordon, whose book is an apology for Peter, wrote that he treated his own friends and co-workers with extreme cruelty, and gave the example of a certain General Goltz, a foreign officer in the Russian army who had performed great services for Peter in a military way as well as securing huge domestic levies for the ruler. 'The Czar often kicked him publicly and beat him like a dog', Gordon wrote, 'so that the bystanders concluded him undone, but always the next morning the peace was made up.'

Peter's court was filled with jesters of all kinds, among them dwarfs, storytellers and buffoons. Though this was nothing new, for the Czars had always kept fools in the Kremlin, Peter's use of them was probably more varied than any other Russian ruler's. In 1694, for instance, at Moscow, he had Turgenev, a court jester, marry a widow. The huge wedding celebration, which Peter planned with great care so that the court would be amused, was described thus by an eyewitness:

'In the procession with the newly married pair were boyarins, high officers of state, and other dignitaries mounted on oxen, goats, swine and dogs; their attire was droll; in bass sacks, dark hats, blue linen kaftans, trimmed with cats' paws, in grey and many coloured kaftans trimmed with squirrels' tails, in straw boots, mufflers of mouse skin, and hats to match . . .'

On another occasion, also a wedding, this time of two dwarfs, Peter ordered that dwarfs from all over Russia should attend the ceremony. An imperial order was issued, seventy-two dwarfs were assembled, and a riotous wedding was held.

Even as late as 1723, two years before his death, Peter indulged himself in one of his most extravagant practical jokes. In St. Petersburg, which like Moscow was very susceptible to fire, he had the tocsin sounded late at night, causing the city's population to leave their beds and hurry into the streets. According to one witness, Peter 'could not contain himself for joy, when, rushing half distracted in the direction of the supposed disaster, they came upon a brazier, lighted, by his orders, in a public square, by soldiers, who laughed in their faces, and greeted them with shouts of "April Fool's Day!"'

From his early youth Peter enjoyed forming various societies whose purposes were to make fun of authority, such as nobles, the courts of justice, the Church. Peter himself often drew up the by-laws and rules and participated in the tomfooleries of the organizations. These societies, like his jesters, were not always only for amusement. In addition to providing him with fun, they frequently exposed with their buffoonery and nonsense the old-fashioned customs and prejudices that Peter wished to root out of Russia.

In all this clowning there was always present the element of cruelty and force. The nobles were forced, for instance, under threats of dire punishment should they refuse, to admit into their homes the drunken louts that Peter brought into the several societies he had organized and were required to entertain the 'members', feed them, and, in general, show them the warmest hospitality.

Even in carrying out his reforms, such as the Westernization of Russia, terror was often used rather than persuasion. For example, the ukase that beards should no longer be worn was a profound shock to the religious-minded Russians, who believed that the order requiring them to shave their beards off was 'an attempt to disfigure the image of God, after which man had been created, and by which Christ would recognize His own at the Last Day'. Failing to convince the common people—the nobility, by and large, complied with the order—by peaceful means, Peter ordered bearded men to be seized, beaten, and, in some cases, put to death, as an example to others not to defy the wishes of the Czar. There is the story that Peter together with some followers gathered together a group of bearded men in a village and ordered that they be summarily beheaded for failing to obey the order to cut off their beards. While the decapitation was going on a young, beardless lad rushed up and put his head on the block. The soldiers chased him away. The boy returned and again put his head on the block. Peter, who was participating in the executions, walked over to the boy and inquired of him why he insisted on having his head cut off. 'These men are innocent of any wrongdoing and are being killed. I'm innocent also, and therefore I should be killed, too.' The Czar ordered the men to be freed and walked away.

The reign of terror continued to the very end of Peter's life, and Russia during his reign was a police state in the most absolute sense. Peter had proclaimed himself the head of all that transpired in the state, fully believing that he had the right to bring, as one writer phrased it, 'all other wills, all other intelligences and passions, without distinction, and without favour, under his rule'.

The arrest of one suspect usually set off a chain reaction in which dozens of other individuals were incarcerated. Oftentimes, the arrested 'accomplices' had no connection at all with the suspect who, under torture, had blurted out names at random. A memoir written during Peter's reign stated that 'When his [the suspect's] memory failed him, a sort of coarse canvas hood was put over his head, and he was led through the streets, in search of passersby, whom he might point out to the officers of justice. Then a shout would rise, more terrible even than the call of "fire", and the most populous quarters would straightway become a desert. "The tongue, the tongue", thus the populace designated the involuntary, but generally docile instrument of this hunt for culprits, and forthwith there was a general *sauve qui peut*'.

A series of ukases, issued between 1705 and 1722, provided for secret accusations in which the accused was denied the right to know the identity of his accuser. They also provided rewards to informers, and threatened that anyone who had knowledge about anything that threatened the Czar or the empire and did not report such knowledge to the authorities would be subject to severe punishment. The usual reward was six roubles, but if the information was thought of great importance, the reward was more. Numerous records of the time, gathered from official sources, reveal that crimes for which people were punished were often of a trivial nature, such as an imprudent word or two, or a suspicious facial grimace or bodily movement. A peasant was put to torture and then exiled for doing, while drunk, obeisance to the Czar 'in an unusual manner'. Another was tortured for being unaware that the Czar had the title of 'Emperor'. A student, also drunk, spoke disrespectfully of the government; he was given thirty lashes with the knout, his nostrils were torn out, and he was sentenced to a lifetime of hard labour.

Towards the end of his reign, fear and suspicion were so widespread among Peter's most intimate friends and advisers that life in the court became intolerable. Everything was conducted with great secrecy, and Peter, himself suspecting everyone of treachery, insisted on keeping even the smallest details of government to himself. The most innocuous government matter became a subject of deepest mystery, for each person was afraid to speak for fear of misinterpretation and thus be liable to accusations of treason. Conversations were carried on in whispers so that no third person could possibly bear witness, and the official letters of the time that passed from department to department were filled with vague and ambiguous terms. It was, by and large, a repetition of Ivan the Terrible's régime, in which practically none of his closest advisers survived the executioner, all of them, in Ivan's suspicious mind, being guilty of treason. An old Russian proverb, 'Near the Czar, near death', was only too true, and many noblemen preferred to live isolated lives rather than be near the court. As a result, the court was filled with men of the lower classes, such as Peter's chief adviser, Menshikov, who had been a pastry cook's helper. Though a number of writers have pointed out that Peter preferred lower-class aides because the Czar was 'democratically minded', another and probably more cogent reason was that men of the upper classes, valuing their necks, preferred the boring but relatively safe life on their estates rather than the more interesting but precarious existence at court.

Throughout his life, Peter surrounded himself with male companions, whose company he enjoyed much more than women's. Some of his relationships with these companions were suspect, and even in his lifetime there were persistent rumours about his unnatural relationships with them. Nevertheless, whatever his relations with his male friends, Peter did not ignore the distaff side; in fact, from his earliest youth a series of women from all walks of life found their way to the royal bed. Gordon commented that the Czar's 'great foible was the love of women, [though] he was not profuse, nor even generous in his amours'. Peter was not partial in his choice of mistresses, often preferring girls from the lower classes, whom he found to be more passionate and agreeable to his reputedly violent lovemaking than upper-class girls. One of the most famous paintings of Peter, in the Peterhof Palace, showed him with a common wench in his arms in a public drinking place in Holland. On one occasion, Peter saw a pretty girl working in a garden, was attracted to her, and then and there started making advances to her, when the gardener, obviously unafraid of losing his head, threw a hoe at the Czar to keep him away from his helper. It is not known whether the Czar won the girl or the gardener lost his head.

One of his longest amours—most of them rarely exceeded the time it took to accomplish the amorous task at hand—was with Anna Mons, who was the first mistress of any consequence in Peter's life. She was a wine merchant's daughter of Livonian descent, described by Korb as 'exceedingly beautiful and taking'. But Peter wearied of her, as he did of all his women with the exception of Catherine, and soon, accusing her of infidelity, which was, judging from what is known of Anna Mons, most likely true, he sent her packing.

Peter was tightfisted, and it was rarely that his mistresses received any substantial rewards for services rendered. In an exchange of pleasantries with the King of Denmark, the Danish sovereign is reputed to have said, 'Ah, brother, so I hear you have a mistress?' 'Brother', Peter replied, 'my harlots do not cost me much, but yours cost you millions of crowns, which might be better spent.' Even Catherine, when she first made the acquaintance of Peter's royal couch, was enriched only to the extent of a single ducat by the thrifty Czar. As in all things, Peter insisted that his example be followed, and he is said to have fixed the price of favours shown to his soldiers in St. Petersburg by the 'girls' as one kopeck for three kisses.

The wily Catherine, however, even though her initial payment 'for kindness to the Czar' was only a single ducat, was destined to fare much better than the hundreds of other women who also showed him 'a kindness', winning in time not only Peter's hand in marriage but after his death the throne of Russia. Her story is one of the most bizarre in the annals of Russian royalty, if not in the annals of royalty anywhere.

The facts about Catherine are vague and often contradictory, for the annalists of the time were hard put to reveal the true story of how a camp follower, actually a prostitute, finally became the Czarina of Russia. Nevertheless, the story of Catherine has been more or less pieced together, and though there is no certainty as to the facts, there is no doubt that her rise to power was the most spectacular of any woman's in Russian history.

Catherine Skovronsky, or Skovoroshtchenko or Skovorotsky, was probably born somewhere in Livonia, in or about the year 1685, the illegitimate offspring of a high-born Livonian father who had taken her mother, a peasant, as his mistress. Practically nothing is known about her childhood, except that she was orphaned at an early age and was later taken into the house of a pastor by the name of Gluck, where she performed the duties of a servant when she was not entertaining gentlemen. During one of her liaisons she was supposed to have given birth to a child who died in infancy, and the pastor decided that his high-spirited servant would be better off married. He therefore married her to a soldier who, almost as soon as they were wed, was captured by the Russians during the Livonian campaign of the Swedish war. It was during this campaign that Catherine's 'career' began.

When the town of Marienburg in Livonia was captured by a General Sheremetieff, many of the people fled. The buxom Catherine, however, was detained by the regiment, which found her a most pleasant person to have around. Her rise through the ranks was rapid and she was soon the mistress of the General himself. He quickly tired of her, and somehow or other she found her way into the household of Menshikov, Peter's favourite, where, during the day at least, she was employed as a laundress.

It was in Menshikov's house that Peter first saw her. Peter is supposed to have complimented Menshikov for the neatness and cleanliness of his linen, whereupon Menshikov, without saying a word, opened a door to another room and pointed to Catherine, who at the time, aproned and with a sponge in her hand, was busy cleaning. Her robust figure attracted the Czar and he prevailed upon Menshikov to let him have her. She was installed in the Czar's quarters, together with the other women who formed his—and his friends'—'harem', and for some time she seems to have been just one of many. Menshikov himself for a while shared Catherine—as he shared other women—with the Czar. In time Peter became more and more attracted to her, and by 1706 she was his favourite, if not, as there is reason to believe, his wife by a secret marriage. By 1709 she had already had several children by Peter and rarely left his side, though officially she was still only his mistress. However, in 1712, without Church sanction to dissolve his first marriage to Eudoxia, who was still alive, he married Catherine. The ceremony was performed without too much fanfare, with their own daughters, one five years old and the other three, acting as bridesmaids. The marriage, for obvious reasons, was not performed in the Cathedral of the Annunciation in the Kremlin, which was the usual place for Czars' weddings, but in a small chapel that belonged to Prince Menshikov.

Twelve years later, however, Catherine, at Peter's insistence, was formally crowned as the Empress of Russia in the Cathedral of the Assumption, in spite of the fact that Eudoxia was still alive. Unlike the small, almost private wedding that had taken place years before, this ceremony was held with extraordinary splendour and all the pomp of a typical crowning of a Russian ruler.

Early in the morning of May 7, 1724, a cannon in the Kremlin was fired, summoning all those who were to attend the coronation to come to the fortress. At the ceremony Peter himself set the crown on Catherine's head and personally invested her with the orb, the symbol of sovereignty, though he made sure to keep the sceptre, the token of power, in his own hand.

Catherine's crown was the most splendid ever worn by a Russian sovereign. It was copied after the old Byzantine imperial crown and was covered with almost three thousand precious stones, the most resplendent of the jewels being a ruby, the size of a pigeon's egg, which was immediately under the cross of brilliants at the apex of the crown. Her imperial mantle, too, was breathtaking; it was encrusted with jewels and was of such heavy material and had so much ornamentation on it that it weighed a hundred and fifty pounds. But Catherine, if anything, was a woman of great strength and was able to wear it.

Outside the cathedral, decorated for the occasion with scarlet and gold cloth, people from all walks of life gorged themselves on roast ox, game and poultry and became roaring drunk from wine that was freely dispensed from two fountains in the square, one spouting forth white wine and the other red.

Only once before in Russian history—during the Time of Troubles when Marina, the wife of the first False Dmitri, had been crowned—had a Czarina become an empress in her own right. Heretofore, she had always been merely the Czar's wife.

Catherine's coronation assured her of favoured consideration for the throne should the Czar die before her, for Peter, like Ivan the Terrible, had put to death his son and heir, Alexi, in 1719, and had thus brought into sharp focus the question of his successor.

The story of the life and death of Alexi, the son of Eudoxia, Peter's first wife, is probably the most famous, as well as infamous, story of Russian czardom. It began when Eudoxia was put into a nunnery, and the young Alexi, the Czarevich, was handed over to relatives. Throughout the boy's childhood, Peter ignored him, allowing others to take care of his education. Finally, when Alexi was about eighteen, Peter decided to put him to work, 'to make him serve', as Peter himself phrased it. The young man balked, saying that he preferred a more leisurely life. For the next several years a severe friction grew between them, with Peter becoming more and more insistent that Alexi give up his idle ways and Alexi more and more determined to retain his leisure, his bottle and his mistress, a Finnish girl by the name of Euphrosine. Finally, Peter sent him a letter, 'a last summons' as the Czar put it, to return to Russia from Carlsbad, where with Euphrosine he was taking the cure. 'Thou wilt do nothing, and thou wilt learn nothing', Peter wrote, 'when thou comest to power, thou wilt have to be fed like a little bird. . . . I do not spare my own life, nor that of any of my subjects; I will make no exception in thy case. Thou wilt mend thy ways, and thou wilt make thyself useful to the State, otherwise thou shalt be disinherited.'

Alexi, much to Peter's chagrin, agreed to be disinherited, and agreed, too, to disappear from the political scene and live in a monastery. In the meantime, a cloud of suspicion began to hang over Alexi —that he was the head, or at least the tool, of Peter's enemies. Alexi, now fearing for his life, sought sanctuary with various royal families in Europe. Peter dispatched agents to bring the rebellious son back to Russia. The chase covered a good part of Europe—Libau, Vienna, Naples. The agents promised the Czarevich that if he returned he would be treated fairly, but Alexi was suspicious. Euphrosine, bribed by the agents with valuable gifts, prevailed upon him to heed his father's advice and promised that she would follow him later. Finally, Alexi gave in and handed himself over to the agents. Early in 1718, Alexi returned to Russia.

A few weeks later, the high clergy and lay officials were called together in solemn meeting at the Kremlin. Peter was furious; Alexi begged forgiveness. In the Cathedral of the Assumption, Alexi, fearful of the rack, agreed to relinquish his rights to the throne in favour of Catherine's son Peter. Trying to prevent a criminal trial for his acts, he gave one name after another, whatever ones came to his mind, of his supposed fellow-conspirators. By his confession Alexi seemed, for the moment at least, out of danger. But he wasn't. Now that the persecution had begun, now that he had become a symbol of opposition to the Czar, Peter could not rest the case. Likewise, Catherine, thinking of her own chances for the succession, or of those of her son Peter, pressured Peter to rid Russia of Alexi. The Czarevich was again called before the court, and again confessed to conspiratorial acts. In spite of his admissions, however, he was put to the knout, receiving twenty-five lashes. The knout extracted from him the further admission that he had wished for his father's death so that he could become Czar.

After still further tortures, Alexi confessed the following in court, in a speech that has a contemporary ring to it:

'I was brought up by women, who taught me nothing but hypocrisy, to which, indeed, I was naturally inclined. I did not want to work, as my father desired I should work. Viaziemsky and Naryshkin, in their turn, only encouraged me to gossip and get drunk with popes and monks. Menshikov was the only person who advised me well. So by degrees, not only everything about my father, but his very person, became odious to me, and my stay in foreign countries,

whither my father sent me for my own good, did not suffice to cure
me. It was my own wicked nature which prevented me from fearing his just wrath. Since my childhood, I have been far from the
right path, and as I wouldn't follow my father, I was obliged to seek
my way elsewhere.'

This confession was not complete enough, and Alexi was returned
to prison where he was knouted mercilessly. In the meantime a
violent purge took place, with hundreds of people, suspected of
being in league with the Czarevich, being tortured. His very servants
were knouted and then sent to Siberia. A Frenchman, La Vie, wrote
at the time: 'There have been so many accusations in this town that
it seems like a place of disaster; we all live in a sort of public infection, every one is either an accuser, or an accused person'.

Finally, in the midst of the purge, the High Court of Justice, composed of the Senate, the Ministers, the officers of the crown, and the
Staff of the Guard, altogether comprising a hundred and twenty-
seven judges, pronounced a unanimous verdict—death.

Even the carrying out of the sentence, however, was clouded in
mystery, and the farce-tragedy continued, in a sense, after the
Czarevich's death. For a long time all sorts of stories circulated as to
how the Czarevich died.

The official version ran as follows: 'The Czarevich, when the
verdict was read to him, was seized with a sort of apoplexy. When
he recovered his senses, he asked to see his father, confessed his
faults in his presence, received his pardon, and, in a few moments,
breathed his last'. Peter was disposed to be merciful, the document
further read, but 'in the midst of this uncertainty and distressing
agitation, it pleased God Almighty, whose holy judgments are
always just, to deliver the person of the Sovereign and his Empire
from all fear and all danger, by means of His all-divine goodness'.

Lefort: 'On the day of the Prince's death, the Czar, accompanied
by Tolstoi, went to the fortress, and into one of the vaulted dungeons, furnished with gallows, and all the other necessary preparations for applying the knout. The unhappy wretch was brought in,
and having been fastened up, he was given numerous blows with
the knout, and—though I am not sure of this—I have been assured
that his father struck the first blows. The same thing was done at
ten o'clock in the morning, and towards four o'clock he was so ill-
treated that he died under the lash'.

Count Rabutin, the Czar's Resident: '. . . Peter struck his son so hard [with the knout] that the poor wretch fell swooning to the ground, and the Ministers thought he was dead'. Catherine, who Rabutin averred was present during the scene in the prison, 'then sent for the Court physician, a certain Hobby, who opened Alexi's veins'.

The journal of the military garrison: 'On the 14th of June, a special torture chamber was arranged in the Troubetzkoi Bastion, in a casemate close to the dungeon in which, on that same day, the Czarevich had been shut up. On the 19th, two visits were paid to the chamber [the journal then lists other visits that took place during the next few days]. . . . On the 26th, there was yet another sitting, in the Czar's presence, from eight o'clock in the morning till eleven; and that same day, at six o'clock in the evening, the Czarevich died'.

For years many other versions of Alexi's death made the rounds of European capitals—that Peter himself chopped off his son's head, and then had it sewn on again when the body was on public view; that Catherine herself poisoned Alexi; and even the story that Alexi had not been killed but had somehow managed to escape (for years afterwards False Alexis appeared in various parts of Russia). In whatever manner he died, the Czarevich's death by Peter's order, or hand, opened up the way for a long series of domestic and foreign adventurers who plagued Russia for years even as Ivan the Terrible's murder of his son opened the way to the horrendous Time of Troubles more than a century before.

Throughout this tragic affair, Catherine was a bulwark for Peter, supporting him and possibly egging him on to excesses. As previously noted, Catherine had a good reason to want to be rid of Alexi: his death would put her or her offspring in a most favourable position as Peter's successor.

The reasons for Peter's attraction to Catherine, which increased over the years, are not always too clear. One reason, ostensibly, was the fact that the former Livonian whore and laundress was the only one capable of comforting him when he was seized with convulsions. Count Bassewitz, the Minister of Holstein to the court of Russia, wrote: 'The Czarina . . . was necessary to the preservation of his life. This prince was unhappily subject to very painful convulsions, which were thought to proceed from a poison given to him in his youth. These pains Catherine had found the secret of removing by studied succours and laborious offices, of which she alone was capable, giving herself entirely up to the preservation of a health, equally important to the state and herself. Thus the Czar could not live without her, and thus he promoted her to his bed and throne.'

When the Czar was seized by fits, they were usually accompanied by violent headaches. At such times the Czar would pass from a state of prostration to one of extreme violence, almost madness, and out of fear for their lives, everyone near him would run away. Catherine, however, would approach him and, half tenderly and half commandingly, calm him. She would cradle his head in her lap, run his fingers through his hair until he became drowsy, and then, when he fell asleep, she would sit with his head in her lap for hours until he finished sleeping. When he awoke the Czar was usually refreshed and well again.

In addition to her being a capable nurse there was another, and probably more important, reason why Peter was so fond of Catherine. In her way she was the feminine counterpart of the tough, vulgar, violent and headstrong Czar. She was a *pahodnaia ofitserskaia jena*, a typical officer's wife, capable of bearing the most severe physical tests of endurance. Oftentimes, she went with him, sharing the hardships of the battlefield, long journeys, backward conditions. If need be, without complaint, she would lie on the cold, hard ground, live in a tent, or ride all day on horseback. In the Persian campaign, for instance, she shaved her head and wore a grenadier's cap. She would review the troops for hours at a time, dropping a cheerful word here and there, and even visit the barracks of the soldiers, where she would personally give them brandy. Throughout her life her peasant-stock background was in evidence; she was physically tough, mentally strong and morally weak.

In spite of her masculine qualities, she was at times extremely feminine, capable of great tenderness, especially towards Peter. She did not lack feminine vanity and dyed her fair hair black to enhance her high-coloured complexion. She also forbade the ladies of the court to copy the cut of her clothes. She loved to dance, and was an expert at it, being able to execute the most complicated pirouettes.

There seems to have been a real passion between Catherine and Peter, and their letters to each other are filled with protestations of love and quite often, too, with extremely frank references to sexual activities. 'Oh, if you were with me here', she wrote to him during one of his long absences, 'we would make another *Shishenka*!' Many of their letters refer to their passion for each other in less coy terms.

In appearance Catherine was not beautiful, especially after she had passed the first flush of youth. A few contemporaneous descriptions of her are kindly, but most of them, as well as the portraits of her that still exist, reveal her as being quite unattractive. Baron von Pollnitz, one of the people of the time who described her kindly, wrote in 1717:

'The Czarina was in the prime of life, and showed no signs of having possessed beauty. She was tall and strong, exceedingly dark, and would have seemed darker but for the rouge and whitening with which she covered her face. There was nothing unpleasant about her manners, and any one who remembered the princess's origin would have been disposed to think them good. . . . It might fairly be said that if this princess had not all the charms of her sex she had all the gentleness.'

A more frank description, and less kind, is the one by the Margravine of Bayreuth, who wrote in 1723:

'The Czarina was short and huddled up, very much tanned, and quite devoid of dignity or grace. The very sight of her proved her low birth. She was muffled up in her clothes like a German comedy actress. Her gown had been bought in some old clothes' shop, it was very old-fashioned, covered with heavy silver embroidery, and with dirt. . . . She had a dozen orders, and as many portraits of saints and relics, fastened all along the facings of her dress, so that when she walked she jingled like a mule.'

A portrait of her that was displayed in the Winter Palace in St. Petersburg showed her as being far from attractive. In describing it one writer said that the portrait revealed a face that was large and round and common, a nose that was hideously turned up. 'She had goggle eyes, an opulent bust, and all the general appearance of a servant girl in a German inn.'

Catherine was bold enough to have lovers throughout her life with the Czar, in spite of the fearful danger she ran should Peter decide to punish her for cuckolding him. Peter seemed to tolerate, or was unaware of, her extra-marital relationships until her liaison with William Mons, the brother of Peter's one-time mistress Anna Mons.

Late in 1724 Peter discovered that Catherine was having an affair with Mons, ordered him to be arrested, and, after extracting a confession from him, had him executed. The next day Peter insisted that Catherine drive with him past the scaffold that contained Mons' body. When they did so, Catherine never turned her head to look at her lover's corpse. Vengefully, Peter then had Mons' head cut off, had it put in a vessel containing wine, and placed in a prominent position in the Czarina's apartment.

Catherine tried desperately to win her way back into his good graces, but the rupture was deep. In fact, there is evidence that points to the possibility that because of the Mons affair Peter was contemplating a complete break with Catherine, but whatever action, if any, the Czar was considering never materialized for, a few weeks after Mons' death, Peter himself passed away on February 8, 1725.

Though the cause of Peter's death has been attributed by certain historians to a severe fever he contracted when he flung himself into ice-cold water to save some shipwrecked sailors, the truth appears to lie elsewhere. Campredon, the French Ambassador to Russia at the time, in a dispatch to his government wrote that the Czar died of 'a sickness caused by a poorly healed venereal malady'. Even Pokrovsky, the dean of Soviet historians, who echoed the Bolshevik viewpoint that Peter was a most admirable and enlightened Czar, 'the real one' as the Communists call him, believed the Czar's death was due to disease and excesses and not the result of a heroic action. 'As is well known', Pokrovsky wrote, 'Peter died of the effects of syphilis, probably contracted in Holland and ill-cured by the doctors there. For that matter, given the Homeric drunkenness of Peter's court, the best doctors could scarcely have helped him.'

The news of the death of the Czar, the greatest ruler and possibly the most cruel that Russia had had until that time, did not unduly stir the mass of the people. They took the news of his passing away with equanimity and, to a certain extent, with relief. Several contemporaries even wrote that there was 'general rejoicing' among the people. At least one of Peter's followers, however, the non-Russian Gordon, was deeply affected by the Czar's death, and in the manner of the time he wrote the following epitaph:

'Here deposited is all that could die of the immortal, Peter Alexowitz. It is superfluous to add, Monarch of the Great Empire of Russia: That crown, far from giving any lustre to him, became illus-

trious by his wearing it. Let antiquity be silent: Let her boast no more
her Alexanders, or her Caesars: It was easy to conquer, where every
soldier was a hero. But he, who never knew rest till now, found not
subjects skilled in war, souls who preferred fame before life: His
people might be said more to resemble the bears of their country
than men; yet even these, untractable and barbarous as they were,
he civilized and polished. He, like the rising sun, dispelled their
hereditary darkness; and by the force of his innate genius taught
them to conquer the conquerors of Germany. Other princes have
led victorious armies: His army he made himself. Blush thou Art,
to see a hero who owed thee nothing! Exult O nature! This prodigy
was all your own.'

XVII

St. Petersburg: the New Capital

THE KREMLIN was always an anathema to Peter, and during his lifetime he shunned it, preferring to live in a number of other places rather than within its cold, forbidding walls. The fortress represented to him not only the place where as a child he had witnessed the horrors of the *streltsy* riots, when the soldiers had dragged him through the blood of his own relatives and friends, but it also represented to Peter all that was outmoded and that should be changed in Russian life. He was repelled by its virtual storehouse of relics; its bewildering maze of corridors and court apartments; its *terem*, where the distaff side of the royal family languished in idleness; its multitude of Church dignitaries and attendants, gloomy-looking in their black robes and long beards; and its formal, humourless Byzantine ritual.

Peter's very nature was that of a man who had to break down barriers, try new methods, and visualize new goals, and the stolid Kremlin symbolized to him Russia's very lack of flexibility, fluidity and forward movement. The citadel symbolized, too, the East, with its tradition of Byzantium and the Tartars, for which Peter had neither sympathy nor understanding. Even the colourful city of Moscow, with its market-places in the Oriental style, its narrow, confining, crooked streets, and its Eastern atmosphere, did not fascinate him.

It is not surprising, therefore, that in time Peter entertained the revolutionary idea of moving the capital of Russia away from the Kremlin, which he hated, and Moscow itself, which he disliked. The question was—where? For a while he considered Nizhni Novgorod for his new capital, and some plans still exist in the Russian national archives relating to this project. But this city on the upper Volga was no more European than Moscow and in many ways just as Oriental in its appearance and outlook, and Peter soon abandoned the idea of moving the capital there. Other Russian cities were considered, but none was acceptable. And for good reason. For what Peter really wanted was not only to get away from the Kremlin and Moscow *per se* but to have a Western European type of city as the capital, and none of the cities then in existence in Russia could possibly qualify.

This desire for a typically European city as the capital of a 'new' Russia had been in Peter's mind for a long time, possibly since he was a young man, when he had been so fascinated by the *sloboda*. And this desire was strengthened, too, by his travels through Europe where, unlike any Czar who had preceded him, he had personally seen new and different ways. In addition to his famous grand tour, not a year had passed after 1701 that he hadn't crossed the European frontier of Russia at some place or other, each time returning from his journeys more and more convinced that the face of Russia should be turned towards the West.

Finally, during Russia's war with Sweden, Peter made a bold decision: at the mouth of the Neva River he would build an entirely new city—a city that would be not only Russia's new capital but would be 'a window open to the West'.

Though the actual location for the new city was in the worst conceivable place from a structural and health point of view, for the site consisted of marshes surrounded by vast stretches of desolate land, psychologically it was a sound choice; the capital of Russia was to be as close to Western Europe as possible—actually only a scant few miles from the frontier—an ideal spot for Peter to pursue his aim of Westernizing Russia.

At the time Peter was severely criticized for choosing such an area. In addition to the treacherous marshes on which the city was to be situated, his critics claimed that the new capital was strategically vulnerable to enemy attack; that by removing the capital to the frontier he was neglecting the interior provinces; and that tradition was being flaunted by having the capital on what many people considered to be not Russian soil but Finnish. More than a hundred years later there were still many Russians who angrily denounced Peter for moving the capital, and one of them, Konstantin Aksakov, in an apostrophe to Peter, wrote: 'Thou hast despised Russia and all her past. Therefore a seal of malediction is imprinted on all thy senseless work. Pitilessly thou hast repudiated Moscow and hast gone out to build, apart from thy people, a solitary city. For thou and they could no longer live together'.

The building of St. Petersburg was carried out with utter disregard of expense; in fact, the costs were so great that the national treasury was depleted. Tools were pitifully inadequate or, in some instances, non-existent. For a while there were no wheelbarrows, and the labourers carried dirt from one spot to another in the corners of their clothing. Nevertheless, what was lacking in tools was somewhat countervailed by a forced draft of manpower; by the hundreds of thousands, serfs and labourers from all parts of Russia were sent to St. Petersburg. When the job of transforming the pestilential marshes into a city was finally completed, more than two hundred thousand of them had died of disease and exposure.

The job of filling in the marshes and building quays seemed endless, and time and again floods inundated the city. In 1705 nearly the whole town was under water, and as late as 1721, nine years after St. Petersburg had formally been declared the capital of Russia, the streets of the city were navigable. Peter himself once almost drowned on the Nevsky Prospect, the main street of the city, and on another occasion the cottage he was living in at the time was under two feet of water, a not uncommon occurrence in those days for houses in St. Petersburg. The critics of Peter's new capital were overjoyed whenever there was an inundation, and they predicted that one day this city defiled by foreign ways would sink for ever under the water.

St. Petersburg represented the 'new' spirit in Russia just as Moscow represented the 'old'. For example, Peter's campaign to get the women out of the *terem* and into a more advanced social life was carried out in the new capital to a greater degree than anywhere else in Russia. In St. Petersburg some women mingled freely with men and were no longer confined to haremlike quarters. By means of a ukase issued in 1718, periodic receptions called 'assemblies' were ordered to be held in various private homes in which women were to join men in social activities such as dancing and games. The ukase listed the procedure to be followed down to the minutest detail.

In order to introduce Western social graces into Russian court life, Peter himself often set a personal example, insisting that his dance steps, for instance, be imitated, as well as the various Western manners and mannerisms he had observed in Europe.

Court life at St. Petersburg, however, was a far cry from that at Versailles, and the attempted aping of Western ways in the court and in the homes of the aristocracy was often more ludicrous than instructive. Many of the men and women, for example, were embarrassed by this new disturbing relationship between the sexes, and attended court receptions, especially the newly organized assemblies, only under the greatest official pressure. Ill at ease, the men refused to mingle with the women, and vice versa; they conversed among themselves or sat alone in brooding silence. To break down the reserve between the sexes at social functions, Peter initiated various ice-breaking amenities, one being a dance in which he insisted that the men kiss the women on their lips when certain figures of the dance were excuted. (It may be noted, in passing, that the women of the time for beauty's sake still blackened their teeth.)

The manners of the aristocracy of the time were scarcely more refined than the common people's, and the Czar himself was often as boorish as the most ignorant peasant. Nevertheless, Peter had seen enough during his travels through Europe to realize that certain amenities of Western civilization would have to be introduced into Russia before the Russian, too, could be considered Westerners. As a result, Peter ordered a book to be issued on social behaviour, in which correct manners were prescribed; among other things, the Russians were instructed to be modest, friendly and respectful, to look people squarely in the face when they were speaking or being spoken to, to take their hats off when conversing with women, not to wear heavy boots on a dance floor, not to spit on the floor, not to pick dirt from the nose, to sing without shouting, not to rub the lips with the hands, not to lick the fingers after dining or gnaw bones during a meal, to talk with the mouth full, not to scratch the head. In many ways the book on etiquette was Peter's *Domostroy*.

By and large Peter's desire to build a Western European type of city was successful, and over the years St. Petersburg, because of the numerous canals, quays and bridges, was often compared to Venice. Still, it was not the layout of the city, which differed so greatly from other Russian cites of the time, that made St. Petersburg unique; it was its spirit. As Peter planned it, the new capital was not only 'a window open to the West' but a truly Western city. Here foreigners were not confined to a segregated area as they had been in Moscow's *sloboda*, but they lived together, and also mingled freely, with the Russians. In St. Petersburg the Czar had his greatest success in convincing the people to wear Western-style clothes, to learn European languages, to cultivate various arts and sciences, and to break in general with the tradition-heavy past, with its prejudices and superstitions.

6—TK

Though Peter was miserly, he spared no expense in building fine palaces in St. Petersburg, so that everyone, native and foreigner alike, would be impressed by the magnificence of the new capital. However, Peter himself disliked large buildings as living quarters and rarely lived in them; instead, he chose to live nearby in a modest Dutch-style house which had only a minimum of luxuries, though it was not as mean as his cottage at Preobrazhenskoe. In time he used several other cottages in and near St. Petersburg, as well as in other areas. One of them, in Revel, was quite typical of his housing tastes, consisting as it did of only four rooms—a bedroom, dining-room, bathroom, and kitchen. Thus, just as he had shunned the opulent but depressing Kremlin, he now refused to live permanently in Peterhof, the new palace in the new capital that was copied from Versailles and rivalled it in beauty, opulence, majesty and size. Though Peterhof did not remind him as the Kremlin did of indelibly bitter memories of a blood-soaked childhood, it still did not intrigue him, in spite of its sparkling fountains and spacious parks and sumptuous rooms.

Peter insisted that elaborate balls be held in the palace, so that the 'new' Russians could display themselves in their newly adapted European dress and dance their recently learned Western steps. Although he attended them and often took the lead in various ball-room activities, he would, if he was not too drunk, leave the palace with the other invited guests when the affair was over and return to his small cottage, where he could see from his bedroom window the bay and the ships of his tiny fleet.

Peter's hatred for the Kremlin was so intense that, from the time St. Petersburg became the capital, he rarely entered its grounds, and then only because it was necessary to carry out state affairs or because he wanted to take advantage of its time-honoured traditions. In 1722, for instance, after the war with Sweden, he made a triumphal march into the Kremlin, imitating the Czars before him who also had returned from victorious wars and had been acclaimed at the ancient citadel. In 1724, when he insisted that Catherine should be crowned empress in her own right, he again took advantage of the traditions of the Kremlin, where the Czars before him had been crowned in the Cathedral of the Assumption. Peter realized very well that in the eyes of the people, and of the clergy and nobility, too, the crowning of Catherine in the same cathedral where other rulers had been crowned would add weight and prestige to his unique step of having a Czar's wife invested with the title of 'Empress'.

Peter's abandonment of the Kremlin was a logical step for him; it was a direct result not only of bitter memories but of a burning desire to liberate Russia from outmoded traditions and practices, which, he felt, were stifling her. Moreover, like the desertion of the capitals of Kiev and Vladimir in the late Middle Ages, it was necessitated by the vision of new horizons. No other action that Peter undertook in a lifetime filled with precipitous actions was as symbolically meaningful as the move to St. Petersburg. Henceforth, Russia was not only to have a window that faced Europe but in time was to be an integral part of Europe itself.

XVIII

The Reigns of the Czarinas

THE list of Peter's achievements is legion—a new script, improvements to the language, the establishment of the first Russian newspaper, translations of foreign books into Russian, canal building, sheep breeding, grape planting, increased potato cultivation, development and protection of natural resources, a strengthened governmental apparatus, to name but a few. However, by the execution of his son and the crowning of Catherine as empress, so that she had a strong claim to the throne after his death, he failed to achieve a most important goal—a strong line of successors to carry out his work. Of the six rulers who followed him, one was an illiterate hoyden, two others were women who were dominated by their self-seeking foreign lovers, one was an immature boy, another was a mere infant, and still another was an imbecile.

Many people at the time believed that after Peter's death Moscow would again become the capital. But Catherine, who now ruled in her own right as Catherine I (1725–27), had no intention of leaving the spanking-new palace at St. Petersburg for the austere fortress in Moscow. And for the next two years or so, until her death in 1727, the Czarina, who has been described as 'a Livonian by birth, a Lutheran by faith, a servant by trade and a harlot by avocation', threw herself into a series of wild orgies, completely neglecting her duties as ruler. When she died, ostensibly from a lung ailment but more probably from the same venereal disease that caused Peter's death, she was, according to contemporaries, a fat, blotchy-faced, dissolute-looking hag. Of the eleven children she had borne Peter, only two survived her: Anna, born in 1706, and Elizabeth, born in 1709.

Catherine was succeeded to the throne by the twelve-year-old Peter II (1727–30), the grandson of Peter the Great and the son of Alexi. The young Czar earnestly wished to turn Russia back to pre-Petrine times, for he had little sympathy for his grandfather's new ways, and though there were few official acts during his short reign that put into practice his beliefs, there is no doubt that had he lived he would have tried, as the young Czar himself said, 'not to sail the same seas as my grandfather did'.

St. Petersburg was antipathetical to Peter II for, among other things, it represented to him not only the most visible symbol of Peter the Great's de-Russification programme but was also the city that had been dear to the heart of his father's murderer. Therefore, soon after he became Czar, Peter II decreed that Moscow would again become the capital of Russia and that the government as well as the royal family would move back into the Kremlin. It was a decision that was met with rejoicing by the traditionalists. But Moscow and the Kremlin's return to glory was short-lived, for scarcely three years after Peter II became Czar he died of smallpox at the age of fifteen.

In 1732, two years after Anna I (1730–40), the eldest daughter of Peter and Catherine, became Empress of Russia, the court returned to St. Petersburg, where it remained for almost two hundred years. Though the court and the government offices were never officially moved back to the Kremlin from St. Petersburg during these two centuries, the Kremlin was used from time to time as the residence of the royal family whenever it decided to go to Moscow for a holiday or for various official ceremonies such as coronations, which were still held in the Cathedral of the Assumption.

Anna herself, after she left Moscow for St. Petersburg, never returned to the Kremlin. A disgustingly fat, dull and vulgar woman filled with envy and spite, she ruled her St. Petersburg court with German adventurers guiding her, as though she were a provincial baroness in a tiny German duchy, rather than the ruler of a great empire.

It was during Anna's reign that Moscow was devastated by the worst fire since the end of the sixteenth century; flames swept through Moscow, burning down a good part of the city and suburbs and a number of buildings in the Kremlin, including the arsenal and the mint, and seriously damaging the palace and many of the ministerial buildings. In addition to the loss of great sums of currency, huge stores of military supplies, records, registers and historical items of all kinds were irretrievably lost. It was during this fire that the Czar Bell reputedly fell and lay embedded in the ground for almost a century, until 1836, when it was raised to its present position.

Upon Anna's death in 1740, she was succeeded to the throne by Ivan VI, the infant son of a niece, also named Anna. Within a year, however, Peter the Great's youngest surviving daughter, Elizabeth, through a *coup d'état*, seized power and had the infant Czar imprisoned in the fortress of Schlüsselburg.

Elizabeth I (1741–61) was in many respects a female counterpart of her father, Peter the Great. She was a large-framed woman, pleasure-loving to the point of sexual gluttony. As robust as a grenadier, she enjoyed mannish diversions and even dressed as a man on many occasions, and she loved to do things on a lavish, gigantic scale. On the other hand, she was also lazy, self-indulgent and inordinately vain. She was an extremely complex person, unpredictable and contradictory in her actions and her beliefs. As a result, contemporaneous and modern writers have varied widely in their interpretations of her, some viewing her as little more than a disgusting voluptuary while others compare her to the great woman monarchs of all times.

Though Elizabeth appeared to have the inherent intelligence necessary to be a great monarch, she wasn't, for her character was such that she frittered away her powers on extravagant personal indulgences. Even so, she did accomplish a great deal, many of her achievements being of great importance. She founded the first Russian university, in Moscow in 1755, and furthered the introduction of Western culture, especially French, into Russian life. During her reign the first real beginnings of Russian scholarship and belles-lettres were made, with the poet Lomonosov leading the way. She appears to have had a sense of justice and, on occasion, fulminated against government officials who did not do an honest job. 'The laws are not carried out because of common enemies inside who prefer their lawless gains to their oath, duty, and honour', she said in a letter of complaint. 'The insatiable pursuit of gain has gone so far, that some of the courts established for justice have become a mockery.' Unlike her father, she opposed the concept of *lex talionis* and in 1753 abolished the death penalty, being the first monarch in relatively modern times to do so.

Though Elizabeth like Russian rulers before her, with the exception of Peter the Great, was a very religious person, she did not—again like so many other Russian rulers—allow this to interfere with her penchant for carnal pleasures. The Czarina, according to the then Spanish Ambassador, Duke de Liria, 'shamelessly indulged in practices which would have made blush even the least modest person'. Until the very end of her life, a steady flow of lovers, estimated to be in the hundreds, found their way to her royal bed. Like her father she loved to have a 'good time', and throughout the two decades she ruled Russia her life was filled with round after round of balls, masquerades, pageants, and pleasure excursions of many kinds that were more elaborate than anything that had been attempted in the Russian court up to that time.

Early in her reign Elizabeth brought to her court her nephew Peter, the son of her deceased sister Anna, and soon thereafter arranged for him to marry the fourteen-year-old Princess Sophia Augusta of Anhalt-Zerbst, who later ruled as Catherine II. An independent, alert young woman, Catherine chafed under the domineering attitude of Elizabeth, complaining in later life that 'neither he [the Grand Duke Peter] nor I, during the Empress's reign, dared to go to town or even to leave the house without first getting her permission'. In her memoirs Catherine gave her impression of Elizabeth, and though she was far from an impartial observer of the Czarina, her comments do point up Elizabeth's character.

'The Empress Elizabeth had keen natural intelligence, was of a gay disposition, and indulged in excessive pleasures. I think she was kind at heart; she had great high-mindedness and much vanity; she wanted to shine and was fond of admiration. . . . Her extreme preoccupation was that her beauty should not be dimmed by any other's. This inspired her extreme jealousy, which often drove her to a pettiness unworthy of majesty. Her laziness prevented her from cultivating her mind, and her early youth had been very much wasted. . . . As she possessed no principles and had no serious matters with which to occupy her mind, her life dwindled into such tedium that in her last years she found nothing better to do than sleep as long as she could. For the rest of the time, a woman, expert in the art, would tell her stories.'

Catherine's opinion of Elizabeth was quite typical of other contemporary viewpoints, which insisted that Elizabeth was so intellectually lazy that though she was often shown a map of Europe, she never bothered to study it and till the end of her life believed that England could be reached by dry land.

Though Elizabeth had the sumptuous Winter Palace built in St.

Petersburg at the cost of ten million roubles—a staggering sum in those days—she was not a great partisan of the new capital, deserting it periodically to visit Moscow which intrigued her and for which she had a great affection. In fact, her visits to Moscow were so numerous and of such long duration—she occasionally stayed there as long as a year at a time—that, for all intents and purposes, there was a dual capital during her reign.

Whenever she left St. Petersburg for Moscow, or vice versa, the various branches of the government—the War Office, the Treasury, the Foreign Office and others—moved with her, as well as the court personnel itself, which numbered many thousands. In order to supply transportation for so large a number of people, nineteen thousand horses were used, which transported as many as twenty-four thousand people. Elizabeth insisted that a good part of her personal and household possessions also be taken along, with the result that dresses and uniforms, favourite chairs and beds and mirrors and curtains, wines and liquors, and even pots and pans were hauled over the four-hundred-mile-long road. Influential members of the government insisted that their personal possessions be transported too, with the result that each journey took on the appearance of a huge army on the move.

The road between the two cities, although the best in Russia at the time, was still a treacherous one. In parts it was sandy but there were many stretches that were soft and marshy, and though attempts were made to make the road more solid by laying a track of logs over the worst sections, the journey was usually extremely difficult and it would often take as long as a week. Wintertime, when sleighs could be used, was a much better time for travelling and the trip would often be made in as little as three days. Some of the sleighs were huge affairs, containing a completely furnished room, bed and all. Elizabeth's personal enclosed sleigh, which she used for her coronation in 1742 and which is still preserved in the Kremlin, was equipped with, among other conveniences, a stove, a table, and divans, and was luxuriously decorated with green cloth.

When Elizabeth decided upon one of her frequent journeys, thousands of labourers were dispatched to the St. Petersburg-Moscow highway to level the road, lay logs if need be, and, in general, put it in as good condition as possible. Then the thousands of horses that were needed for the trip were put on special rations of oats to build them up for the arduous journey. Finally the army set off, stopping now and then to effect a change of horses. However, the horses were driven at such high speeds and for such long periods of time without rest that many of them died along the way, and were replaced by others from spare teams that were always taken along. On one occasion, at the insistence of the Empress, the four-hundred-mile trip was made in twenty-four hours, with the result that hundreds of exhausted horses were left to die all along the road. (Driving horses at top speed for long distances was a common sport of Russian royalty, in spite of that fact that this 'sport' often killed the animals. The road, for instance, between St. Petersburg and Czarskoe Seloe, the town some miles away that housed the summer residences of the royal family, was dotted with the carcasses of horses that had been literally driven to death, and many foreigners at the time complained that it was almost impossible in the summer-time to drive along the road without being made sick by the stench of rotting horseflesh.)

While in Moscow, Elizabeth stayed in the Kremlin palace or in various other royal residences in and around the city. She appears to have been quite popular with the people of Moscow, especially with upper-class ladies, for whom every Sunday she held open house.

Since Elizabeth was devout, she made frequent pilgrimages to the various holy places in the vicinity of Moscow. To prove her piety she often insisted on making them by foot, but since she was by nature quite lazy, after a mile or so she would give orders to stop for the day and the entire company, consisting of a large entourage of court ladies and gentlemen, would then be quartered in an enormous camp that was pitched by the side of the road. On one such pilgrimage to the Troitsko-Sergievskaia Monastery, about forty miles from the Kremlin, the expedition's progress was so slow that more than half the summer was spent in getting there.

Though Elizabeth was fond of Moscow, most of the court, and especially the foreign embassies which were forced to move to Moscow whenever the Czarina did, intensely disliked the city because of its inconveniences, for Moscow since the capital had been moved north had fallen into disrepair. During the building of St. Petersburg, Peter had given strict orders that construction everywhere was to cease and all available material and men be shipped to the site of the new capital on the Neva. Later, Peter had made a half-hearted attempt to improve the erstwhile capital, but little had been done. As a result the buildings of Moscow had become dilapidated. Streets were often impassable, with mud so deep at certain times of the year that people had to carry with them portable bridges in order to cross them. Time and again carriages would overturn as they rattled over the poles that had been laid in the mud, and their occupants would be thrown into the muck. The sanitation system, whatever little there had been in former days, was neglected, so that in addition to the mud and muck refuse littered the city.

Moreover, the bitter cold of the Moscow winters was another complaint, especially of foreigners attached to Elizabeth's court. One foreign diplomat wrote home to his government that 'the weather is at present so excessively cold that the timber, of which the houses are built here, cracks as if there was cannons a-firing'.

In spite of the foreigners' complaints about Moscow's living conditions, life in St. Petersburg was not too agreeable either. For instance, the Winter Palace during Elizabeth's reign was a weird combination of extraordinary sumptuousness and extraordinary squalor. The main salons were huge and lavishly decorated, so that their appearance to the outside world was one of great opulence, befitting a powerful monarch of a powerful country such as Russia. But apart from the main salons, the other quarters in the palace (which remained unfinished even at the time of Elizabeth's death because she could not raise additional money to have it completed) were in a shocking state. The doors would not shut, draughts blew in through poorly hung windows, water trickled down the walls so that the hangings were constantly mildewed. Since the Winter Palace was unfinished and many of the rooms were uninhabitable, there was a shortage of space. Catherine, when she was still a grand duchess, complained that as many as seventeen of her personal servants had to sleep in one small room next to hers, while she herself had to sleep in a room in which there were large, gaping cracks in the stove.

The robust Elizabeth, however, did not appear to mind too much the discomfort of either the gilded squalor of her St. Petersburg residence or the frowsy disrepair of her Moscow ones. She was much more interested in her personal appearance, upon which she spared no expense. (Upon her death she left behind her more than fifteen thousand gowns, dresses and uniforms and two chestfuls of silk stockings, among a mountain of other personal effects.) She had a magnificent figure, knew that she did, and made sure that everybody else knew it too. For this reason, and also because she loved to have a good time, court life whether in free and easy St. Petersburg or in dour Moscow consisted of innumerable parties, especially masquerades, during which Elizabeth, often costumed as a man, could display her succulent charms. Catherine in her memoirs gave a picture of one such occasion, in which, incidentally, she could not help but reveal her admiration for the domineering Empress:

'In 1744, in Moscow', Catherine wrote, '. . . the Empress had a fancy to have all men appear at the Court balls dressed as women and the women as men, without masks; it was like a Court day metamorphosed. The men wore whaleboned petticoats, the women the Court costume of men. The men disliked these reversals of their sex and were in the worst possible humour, because they felt hideous in their disguises. The women looked liked scrubby little boys, while the more aged had thick short legs which were anything but attractive. The only woman who looked really well and completely a man was the Empress herself. As she was tall and powerful, male attire suited her. She had the handsomest leg I have ever seen on any man and her feet were admirably proportioned. She dressed to perfection and everything she did had the same special grace whether she dressed as a man or as a woman. One felt inclined to look at her and turn away with regret because nothing could replace her.'

As for the staid Kremlin, no ruler for a long, long time did replace her, for she had transformed the fortress that had always symbolized all that was austere and forbidding and traditional in Russian life into a place of pleasure, where madcap royalty, led by a woman, indulged themselves in wild, orgiastic revelries. The days of the *terem* seemed far away indeed.

XIX

Catherine the Great

DURING the two centuries that the capital of Russia was St. Petersburg, the Kremlin, though for the most part abandoned as an administrative centre and the home of the Czars and Czarinas, remained the ritual and spiritual centre of the country. In its cathedrals the Czars were married and crowned, and in its vaults deceased members of the royal family were entombed. The Church did not consider any other place but Moscow its headquarters and the Kremlin churches retained their supremacy over all others, even over the largest and most elaborate churches in Russia, such as St. Isaac's Cathedral in St. Petersburg.

According to the personal wishes of the particular Czar or Czarina at the time, the Kremlin was either occupied by royalty during visits to Moscow or, as was more common, completely ignored, the rulers preferring other, more comfortable quarters in Moscow. Some of the Czars and Czarinas not only bypassed the Kremlin during their visits to Moscow but also refused to spend any money on its upkeep and refurbishing.

Elizabeth, whose visits to Moscow were so frequent and who often resided in the Kremlin, was one of the few rulers during this two-hundred-year period who was willing to allocate funds for alterations and, moreover, additions to the fortress. In 1753 she commissioned Bartolomeo Rastrelli, one of the most famous architects of the time and one of the founders of the baroque school of architecture in Russia, to build a small palace (the Elizabeth Palace) for her within the Kremlin grounds and facing the Moscow River. However, her attempts to keep up the general appearance of the Kremlin grounds and buildings were not successful. In 1750 she appointed a commission to clean up debris that had accumulated over the decades and to make certain repairs on the buildings, but the commission did next to nothing. No other action of consequence was taken to renovate the Kremlin, and by the time of her death on December 25, 1761, the fortress having been neglected for half a century was in a dilapidated condition, with many buildings in a partial state of deterioration.

Catherine II (1762–96), who succeeded her husband, Peter III (1761–62) to the throne, had spent a great deal of time in Moscow during Elizabeth's reign, but she had not been particularly impressed with the former capital, and even many years later when she wrote her memoirs complained bitterly about the poor accommodation. Concerning one of her stays there she wrote:

'We were living in a wooden wing. . . . Water flowed down the panelling and the rooms were singularly damp. . . . My bedroom [was] filled with every kind of insect preventing me from sleeping. . . . Nothing could be more uncomfortable. The wind blew in on all sides, the windows and doors were half rotten, the floor had cracks and gaps three or four fingers wide, and it was filled with vermin.'

Experiences of this kind, plus the fact that the young Teutonic Catherine felt strange in the city that was the heart of Orthodox Russia, contributed at the time to her intense dislike for Moscow, and she continued to harbour this dislike, almost an aversion, for the ancient city for the rest of her life. On the other hand, she had a deep affection for St. Petersburg and was not loath to say so. The condemnation of Peter for moving the capital away from Moscow continued up to—and after—the reign of Catherine, and in her autobiography the literate Empress frankly set forth her views on the Moscow v. St. Petersburg question:

'There have been many outcries in the past about it [the removal of the capital from Moscow] and even now the matter of the construction of Petersburg and the transfer of the Court from Moscow is a topic of violent, though less acid, discussion. It is said (and it is partly true) that several hundreds of thousands of men died in the process from scurvy and other diseases, that the workmen who came from the provinces never went back, that the cost of living in that town compared to Moscow was ruining the nobles, etc. This operation by Peter the Great was compared to that of Constantine who, by transporting the seat of the Roman Empire to Byzantium and abandoning Rome, destroyed the Romans' sense of patriotism, so that the virtues of their country began to disintegrate and were gradually annihilated.

'I do not like Moscow, I have nothing against Petersburg, but in my appraisal of them both I shall be guided by the good of the

Empire. Moscow is the seat of sloth, partly due to its immensity: one wastes a whole day trying to visit someone or getting a message across to them. The nobles who live there are excessively fond of the place and no wonder: they live in idleness and luxury, and become effeminate; it is not houses they own there, but regular estates. Apart from that, the town is full of symbols of fanaticism, churches, miraculous icons, priests and convents, side by side with thieves and brigands. Nor must one overlook the number of large factories which create an excessive accumulation of workmen.

'Yes, it is true that the construction of Petersburg cost much money and many lives; it is a costly city to live in, but in forty years it has given more circulation to money and commerce than Moscow in the five hundred years she has existed; the inhabitants are more docile and polite, less superstitious, more accustomed to foreigners, from contact with whom they always acquire something valuable.'

Still, in spite of her self-confessed dislike for Moscow, no ruler since the days of the two great Ivans planned such large-scale alterations of the Kremlin. The plans that were made under Catherine were so grandiose that if they had been carried out they would have completely changed the Kremlin's appearance; the remnants of the first Kremlin—the wooden one—would have completely disappeared, and the second Kremlin—the stone and masonry one that exists to this very day—would have been changed almost beyond recognition.

The plans for the third Kremlin were made by Vasili Bazhenov, a young architect, and presented to Catherine the Great for her approval. Catherine who was attracted, albeit in a superficial way, to artists, philosophers, and aesthetes, and who had dreams of great glory for herself as an architect of Russia's future, agreed to the elaborate plans, the carrying out of which, she hoped, would make the Kremlin so magnificent that her name would always be remembered as the builder of one of the greatest monumental structures of all times.

A model for the proposed reconstructed Kremlin was examined by Dr Edward Clarke who described it as follows:

'The plan was to unite the whole Kremlin, having a circumference of two miles, into one magnificent palace. Its triangular form, and the number of churches it contains, offered some difficulties; but the model was rendered complete. Its fronts are ornamented with ranges of beautiful pillars, according to different orders of architecture. Every part of it was finished in the most beautiful manner, even to the fresco painting on the ceilings of the rooms, and the colouring of the various marble columns intended to decorate the interior. It encloses a theatre, and magnificent apartments. Had the work been completed, no edifice could ever have been compared with it. It would have surpassed the Temple of Solomon, the Propylaeum of Amasis, the Villa of Adrian, or the Forum of Trajan.'

The estimated cost to re-do the Kremlin was astronomical for those days—twenty to fifty million roubles or, in present-day figures, from two hundred to three hundred and fifty million gold roubles.

In 1769 work on the new project began, and to clear the site several buildings were razed, such as the fifteenth-century Treasury Building, the seventeenth-century administrative buildings, a few churches, and even some towers (the Secret and the two Nameless Towers) and a section of the Kremlin wall. In August, 1772, a formal excavation ceremony was held, and the following year, on June 1, with great fanfare the cornerstone was formally laid.

Shortly thereafter, however, Catherine gave orders that work on the Kremlin was to stop, giving as the official reason the explanation that the Kremlin soil could not support such a massive structure as the one planned by Bazhenov. No amount of pleading by Bazhenov and others interested in the new Kremlin could sway the Empress, and the grandiose plan was abandoned. The excavations were filled in, the wall and towers were rebuilt, and, in general, everything was reconstructed to appear as it had once been. All that finally remained was the large wooden model, which had been built on a scale of 1 : 48 by the German woodcarver Witman at the huge cost of fifty thousand roubles.

Catherine's actions with regard to the Kremlin were quite typical; throughout her life she planned great projects and then did nothing about them or, after initiating them, abandoned them. Catherine had great intellectual pretensions, often of a liberal nature, but she was an autocrat above all. She was perfectly willing, for instance, to titillate herself with French philosophical thought of the period, but when that philosophy spurred on the French Revolution, she abandoned her predilection for it and became not only the most violent and bitter opponent of the Revolution but also of the philosophy and the philosophers. She ordered the bust of Voltaire to be removed from the gallery and, as one of the courtiers of the time expressed it, 'thrown among the lumber'. At the time of the American Revolution, she called Washington 'a rebel', and declared that if she, like King George of England, had lost the thirteen colonies, she would have 'put a bullet into her forehead'.

The impoverished German princess who had come to Russia as a bride-elect with, as she later confessed, 'twelve bodices and three or four skirts only', actually had but two great passions, neither of them intellectual ones—she loved to love and she gloried in glory. The stories of her lovers are well known, and as for glory, she herself said on one occasion that she would not have kept her head on her shoulders for very long had she been a man, for she would have rushed into battle in search of honour and fame. However, she was not adverse to taking heads off of other people's shoulders, to achieve and maintain power. Her husband, Peter III, was one of her victims, and towards him as towards others that she either did away with or sent to Siberia, she had little compassion. Upon viewing her dead husband's body she is said to have cynically remarked that Peter's heart 'was very small'. It would have been superfluous for her to comment on the well-known fact that his brains were miniscule, too.

Catherine's reign with regard to the Kremlin was not completely devoid of accomplishment, in spite of the Bazhenov fiasco. Matvei Kazakov, Bazhenov's co-worker, was commissioned to draw up plans for the erection of buildings in the Kremlin area, and of the number he submitted Catherine accepted two of them. This time the work was actually completed. In 1775 the Archbishop's House was built, and in 1784 the Senate Building was completed. The latter, one of the prime examples of the early Russian classical school of architecture, has a sumptuous interior and an unpretentious, dignified exterior, with an immense circular domed senate chamber (eighty-three feet in diameter and ninety feet high) at the apex. Its most striking decorative features are a Corinthian colonnade supporting a cupola with a coffered ceiling, and allegorical bas-reliefs portraying significant events of Catherine the Great's reign.

These two buildings were the last structures of any consequence to be erected in the Kremlin for the next fifty years. However, the citadel was destined to become, within fifteen years after Catherine's death, the scene of far greater activity and import than the construction of buildings; it was to become, together with the city of Moscow itself, the focal point of that most dramatic and meaningful event in Russia's history—the Napoleonic invasion.

XX

Napoleon Occupies the Kremlin

ON THE NIGHT of June 23, 1812, the troops of Napoleon crossed the Niemen and invaded Russia. Less than three months later the French were on the outskirts of Moscow. Czar Alexander I (1801–1825), who was in St. Petersburg, insisted for the benefit of public opinion that Moscow be defended. Military wisdom, however, prevailed over Alexander's appeal to 'the faithful sons of Russia to combat [the enemy] with all their force . . . and to break the jaws of the lions which are open to devour you!', and the Russian army at the order of its commander-in-chief, Kutuzov, withdrew a hundred and twenty versts beyond Moscow, leaving the city defenceless. Nine-tenths of the city's population also abandoned the city. The handful of people who, for one reason or another, decided to remain, waited resignedly for the French to occupy Moscow.

Napoleon, who had halted at the Sparrow Hills near the city, ordered that influential boyars or important municipal officials be presented to him, with the keys to Moscow. None could be found. The city, for all intents and purposes, as Tolstoy wrote in *War and Peace*, was 'deserted as a dying, queenless hive is deserted'.

On September 15, the first of Napoleon's troops, under Murat, entered Moscow. The French General Ségur wrote that they were 'struck with profound astonishment at the sight of this complete solitude. They replied to the taciturnity of this modern Thebes with a silence equally solemn. These warriors listened, with a secret shuddering, to the steps of their horses resounding alone amid these deserted palaces. They were astonished to hear nothing but themselves amid such numerous habitations'.

Murat headed for the Kremlin, which Napoleon had decided would be the headquarters of the Army as well as his own dwelling place. When Murat reached the Kremlin gate there was a barricade across it. Murat and his guards halted. From behind the barrier a few shots were fired at the French, who retaliated. The barricade was quickly destroyed, and the defenders of the Kremlin—nine nondescript Russian civilians—were routed; three were wounded, four were killed, and two, dressed in peasant clothes, ran away. The French statesman and historian Thiers, reflecting the embarrassment of Napoleon and his staff whose only opposition in Moscow had come from such a motley band, wrote: 'These wretches had invaded the sacred citadel, had taken possession of the guns of the arsenal, and fired on the French. Some of them were sabred, and the Kremlin was purged of their presence'. These 'wretches', however, had provided a most ludicrous touch to the long march of the Grand Army across Russia and to its triumphal entry into the very heart and soul of Rus itself—the Kremlin.

With the 'enemy' dispatched, Murat gave the order to march into the fortress. Inside the citadel the soldiers encamped in the squares, while their officers found quarters in various buildings. The next day Napoleon himself entered the Kremlin through the Trinity Gate and made his way directly to the Czar's Palace. There he mounted the famous and infamous Red Stairway—where Ivan the Terrible had stood when he threw his iron-pointed stave through the foot of Prince Kurbsky's messenger and where Peter the Great as a boy had seen the *streltsy* murder his friend Artamon Matvyeev —and established himself in the apartments of the Czar, choosing one of the tiny Byzantine arch-roofed rooms as his bedroom.

Napoleon's stay in the Kremlin was brief, for on the night of the sixteenth, fires, which had broken out sporadically from almost the first hour after the French occupation, now raged throughout the city. Looking out of the window in his apartment in the palace at the burning metropolis, Napoleon is said to have exclaimed, 'What a tremendous spectacle! What extraordinary resolution! What men! These are indeed Scythians!' A rumour spread that the Kremlin itself was in danger from mines that the retreating Russians had set under it, but Napoleon was unimpressed by this bit of alarming news and refused to evacuate the palace. However, later, when the fire actually spread to the immediate environs of the Kremlin, threatening the arsenal itself, Napoleon, his generals and his guards, fearing that the fire would set off the vast stores of ammunition there, evacuated the Kremlin and headed for quarters in the Petrovsky Palace on the outskirts of the city.

When the fires finally died down four days later, two-thirds of Moscow had been levelled. Of the 2,567 stone houses in Moscow, only 526 remained; of the 6,591 wooden houses, all but 2,100 were destroyed. The Kremlin itself was scarcely touched, and Napoleon moved back into it. The loss of life was relatively small for such a widespread conflagration, since most of Moscow had been evacuated, but the fire had brought out of hiding more than twenty thousand Moscow residents who had remained behind and who now had to seek refuge in the few remaining unburned buildings or in the camps of the French soldiers.

The question of who started the fires that all but destroyed Moscow has never been definitely ascertained. The Russians blamed the French; the French accused the Russians. Count Rastoptchin, the governor of Moscow, was the one most frequently accused of having given orders to fire the city, but he himself in a pamphlet he wrote in later years never verified the charges, preferring to accuse the French of barbarism rather than to praise the Russians for committing an act of great sacrifice in the name of patriotism. Napoleon denied that the French fired Moscow, and in general the French defended themselves by pointing out that they were the ones who tried to put out the fires and who punished incendiaries, most of whom were criminals who had been released on orders from Count Rastoptchin from Moscow jails just prior to the French entry into the city.

Probably the best answer to the question was given by Tolstoy, in *War and Peace*, who claimed that neither the French nor the Russians were responsible, but that the fire, under the set of circumstances that then prevailed, was inevitable.

'The French ascribed the burning of Moscow *au patriotisme féroce de Rastoptchine*; the Russians to the savagery of the French. . . .' Tolstoy wrote. 'Moscow was burned because she was placed in conditions in which any town built of wood was bound to be burned, quite apart from the question whether there were or were not one hundred and thirty inefficient fire-engines in the town. Moscow was sure to be burned, because her inhabitants had gone away. . . . A town of wooden houses, in which when the police and the inhabitants owning the houses are in possession of it, fires are of daily occurrence, cannot escape being burned when its inhabitants are gone and it is filled with soldiers smoking pipes, making fires . . . and cooking themselves meals twice a day. . . . *Le patriotisme féroce de Rastoptchine* and the savagery of the French do not come into the question.'

When the fire was finally over, the pillaging began—by both the French and the Russians, many of whom, according to Ségur, were 'well dressed' and 'of both sexes'. Moscow had been left well stocked by the retreating Russian army and the people of Moscow, and now the looters could be seen, as Ségur wrote, 'seated on bales of merchandise, or heaps of sugar and coffee; amidst wines and the exquisite liqueurs, which they were offering in exchange for a morsel of bread'.

Napoleon issued orders that the pillaging should stop, but the orders were never obeyed. One of the official reports of the military authorities, for instance, stated:

'The Emperor is exceedingly displeased that, in spite of the strict orders to stop pillage, bands of marauders from the guards are continually returning to the Kremlin. In the Old Guards, the disorder and pillaging have been more violent than ever. . . . The Emperor sees, with regret, that the picked soldiers, appointed to guard his person, who should set an example to the rest, are losing discipline to such a degree as to break into the cellars and stores prepared for the army. Others are so degraded that they refuse to obey sentinels and officers on guard, abuse them, and strike them.'

To the handful of remaining Muscovites in the city, Napoleon issued proclamations promising them justice and asking them to continue their normal business and trade. His proclamations to the Russians, like his orders on pillaging to the French troops, were ignored; the Russians had little interest in Gallic justice, and nothing that Napoleon could offer them in the way of safeguarding legitimate trade and commerce was as profitable as the rich store of goods in the city that they could illegitimately pilfer.

Hoping to impress the rough Russians with the cultured ways of the French, Napoleon set up theatres both in the Kremlin and at the house of a certain Posniakov, as well as arranging for a few musical events. The attempt of the French to impress the uncouth Slavs was as unsuccessful as most of their activities in Moscow, for the performances in the theatres had to be called off when the performers were set upon by the loot-mad soldiers and their colourful costumes were torn off their backs.

Disorder was the order of the day during Napoleon's stay in Moscow, and the state of affairs was made no better when the Emperor infuriated his own troops by paying them in counterfeit

Russian notes that he had ordered to be printed and which, as it turned out, were unacceptable as payment for goods and services by the hardheaded Russians.

The French stayed in Moscow for five weeks, and during this period, except for the several days of the great fire when Napoleon resided in the Petrovsky Palace, the Emperor lived in the Czar's Palace in the Kremlin. In addition to certain members of his staff who lived in the citadel, many soldiers, too, mostly his guard, were quartered in various buildings or in tents that were pitched on squares within the Kremlin area. The troops within the fortress had little regard for its historic buildings and treasures; priceless furniture was removed from the palaces and buildings and used as firewood by the soldiers camping out-of-doors; in the Church of the Saviour forage for the cavalry was stored above the relics of the first Christian martyr in Russia; and at one end of the Cathedral of the Assumption a furnace was erected to melt down pilfered gold and silver candlesticks, icons and other precious objects.

When, after five weeks of inglorious and frustrating occupation, Napoleon finally decided to abandon Moscow, whatever treasures had not already been pocketed by the French were hastily collected together and carried either on the person of the soldier or in carts. Loaded down with their loot, the army that left Moscow looked more like an army of marauders than of conquerors. There were trains of carriages and vehicles of every sort, even wheelbarrows, piled high with trophies and plunder that the soldiers had accumulated, in many cases pulled by peasants who had been taken prisoner or by the soldiers themselves. How they hoped to lug their piled-high carts and carriages and wheelbarrows across Russia through the snow (which had already begun to fall six days before the beginning of the evacuation), across swollen rivers and over miserable and rutted roads, God only knows! But it was not only the common soldier who had dreams of returning to his native country (troops of twelve European countries were in the invasion army) a rich man, but the staff officers, too, had carried off mountains of loot, as had their commander-in-chief, Napoleon, who had made sure that his own private *trésor* was not left behind.

One of Napoleon's last orders before leaving Moscow was that the Kremlin itself should be destroyed. The task was assigned to General Mortier, Napoleon's governor of Moscow, who was in command of one of the last contingents of troops to leave the city. Mortier ordered that a hundred and eighty-three thousand pounds of gunpowder be placed under the walls of the citadel and various buildings. When the explosion occurred it was frightful but, considering the amount of gunpowder that was used, the damage though severe did not destroy the ancient fortress. In the main the destruction consisted of the wrecking of Elizabeth's Palace and a section of the Arsenal, the cracking of the gates of the Saviour and the Trinity, damage to the Tower of Ivan the Great, and large gaps in the Kremlin walls. Miraculously, the Kremlin, by and large, was saved, even as weeks before gaudy St. Basil's on Red Square had escaped demolition, when in a fit of pique Napoleon had ordered his troops 'to destroy that mosque'. They ignored his order and used the church for a cavalry stable instead.

As soon as Napoleon's army left Moscow for its ill-dated retreat (only fifty thousand soldiers out of the original invasion army of six hundred thousand managed to survive), the Russians hurried back to the city. Cossack soldiers and peasants from the surrounding countryside were the first to return, and they took up the pillaging of Moscow where the French had left off. Another army now left Moscow, this time of Russians who carried away to the surrounding villages cartloads of loot that the French had not been able to take with them. Even within the city itself there was a busy coming and going, the Muscovites themselves looting the homes of absent neighbours, claiming that the items they stole were in reality theirs, which the wicked French had taken away from them.

All through the month of October a state of anarchy prevailed in Moscow, but then order was re-established. Peasants who came to Moscow with their carts, intending to loot, were forced by the authorities to use their carts to carry away the dead; labourers who came for the same purpose were put to work cleaning up the city and rebuilding the burnt-out houses. The merchants returned and set up their shops as best they could, and the nobility returned from their estates in the country where, if Tolstoy's analysis has any validity, by sitting out the occupation the ladies had performed a patriotic act. ('The lady who in June set off with her Negroes and her buffoons from Moscow for her Saratov estates', Tolstoy wrote, 'with a vague feeling that she was not going to be a servant of Bonaparte's, and a vague dread that she might be hindered from going by Rastoptchin's orders, was simply and genuinely doing the great deed that saved Russia.')

The city of Moscow was in a pitiable condition, being described by an eyewitness of the time as 'forlorn . . . street after street greeted the eye with perpetual ruin; disjointed columns, mutilated porticoes, broken cupolas, walls of rugged stucco, black, discoloured with the stains of fire, and open on every side to the sky, formed a hideous contrast with the glowing pictures which travellers had drawn of the grand and sumptuous palaces of Moscow'.

The reconstruction of Moscow was given priority by the Czar, and the rebuilding of the devastated city was energetically undertaken. Many new buildings were constructed, while others were restored; new squares were laid out; streets were made straighter, wider, and more regular; and some of the worst hovels were eliminated, with the result that certain sections of Moscow took on a more European aspect, though the irregular Asiatic outline of the city was still in evidence.

In the Kremlin, the Palace of the Czar was enlarged; the Arsenal was reconstructed; three large buildings were erected for use by the Chevaliers attached to the court; the walls were repaired; the streets within the Kremlin were repaved; and, in general, a fairly thorough job was done in repairing the fortress. However, the Tower of Ivan Velikii, though rebuilt, was askew, and to this very day it is referred to as 'Ivan slightly tipsy'.

And to this day, too, within the Kremlin, lined up alongside the walls of the Arsenal are eight hundred and seventy-five cannons that the Russians captured from Napoleon during his invasion of Russia—a grim reminder of the only European army (with the exception of the Poles during the Time of Troubles) that ever succeeded in occupying the fortress.

XXI

The Grand Kremlin Palace

THE enigmatic Alexander I—who had begun his reign as a liberal, in the middle of his rule had become a Russian hero by conquering Napoleon, and towards the end of his life had evolved into a typical Russian reactionary autocrat—died in 1825. Since Alexander left no children, the succession normally should have gone to his oldest brother, Constantine, but he refused the throne and it passed to the younger brother, Nicholas I (1825–55). Nicholas, like his father, Paul I (1796–1801), was the paradigm of the Russian autocrat—narrow-minded, Prussian-tempered, and an implacable enemy of any form of liberal thought. (During his brief reign, Paul I radically changed the temper of the court as it had existed under his mother, Catherine the Great, whom he despised, from one of liberal pretensions to one of strict Prussianism mixed with Russian autocracy—a most ruthless compound. Under Paul's rule, Russians were forbidden to travel abroad and no foreigner was permitted into Russia unless he obtained a special permit from the Czar. 'In Russia', Czar Paul once said, 'the only great man is the one with whom I am speaking, and that only so long as I am speaking to him.' Understandably, there was great rejoicing in Russia when on March 11, 1801, he was murdered.)

Nicholas ruled with an iron fist, and during the thirty years of his reign the jails were full and the road to exile in Siberia was well trod. It was a period in which Russia, having recently come of age as a powerful European state—the culminating point being her defeat of Napoleon—and as the strong-arm member of the Holy Alliance, actively participated in the Continent's political affairs. It was a period, too, in which there was a flowering of Russian intellectual genius. Even though the censorship was rigid and contact with Western culture was limited, foreign ideas crept in through the back door, and the first of the significant Russian nineteenth-century writers and thinkers emerged—Pushkin, Lermontov, Gogol, Belinsky, Bakunin. The long-standing, vexing problem—which had become acute since the days of Peter the Great—of whether or not

Russia should isolate herself from Europe now became accentuated, and a sharp struggle ensued between the Western-orientated and the strictly nationalistic intellectuals—a struggle that has never been completely resolved in Russia, then or now. The Czar and most of the court supported and fostered the extreme nationalistic groups, who believed that Western ideas and culture were decadent as well as being alien to the Russian spirit and soil, and that they would stifle the expression and development of native art forms.

This struggle had its influence in the field of architecture, as well as in other cultural areas and, as it turned out, acutely affected the appearance of the Kremlin. Under orders from Nicholas, Konstantin Thon, a leading architect of the period and an outstanding champion of a 'pure' Russian style based on the so-called Russian-Byzantine and Russian-Gothic architecture, was given the commission to build the Grand Kremlin Palace (*Bolshoi Kremlevskii Dvorets*) in such a way that it would symbolize the spirit of Russian nationalism. In 1839 work began on what was destined to become the dominant structure within the Kremlin walls, and in 1849 it was completed. However, it fell far short of its purported aim of being representative of native Russian influences, for only in certain respects, and minor ones at that, does it do so—such as in certain decorations of the window architraves and the tentlike covering over the roof. Architecturally, it is a potpourri of many styles and periods, mainly Italian Renaissance and pseudo-Russian.

In order to build the gigantic Grand Kremlin Palace many existing structures were torn down, though an effort was made to preserve some of the historic buildings and churches on the site and, wherever possible, incorporate them into the new palace. Thus preserved and made part of the new palace were the ancient Golden Czaritsa Chamber, the apartments of Czar Alexi, the Palace of Facets, and several old churches.

From the time it was erected over a century ago, the huge rectangular Grand Kremlin Palace, together with the adjoining *Oruzheinaia Palata*, the museum of the Kremlin, has been the focal point of the fortress. The palace staggers the observer by its immensity, for it occupies an area of almost a half million square feet and covers a good part of the Kremlin hill. Many parts of the palace itself are of Gargantuan dimensions; the principal wing, for instance, facing south, which houses most of the huge halls of the palace—St.

Andrew's Hall, Alexander Hall and the southern end of St. George's Hall—is four hundred feet long and ninety-two feet high. The north wing consists of the royal family's apartments in the old Terem Palace; the east wing includes the Palace of Facets, the Hall of St. Vladimir, the Holy Vestibule and the Red Staircase; and the west wing has in it the State Bedroom, the State Drawing Room, the Hall of St. Catherine and the Guard Room.

Facing the entrance to the *Palata* there is an archway that leads to the Kremlin Palace Court, and in the centre of this rectangular court is the most ancient building of the Kremlin—the six-hundred-year-old Church of the Saviour in the Wood (*Spas na Boru*). Though the church itself is the fortress's oldest building, the frescoes in it were done quite recently, most of them executed in the nineteenth century. One mural of ancient times is still in existence—the picture of the Transfiguration which has been ascribed to the Moscow school of the fifteenth century.

The main entrance of the Grand Kremlin Palace is on the façade that faces the Moscow River. The fifty-eight-step granite staircase of the main wing of the palace leads to the State Parade Antechamber, which has a vault sustained by four gigantic monolith columns of grey granite. On the ground floor to the left of the entrance are private apartments which were used by the Czars, beginning with Nicholas I, when they visited Moscow. The reception rooms, dining-room, boudoir, and study of the Czarina, and the bedroom, dressing-room and study of the Czar are all furnished in mid-nineteenth-century style.

At the head of the main stairway is the Antechamber which leads into the great state halls, each of them named after one or another of the Czarist military orders and ornamented with appropriate heraldry, with the walls of each hall draped with silk that is the colour of the various ribbons of the particular military order. The formalistic halls are expensively decorated with marble and alabaster columns, malachite pilasters, crystal chandeliers, magnificent parquet floors made of inlaid work of different coloured woods, and a profusion of gold.

The Hall of St. George (*Georgievskaia Zala*), situated on the site of the former Middle Golden Palace of Ivan IV, is the largest hall in the Kremlin (two hundred feet long, sixty-eight feet wide, and fifty-eight feet high) and was named after the Order of St. George, the highest imperial military order, founded by Catherine the Great in 1769. Inscribed in gold upon the marble tablets that are on the walls of the hall are the names of all the Russian regiments at the time of Nicholas I, as well as the names of honoured knights of the Order. One of the most interesting features of the hall is provided by eighteen alabaster twisted columns that stand in a row along its walls and serve as pedestals for allegorical representations of various conquests in Russian history, from the annexation of Perm in 1472 to that of Armenia in 1828. The colour scheme of the furnishings is black and white, which are the colours of the Order.

Alexander Hall, named after the Order of Alexander Nevsky, has walls of pink imitation marble which are richly decorated in gold. On the walls are six paintings dealing with significant aspects of Alexander Nevsky's life.

The Hall of St. Andrew (*Andreevskaia Zala*), dedicated to the Order of St. Andrew founded by Peter the Great in 1698, is the former imperial throne room, where the secular part of the coronation ceremony took place. It has square columns and a vaulted ceiling, similar to that of a cathedral, which is decorated with flowers of gold and heraldry. The inlaid floor, made of more than twenty varieties of wood, is an elaborate and intricate pattern of scrolls and flowers.

In the west wing of the palace is the Hall of the Horseguards (*Kavalergardskaia Zala*), with its walls of white imitation marble; the Catherine Hall (*Ekaterinenskaia Zala*), the throne room of Catherine the Great, with its two massive malachite pillars; the State Drawing Room (*Paradnaia Divannaia*); the State Bedroom, with two monolith pillars of greyish-green marble; and the Winter Garden.

Beyond the State Bedroom there is a flight of stairs that leads to the Terem Gallery, and farther on to the Chapel of the Holy Virgin's Nativity (*Tzerkov Rozhdestva Bogoroditzy*), which was built in 1514 above another chapel that had been erected in 1395 by the wife of Dmitri Donskoi in commemoration of his victory over the Tartars at Kulikovo. In 1681 the upper chapel was walled up and remained so until 1838 when it was rediscovered. In the restoration process valuable frescoes were destroyed, but externally, at least, it has retained its original outlines.

In the north-east section of the palace is the Zhiletskaia Chamber which was used as a guard room by the *zhiltzy*, who were the guards of the palace. Next to it is the Czaritsa's Golden Chamber (*Zolotaia Czaritsina Palata*) which was used by the Czaritsa as a state reception room.

On the east side of the palace, near the northern end, is the oblong-shaped Holy Vestibule (*Sviatye Steni*) which, during the building of the new palace, was disfigured and later lost its original character when it was decorated with more modern frescoes. A door in the Holy Vestibule leads to the Red Staircase which the Czars used when they went to the Kremlin cathedrals on festival days, and which, as has been mentioned previously, was the scene of many gruesome events from the time of Ivan the Terrible to the time of Peter the Great. Another door in the Holy Vestibule, to the right, leads to the ancient stone facet-shaped *Granovitaia Palata*, the front part of which faces on Cathedral Square, and another door, to the left, leads to the Boyars' Terrace (*Boyarskaia Ploshchadka*) where the boyars assembled before being admitted into the presence of the Czar.

In this same area is the Hall of St. Vladimir (*Vladimirskaia Zala*), dedicated to the Order of St. Vladimir, which was founded in 1782 by Catherine the Great. The room is octagonal in shape, measures fifty-eight feet across, and from the floor to the circular lantern in the cupola is sixty-three feet high. The walls are appropriately faced with a reddish marble, which is the colour of the Order. A large bronze chandelier, weighing eighty-six hundred pounds, hangs from the ceiling, and the parquetry of the floor is star-patterned. The hall is the connecting link between what remains of the old Terem Palace and the new palace of Nicholas I. There is a double staircase that goes from this room into the old palace. From the first landing of the staircase, in the olden days, one could look out upon an open terrace (*Verkhospasskaia Ploshchadka*), but this, during the building of the new palace, was converted into a dark entrance hall. Around the former terrace area is an ornamental gilded railing that was made in 1670 of debased copper coins, which because of their decrease in value touched off an uprising in 1662 and in consequence were withdrawn from circulation.

The entrance into the small Church of the Redeemer Behind the Golden Railing (*Spas za Zolotoi Reshetkoi*), also called the Upper Cathedral of the Redeemer (*Verkhospasskii Sobor*), is to the right of the terrace. The chapel was built above the *Zolotaia Czaritsina Palata* in the seventeenth century by Ogurtsov, Konstantinov, Sharutin and Ushakov, the architects who built the upper floors of the old palace. It is distinguished, among other things, by the coloured tiles on the cornice and cupolas, as well as by its group of eleven cupolas.

Many Russians, as well as many foreigners, have criticized the Grand Kremlin Palace as being architecturally out of place in the ancient fortress. (Some Russians felt, too, that Nicholas had desecrated the Kremlin by ripping it up to build his new palace, disturbing, so to speak, the fortress's holy soil.) One writer has said of the Grand Kremlin Palace that it is 'a vast Renaissance structure which would be impressive elsewhere, but which clashes sadly with its Muscovite surroundings. Its interminable cornices seem wearisome and out of place among these fantastic palaces', or, as Gautier described them, 'this throng of Oriental mosques, darting heavenward their golden forest of domes, spires and bulbous belltowers'. An American journalist commenting on the Grand Kremlin Palace called it 'a kind of period piece. Disrespectfully I was reminded of the United States Hotel in Saratoga'. A late-nineteenth-century writer, however, liked the new palace precisely because, as he put it, 'Amidst the confusion of the numerous small and antique edifices in the Kremlin, the Bolshoi Dvorets has an imposing aspect'. However one views the new palace, the fact is that it is there, dominating the Kremlin. Since its completion in 1849, it has been the very heart of the fortress, and since shortly after the Bolshevik Revolution of 1917, the most important centre of activities of the Soviet government.

Adjoining the Grand Kremlin Palace is the *Oruzheinaia Palata*, or Chamber of Arms, which was erected by Thon in 1849–51; it is probably the most impressive, as well as the oldest and richest, museum in Russia. The beginning of the *Oruzheinaia Palata* dates from the early sixteenth century, when it was founded not as a museum but as an arsenal. Though its prime purpose was the manufacture of arms, over the years it also became a centre for various technical, scientific, and artistic endeavours, and within the *Palata* the most skilled artisans of Russia could be found—silversmiths, goldsmiths, lapidaries, wood carvers, icon painters. After the capital was transferred to St. Petersburg, many of the *Palata's* functions and workers were moved there, too, and the *Palata* became little more than a storage place. In 1737, during the great fire, the building was destroyed, but the various collections were saved and subsequently distributed to other Kremlin buildings. During the Napoleonic invasion most of the treasures that were formerly in the *Oruzheinaia Palata*, as well as other Kremlin treasures, were sent to Nizhni Novgorod for safe keeping; in 1814 they were returned to the Kremlin, but many valuable pieces were missing.

In 1851 when the present-day *Oruzheinaia Palata* was finished, it became the central storehouse and museum of Czarist treasures. Its collections, numbering thousands of pieces, include among other things, royal armour; furniture; coaches; insignia of all kinds; sacred and secular art works in metal, ivory, stone, porcelain, and glass; gold and silver plate; goblets; embroidery; and clothing. Even before 1851 the dispersed collections, according to a catalogue compiled in 1835, contained more than ten thousand items, and after 1851 when the collections were unified in the new building the number of items was even larger.

Under the Soviets, the museum was reorganized and, beginning in 1920, many collections from various sources were added to those of the *Palata*: valuable and unusual tapestries, enamel and silver work, and other art objects from the Patriarchal Treasury; art works from various cathedrals and monasteries in and around Moscow; the priceless items from the Court Treasury which had been transferred from St. Petersburg to Moscow at the outbreak of the First World War; and innumerable objects from the ecclesiastical treasuries which were nationalized in 1922.

Almost all Russian Czars, even the early princes and grand dukes, were avid collectors and, as a result, over the centuries a vast collection of armour and *objets d'art* were gathered together from various sources. Although most of the collections originated in the workshops of the Kremlin, some of the treasures were gifts from domestic and foreign donors, while others were objects seized by conquering Russian armies. The collections were not the result of any plan; they were a haphazard accumulation that grew larger and more valuable over the centuries, reflecting in the main the Russian rulers' penchant for opulence as well as their predilection for objects that were colourful and ornate. The museum's extensive collection of jewels and objects made of precious metals—one of the most valuable in the world—is a veritable history of Russian decorative art as well as a fairly complete picture of the artistic tastes of the rulers.

Since the bulk of the collections in the *Oruzheinaia Palata* is from pre-Petrine days, the Eastern influences—Persian, Indian, Chinese, Mongolian and Byzantine—are most in evidence, though there are certain Western influences, too, such as Roman, Italian Renaissance and Polish-Italian baroque. The smaller number of objects that date from post-Petrine times show a decidedly marked Western influence, especially Frankish and Italian.

In addition to the construction of the *Oruzheinaia Palata* and the Grand Kremlin Palace, another important development affecting the Kremlin during the nineteenth century was the changes made in Red Square. Two years after the fire of 1812, a commission under Osip Beauvais was appointed to reconstruct the burned-out city of Moscow. Along with his design for a radial system of wide boulevards and avenues, Beauvais drew up plans that would make the square into an open parade ground as well as a civic and commercial centre. His plan for the square was accepted and soon thereafter the square was, so to speak, 'opened up' by the elimination of the row of masonry buildings along the Kremlin wall. On the east side of the square, the central unit of the ancient Commercial Rows (*Torgovye riady*) was crowned with a flat cupola, and at the same time a wide Doric portico with a low pediment was added, which gave the square an east-west axis orientated towards the huge Senate Building dome within the Kremlin. By doing this Beauvais not only achieved his desired effect for the square itself but also created an impressive relationship between Red Square and the Kremlin.

Once the ancient masonry buildings along the Kremlin were abolished, the square took on a more picturesque appearance, and certain imposing structures such as St. Basil's Cathedral were more easily visible. To preserve the dominance of the cathedral in the square, the commission ruled that in the future no buildings more than one storey high could be built near the church.

In the eighteen-eighties, however, the Commercial Rows were torn down and replaced by a three-storey-high, pseudo-seventeenth-century sandstone building, which was intersected in each direction by three corridors that had connecting bridges at each floor and all under one glass roof. The new building housed over two hundred and forty small shops.

On the north end of the square the Historical Museum was constructed, between 1875 and 1883, according to the plan of the architect Sherwood. In an attempt to use ancient national forms of architecture, Sherwood designed the building so that it had many elements of the Kremlin, especially the towers with tent-shaped belfries and various details characteristic of church architecture. Voyce, in his discussion of Kremlin architecture, calls the Historical Museum 'one of the more successful attempts of this period' to capture 'the spirit of national Russian art. . . . But the very complex grouping of the masses—the gloomy manner in which towers, tents and roof ridges are arranged—does not truly re-create the beauty of the old Russian architecture'.

South of the Historical Museum a monument was erected in 1818 in honour of Minin and Posharsky, the liberators of Moscow from the Polish occupiers during the Time of Troubles. The monument was cast in bronze from a design by the sculptor I. P. Martos, and shows the figures of Minin and Posharsky standing on a granite pedestal that is decorated with reliefs.

During the reigns of the last three Czars of Russia—the 'liberator' Alexander II (1855–81), the narrow-minded Alexander III (1881–1894), and the weak-willed Nicholas II (1894–1917)—the Kremlin remained, as it had been since the beginning of the eighteenth century, in the background. The centre of Russian official life was in St. Petersburg, and the Kremlin though used for coronations, as a dwelling place when the Czars visited Moscow, and as the centre for certain official and, especially, ecclesiastical functions was, in the main, merely another section of the city of Moscow. The people of Moscow used it, as well as the adjoining Alexsandrovsky Park which was laid out by Beauvais in 1826, as a promenade.

All through this period the ancient fortress was open to everyone, not only Russians but foreigners, who came, saw, and were conquered by its lush, though austere, appearance. Though no longer the centre of Russian imperial power or the home of the Czars, it was an intriguing place, with the memories of its long, violent history adding romance and meaning to the weird conglomeration of buildings within its walls. Even the visits of the Czars, the elaborate coronation ceremonies, and the various conferences that were held from time to time in the Grand Kremlin Palace could not restore the fortress to its former place as the very heart and soul of Russia, for the power of the government was elsewhere—in St. Petersburg— and through the years the Sunday promenaders who roamed over its pleasant park-like grounds, babies in perambulators, and the excitable voices of children playing alongside its hallowed buildings all but wiped away, it seemed, the almost unbelievably horrible events that had taken place there in the past. During these years the Kremlin was no longer the site of ruthless Russian state power, and its glory and gore were relegated to history books and guide books. The Kremlin might have continued being a kind of museum piece for many more years, except for an event that occurred in 1917—the Bolshevik Revolution, which in time not only returned the fortress to its former position as the symbol of state power but also made it into a symbol of emergent and dynamic Russian and world Communism.

XXII

The Communist Kremlin

On NOVEMBER 7, 1917, in St. Petersburg, the Bolshevik Party seized power. It was a swift, relatively bloodless *coup d'état*, but the few desultory shots that were fired by the armed workers and soldiers, as the American Communist writer John Reed prophetically put it at the time, did indeed 'shake the world'.

Two days later a battle for control of Moscow began between the Bolsheviks and their implacable 'bourgeois' enemies, numbering, among others, Junkers (pupils of the higher military schools) and army officers, who entrenched themselves in various parts of the city, and especially in the Kremlin which contained a large store of military supplies in the Arsenal. The Junkers, who had set up machine guns in the bell towers of churches within the Kremlin, fired upon the besieging Red troops, while the Communists after using small arms unsuccessfully to rout the Junkers, finally brought up artillery and shelled the fortress. Within a week, on November 15, the Junkers surrendered on condition of a free retreat, which was granted them. The Red troops entered the Kremlin, and Moscow was completely in the hands of the Bolsheviks.

The battle for the Kremlin had an electrifying effect upon all Russians, Reds and non-Reds alike. 'They are bombarding the Kremlin! The news passed from mouth to mouth in the streets of Petrograd, almost with a sense of terror', Reed wrote. 'Travellers from "white and shining little mother Moscow" told fearful tales. Thousands killed; the Tverskaya and the Kuznetsky Most in flames; the church of Vasili Blazheiny a smoking ruin; Usspensky Cathedral crumbling down; the Spasskaya Gate of the Kremlin tottering; the Duma burned to the ground.'

Though reports reaching St. Petersburg and other parts of Russia concerning the destruction to the Kremlin were, as it later developed, exaggerated, the nation was horrified at the idea that the most sacred historical monument of all Russia was being destroyed, and not by foreign guns and troops but by the Russians themselves. 'Nothing that the Bolsheviki had done could compare with this fearful blasphemy in the heart of Holy Russia', Reed wrote. 'To the ears of the devout sounded the shock of guns crashing in the face of the Holy Orthodox Church, and pounding to dust the sanctuary of the Russian nation. . . .'

To the ears of the non-devout, too, and even to some diehard Communists, who were, it appeared, willing to go to almost any lengths to assure the success of the revolution, the news of the shelling of the fortress by the Bolsheviks was shocking. Lunatcharsky, a top Communist leader and the newly appointed Commissar of Education, wept at a session of the Council of People's Commissars when he heard the news. As reported by Reed, he 'rushed from the room, crying, "I cannot stand it! I cannot bear the monstrous destruction of beauty and tradition. . . ." ' That same day he resigned, and his statement of resignation published in the newspapers read:

'I have just been informed, by people arriving from Moscow, what has happened there.

'The Cathedral of St. Basil the Blessed, the Cathedral of the Assumption, are being bombarded. The Kremlin, where are now gathered the most important art treasures of Petrograd and of Moscow, is under artillery fire. There are thousands of victims.

'The fearful struggle there has reached a pitch of bestial ferocity.

'What is left? What more can happen?

'I cannot bear this. My cup is full. I am unable to endure these horrors. It is impossible to work under the pressure of thoughts which drive me mad!

'That is why I am leaving the Council of People's Commissars.

'I fully realize the gravity of this decision. But I can bear no more. . . .'

Using his great persuasive powers, Lenin, the leader of the Bolsheviks, pleaded with the overwrought commissar to remain in office. Lunatcharsky agreed to do so and immediately issued a statement in which he appealed to the people of Russia to spare their historic and artistic treasures, though he could not restrain himself from once again berating the Bolsheviks, saying, 'That which is happening at Moscow is a horrible, irreparable misfortune. . . . The People in its struggle for power has mutilated our glorious capital'.

The damage to the Kremlin was not inconsiderable, though not as serious as it could have been under such conditions. The little

Nicholas Palace, which had been used as barracks by the defending White forces, was heavily damaged by shellfire, as well as being plundered. The Cathedral of the Assumption was harmed by a shell hole in one of its cupolas, and several feet of mosaic in the ceiling were also damaged. In the Cathedral of the Annunciation some of the frescoes were seriously scarred. The famous Ivan Velikii Belfry was hit by a shell and one corner of it was damaged. The Chudov Monastery, though hit about thirty times, suffered only minor damage, mainly to brick window mouldings and roof cornices. The clock and chimes in the Saviour Tower were destroyed; the Trinity Gate was smashed; and one of the lower towers lost its brick spire. The Beklemishev Tower, on the south-east corner, was partly destroyed, and there were numerous gaping holes in the walls of the fortress. The art works of the Kremlin, as well as the treasures that had been sent from St. Petersburg to the fortress for safe keeping, were not, as had been feared, destroyed during the fighting. The Grand Kremlin Palace, which housed in its cellar the bulk of the Moscow and St. Petersburg treasures, was untouched, as was the adjoining *Oruzheinaia Palata* which contained, among other valuable items, the crown jewels.

One interesting sidelight on the harm done to the Kremlin in the week-long fighting was the destruction of the icon over the Nicholas Gate, which was shot full of holes. According to tradition the Russians believed that nothing could possibly damage the holy picture of the patron saint. Through the centuries it had remained unharmed, though time and again the Kremlin had been damaged by fire, invading armies, and internal disorder. Even the destruction resulting from Napoleon's attempt to blow up the Kremlin when he retreated from Moscow, damaging as it was to some parts of the fortress, did not harm the holy icon, its lantern, and the canopy over the lantern. They could not, however, survive the Bolshevik onslaught, and this age-long Russian tradition, as so many other Russian traditions, was destroyed during the fighting.

Though the battle for Moscow lasted only a week, hundreds of people, mostly Red supporters, were killed. A common grave was dug along the wall of the Kremlin between the Nicholas and Saviour Gates for the revolutionaries who were killed during the first days of the revolution in Moscow, and approximately five hundred of them were buried there in what became known as the Brothers'

Grave. In 1918 on the first anniversary of the revolution, a bas-relief by the sculptor Konenkov was placed on the Senate Tower wall as a monument honouring the fallen revolutionaries. In time it became customary to bury important deceased leaders of the Communist Party, famous writers, explorers, and other prominent individuals—and even leading non-Russian Red leaders—along the Kremlin wall. Some of the people buried there include Sverdlov, Frunze, Krasin, Dzerzhinsky, Karpov, Russakov, Podbielsky, Nogin, Narimanov, Vladimirov, Orjonikidze, Kalinin, Zhdanov, Kirov, and many other top Russian Communist political figures; Maxim Gorky, the well-known writer; the scientist Karpinsky; and Fedoseyenko, Vassenko, and Ussyskin, the explorers of the stratosphere who were killed in 1934. Among the non-Russians buried there are various Communist Party leaders from abroad, such as Ruthenberg of the United States; MacManus of Britain; Katayama of Japan; Landler of Hungary; the German woman Communist Clara Zetkin; the French woman Communist Inez Armand; the American I.W.W. leader Bill Haywood; and John Reed the American Communist writer who died in Russia in 1920. (Reed had the official blessing of Lenin himself for his book *Ten Days That Shook the World*, which is a first-hand reporter's account of the first days of the Russian Revolution. In fact, Lenin was so impressed by the book that he wrote the foreword for it. For this work, as well as for being one of the founders of the American Communist Party, Reed was honoured by having his grave marked by a block of granite.)

The transformation of the Kremlin from a museum piece of autocratic Czarist rule to the stronghold of bureaucratic Communist rule was only a matter of months. In March, 1918, only four months after the outbreak of the revolution, the capital of Russia was transferred from St. Petersburg to Moscow, with the most important government and Party bureaux being installed in the Kremlin. (In December, 1936, when at the VIII Extraordinary Congress of Soviets the so-called Stalinist Constitution of the Soviet Union was adopted, it was officially recorded, in Article 145 of the Constitution, that 'The Capital of the Union of Soviet Socialist Republics is the City of Moscow'. The Kremlin itself was for years prior to 1936 recognized as the 'White House' of the government, and all major acts and decrees of the Soviets were—and are—signed: 'The Kremlin,

Moscow'.) Like the pre-Petrine Czars and high government officials, the top leaders of the government and Party established their personal residences within the fortress too.

The reasons given for moving the capital back to Moscow from St. Petersburg were that in the counter-revolution and foreign intervention that followed the Bolshevik seizure of power, St. Petersburg was too vulnerable to attack, being on the very border of Russia; that the heart of Russia was Moscow, not St. Petersburg, and thus geographically as well as historically it was a more appropriate place for the capital; that Moscow was representative of Russian traditions, and was not tainted by Westernism as was St. Petersburg.

The transference of the capital back to Moscow, as it turned out, was a sound psychological move for the Communists. Since in the years immediately following the revolution the Communists preached and practised austerity, their leaders had a perfect setting in the monastery-like Kremlin. The ornate palaces, such as Peterhof, Czarskoe Seloe and the Winter Palace in St. Petersburg and its environs, with their gilt statues, ostentatious fountains, 'bourgeois' furnishings, lavish display of wealth and extensive park-like grounds and gardens, were inappropriate places indeed for the self-professed defenders of the downtrodden masses to live and work in. Moreover, it was apparent to the Communist leaders from the very first days of the revolution that the very appearance of the impressive Kremlin, fronted as it is by the vast Red Square, is a fortunate one, offering a near-perfect setting for agitational mass demonstrations. For example, the funeral ceremony at the Brothers' Grave, which was attended by thousands of Moscow inhabitants who crowded into Red Square while bands played the *Internationale* and the 'Revolutionary Funeral March' and gigantic banners reading 'Martyrs of the Beginning of World Social Revolution' and 'Long Live the Brotherhood of Workers of the World' rippled in the wind from the top of the Kremlin wall, could not have been staged so dramatically in the more sophisticated surroundings of St. Petersburg.

The Kremlin, which had been the fountainhead of authority at the time of Russia's emergence from obscurity during the days of the two great Ivans and had been the historic symbol of Russia's might, even when Moscow was not the capital, was the logical centre for the twentieth-century prototypes of Ivan the Terrible's all-glorious, all-righteous, all-powerful police state. If the harsh-looking

Kremlin had not existed, the Communists, in order to have a headquarters that represented their mailed-fist rule, would have had to build one.

During the early years of the Soviet régime, when a premium was put on austerity, the leaders lived in almost Spartan quarters which were small, sparsely furnished, and, in many cases, uncomfortable. Lenin, the undisputed Communist leader, occupied an apartment in the former Court of Justice, consisting only of a reception room, two bedrooms, and a workroom. With his wife and co-worker, Nadyezhda Krupskaya, he lived and worked there until his death early in 1924. In the former Court of Appeals, private apartments were made from offices, and in one of them, in a pair of simply furnished rooms, Kalinin lived with his wife and sister. At the far end of the same floor, Trotsky for a time had an apartment which consisted of three rooms and which he shared with his wife and sister.

Though a form of communal living existed within the Kremlin during the first years after the revolution—for instance, the Red leaders and their aides, about three hundred in number, ate in a communal dining hall—the Kremlin was by no means a people's centre; it was, on the contrary, almost hermetically sealed off from the rest of the city, with guards posted at the gates to prevent any unauthorized person from entering the grounds. In fact, during the earliest years, representatives of foreign governments would often meet the Soviet leaders outside the Kremlin walls, rarely if ever being invited into the leaders' quarters and offices within the fortress. The British diplomat Robert Bruce Lockhart, for example complained that at the time when his relations with the Bolsheviks were on an extremely close and cordial basis, he never once was invited into the Kremlin. He spoke with the Communist leaders many times but, as he wrote, 'My interviews with Lenin, Trotsky, Chicherin and other Commissars had always been outside the walls'. (Eventually, Lockhart was arrested by the Communists, accused of conspiring to murder Lenin, spent a month in jail, and was finally released.)

During its first three years in power the new régime was mainly concerned with the retention and consolidation of power and the defeat of the Russian White troops and foreign invasion forces. As a result, nothing was done to repair and refurbish the Kremlin.

However, as early as October, 1918, the Soviet government issued a decree establishing the principle of the state's responsibility for the preservation of monuments of art and antiquity. Under the aegis of the People's Commissariat for Education, a central agency was set up for this purpose, consisting, among others, of a Restoration Commission composed of archaeologists, architects and artists, whose prime function was to repair the walls, towers, churches and various buildings of the Kremlin, and to restore them as nearly as possible to their original appearance.

Two years later, in 1920, the Soviets began to work on the Kremlin, and continued to do so for many years—not only working on the fortress itself but also in the Red Square area. In the square, St. Basil's, which had undergone many alterations over the centuries, was restored to its former appearance. Also, the narrow gates of the Chapel of the Iberian Virgin were torn down so that there could be a wide, unobstructed approach to Red Square.

Within the Kremlin, the buildings, walls, and towers that had been damaged during the 1917 fighting in Moscow were repaired, and many of the innumerable alterations that had been made over the centuries—often in extremely poor taste—to satisfy the particular whim of a Czar or the tastes of some particular school of architecture that had been dominant at the time—were eliminated. Various wings, screens and other additions were removed, and in so doing a great number of original structures and art works were discovered, such as the passageways under the Church of the Twelve Apostles, built in 1656; the portals of the Church of the Consecration of the Priests, dating from 1484–86; and the stone carvings on the Renaissance portals of the Archangel Cathedral. The windows of the Church of the Consecration of the Priests were restored to their original design; the interior arrangement of the Patriarchal Palace, which had been altered in the nineteenth century to make room for apartments, was refashioned in its earlier form; and many unaesthetic decorations and hangings in the various churches and cathedrals were removed, revealing earlier art works of great interest. For example, when the interior of the Uspenskii Cathedral was being restored to its former aspect, the elimination of coatings of lime and cement revealed that underneath these coatings were priceless art works of medieval painters, such as Theophanos the Greek, Andrei Rublev, and Feodosii, the Moscow icon painter.

Beauvais's redesigning of Red Square early in the nineteenth century, so that it was not only a great civic centre but also a magnificent open parade ground, made it, as the Communists fully realized, a perfect convocation area for mass celebrations. Amidst the impressive setting of the high, crenellated Kremlin walls, the elaborate St. Basil's Cathedral, the impressive Historical Museum, and later the huge GUM department-store building, all of them surrounding, so to speak, the immense open area of the square itself, hundreds of thousands of marchers and demonstrators could, in the course of several hours, pass through the square, to be reviewed by high Soviet government and Communist Party officials on the reviewing stand on top of Lenin's Tomb, the focal point of the vast Red Square-Kremlin set up.

After Lenin's death in 1924, the Bolshevik leaders decided to preserve his body and to have it displayed in a mausoleum. A sombre structure, made of wood and painted in red, was erected in 1924 as a temporary shelter. After a design of A. V. Shchusev, it was later redesigned and rebuilt by the same architect as a permanent structure in a style that Soviet architectural authorities refer to as 'the best expression of the techniques of socialist realism'.

The tomb itself is not of great proportions, but its setting in the most conspicuous place in Red Square gives it an impressiveness of location if not of size. Low in height, rectangular in shape, and flat-roofed with setbacks, the structure's design is simple and restrained, and because of its clean, functional lines, it expresses both serenity and power. Enclosed within a low parapet, built of greyish-white, semi-polished granite, the base of the mausoleum is slightly above the level of Red Square. The main part of the tomb is made of highly polished red Ukrainian granite and black and grey labradorite which is flecked with iridescent blue. Surmounting the main structure is a monolith, twenty-six feet high, made of red Carnelian porphyry, and running parallel to the Kremlin wall are rows of tribunes, built, like the parapet, of greyish-white granite.

From the very first day that the mausoleum was opened to the public, there have been long lines of people eager and curious to see the Oriental-looking leader of the Bolshevik Revolution. Often, the double line will extend for a half mile or more, and even in the dead of winter, with the temperature well below freezing, people will queue up for hours to have a two-second look from behind a railing at Lenin in his satin-lined, glass-encased coffin. On each side of the coffin, at attention, stands a grim, tight-lipped, eyes-front soldier. For many years, on the western side of the vault, were displayed the banners of the Communist International and the war banner of the Paris Commune of 1871, which was presented in 1924 to the Russian Communist Party by the French Communists.

With the Bolshevik leader embalmed in a mound-like shrine, like a king or high priest of some ancient civilization, and the thousands of reverential men and women who daily come to pay him their respects or, in some cases, to satisfy their curiosity, Lenin's Tomb points up, probably more than any other single feature of Soviet life, the new religion—the mystique—that has arisen in Russia under Communist rule. The very appearance of the amazingly well-preserved body of Lenin, the prophet if not the god of the new religion, adds a supernatural note to this most materialistic of faiths, for it is the almost unanimous opinion of people who have seen Lenin in the mausoleum that he appears not to be dead but merely resting or, as one foreign visitor to the tomb expressed it, 'contemplating'.

When Stalin died in 1953, he, too, was embalmed in the same shrine, which then became known as the Mausoleum of Lenin and Stalin. Whether Stalin, whose Communist status in death is much shakier than it was during his life, will remain in the same mausoleum with Lenin, or whether in time his presence there, even in death, will be considered a corrupting influence and he will be removed, remains to be seen.

The various buildings within the Kremlin, in addition to being used as dwelling places for high-placed Soviet leaders, have since 1918 served as offices and assembly places for various governmental and Party organizations, though over the years as the bureaucracy grew, more and more official bodies as well as Party officials themselves took up quarters in other sections of Moscow. The highest Soviet bodies have their headquarters within the Kremlin, such as the Central Executive Committee of the U.S.S.R., which meets in the Hall of St. Andrew, though for many years it met in the Kremlin Senate Building, as did the All-Russian Central Executive Committee and the Council of the People's Commissars of the Soviet Union and the R.S.F.S.R.

The headquarters of various official and semi-official governmental agencies have been changed from time to time within the

Kremlin buildings themselves. The Nicholas Palace, for instance, built at the end of the eighteenth century, at one time housed the Sverdlov Club, the club of the Kremlin military school, and later the Soviet of Nationalities. The Barracks, too, have had several changes of occupants, at one time being used by the Red Officers' School for training in what one Soviet publication euphemistically referred to as 'Kremlin courses'.

There has been a great deal of coming and going, too, on Kommunisticheskaia (Communist Street), the only 'named' street in the Kremlin, where many officials have their dwelling places in houses that formerly were residences of court officials. Even the very top leaders have shifted their residences, often as a result of promotions or demotions in the Party hierarchy. Molotov, for example, when he became one of the most powerful Communist leaders, occupied Lenin's former quarters in the old Court of Justice, where, incidentally, the Nazi-Soviet Pact was signed and over whose dome (as well as over other Kremlin buildings) the Red flag flies day and night, 'fluttering like a flame above the sombre outlines of the Kremlin walls . . . a symbol of the Soviet's dominion over the former Russian Imperial realm', as a guidebook issued to foreign travellers in Russia in the nineteen-thirties proudly stated.

For long periods of time since 1918, entrance to the Kremlin was barred to all but official personages. Depending upon the extent of the suspicions of the top leader—Lenin, Stalin, or, in recent years, Malenkov and Khrushchev—the gates were open or shut. After the revolution, they were closed for a long time. In the early thirties they were opened so that the museums and palaces could be visited by natives and foreigners alike. About the time of the Stalin purges, the Kremlin gates were again closed, and remained so, though foreign dignitaries were often allowed to visit the museums and palaces, as well as to attend various social functions within the fortress. In the mid-fifties the Kremlin was again opened to tourists when after years of keeping the Iron Curtain tightly drawn the Soviet government as part of the new post-Stalin 'friendly face' policy initiated by Khrushchev and Bulganin decided to open it slightly and permit tourists to enter Russia. It is difficult to foretell with certainty whether the Curtain will remain somewhat open or again be tightly closed; however, it may be assumed from the numerous about-faces of the Soviet government during the past forty years—and, for that matter, the millennium-long history of Russia itself—that the frontiers of Russia will again be sealed when it is to the advantage of the Communist leaders to capitalize on the time-worn suspicion of Russia towards the outside world.

For six years after the revolution—when Lenin held the position as top leader of both the government and Party—the Kremlin though a meaningful symbol of Russian and Communist power, did not as yet appear to the outside world as the powerful and mysterious symbol of Russian and world Communism that occurred during Stalin's quarter-century-long dictatorship. Under Lenin, the revolution was too new, the state too weak, the policies too flexible (viz. the New Economic Policy, in the early twenties, which, because of the deplorable state of industrial and agricultural affairs in Russia, allowed for a partial return to a capitalistic economy), and the purported ideals too sacrosanct.

During Stalin's régime the Kremlin became a place of terror, mystery, and ruthless power, as it had been in the time of Ivan the Terrible. The methods—and even the personalities—of the two rulers were similar, and it is no wonder that in Stalin's era Ivan was officially regarded as a 'progressive phenomenon', and his reign as 'a glorious page in the history of Russia'. Though Stalin's policies were carried out under the ideological cloak of the dictatorship of the proletariat, rather than under Ivan's self-professed ideological cloak of being chosen and directed by God to be His scourge on earth, as well as the more modest justification that he was, through his extreme measures, breaking up the outmoded feudal system of Russia, both régimes were police states, each with their bullyboys, periodic purges of top government advisers, mass deportations, torture chambers, murder of political enemies, pathological suspicion of foreigners, glorification of one-man rule, dictatorial dealings with state functionaries, and self-deification.

Like Ivan, Stalin during his latter years in power was regarded as 'the sick man of the Kremlin', and his purgings of high officials of the government, army and the Party were regarded, among other things, as signs that he was suffering from hysteria brought about in part by a pathological fear for his personal safety. This was denied by Communists, who called it 'typical capitalist slander of our beloved leader Stalin', when it was made by various writers, and even by diplomats such as Joseph E. Davies, the former American

Ambassador to Russia, in his book *Mission to Moscow*, but the
explosive, idol-smashing speech by Khrushchev in 1956, when he
spelled out the long list of Stalin's crimes before a stunned assemblage of leaders at the Russian Communist Party convention, verified this point of view.

All during his reign Stalin rarely left the Kremlin, and when he
did it was usually to his *dacha*, his country place near Moscow which
was surrounded by a high palisade and guarded by soldiers. Even
during World War II when the Nazis approached to within a few
miles of Moscow, causing the government to flee to Kuibyshev on
the Volga, Stalin insisted on remaining in the fortress. Isaac Deutscher, one of his biographers, wrote:

'His presence in the Kremlin in this late hour was indeed a
challenge to fate. It was as if the fortunes of the world had been
balancing on the towers of the old fortress. To both Stalin and Hitler
the Kremlin became the symbol of their ambitions, for while Stalin
was refusing to leave its walls, Hitler issued an order that "the
Kremlin was to be blown up to signalize the overthrow of Bolshev-
ism". It was in the setting of the Kremlin that Stalin's figure had
grown to its present stature. He had become one with the setting and
its historical associations and he was as if afraid of detaching himself
from it. . . . He was, incidentally, to remain thus voluntarily
immured in the Kremlin throughout the war. Not once, so it seems,
did he seek direct personal contact with his troops in the field.'

Like Ivan the Terrible after the victory over the Tartars at Kazan,
when he avoided front-line battle, Stalin after the war posed as the
conquering military hero of the Germans, just as he had posed as
the military genius who had substantially contributed to the defeat
of the Whites after the revolution. Stalin, like almost every Russian
ruler before him, either fled from the scene of battle or isolated himself from it, though, again like the Russian princes and Czars who
preceded him, he insisted that after the enemy's defeat the victor's
mantle be draped around his shoulders.

During Stalin's lifetime, and after, the Kremlin itself was kept in
excellent condition, without the faintest trace of the shabbiness that
exists in most Russian cities and even in the capital city of Moscow.
Almost every visitor to the Kremlin, to this 'prison of luxury', as
ex-Ambassador Davies called it, who has written of his visit, has
remarked favourably upon its appearance in recent years. The

American writer Lydia Kirk, after visiting the Kremlin in 1949, wrote: 'The various buildings and grounds inside the Kremlin are as neat and polished as tiled bathroom fixtures, the only really well-kept spot I've seen in the Soviet Union. Even the blades of grass looked as though they had been straightened that morning'. Another recent visitor to the Kremlin wrote that the fortress 'is an expanse of broad, well-kept lawns, prim borders planted with young shrubs, and official-looking stuccoed buildings with wide windows. . . . One was reminded of the courtyard of a college in one of England's ancient universities'.

In addition to keeping the Kremlin buildings and churches in good repair and the grounds spick-and-span, the invaluable historic items have been carefully preserved and catalogued, and every article is tagged with a serial number and an historical description. Though certain Czarist trappings in the Kremlin have been super-seded by Communist ones—such as the old imperial arms on tower spires that were replaced by revolving five-pointed red stars, ten feet across from point to point, in 1937, in commemoration of the twentieth anniversary of the Bolshevik Revolution—the general state of the fortress, and the impression one gets upon viewing it, especially from the outside, is of a well-preserved monument of olden days.

Within the buildings themselves, though, there have been many instances in which old-fashioned items have given way to modern ones, especially with regard to comfort and convenience. The Kremlin now has in many of its buildings fluorescent lighting, modern heating appliances, and air-conditioning, not to mention, of course, typewriters, telephones, and other modern office equipment.

The introduction of modern conveniences has not lessened the splendid appearance of the more elaborate halls, apartments and churches, which have retained or, in those cases where they had been neglected, have been restored to their former grandeur. St. George's Hall, for instance, where most of the large official Soviet government receptions are held, is kept in perfect condition, and few visitors to it would disagree with the New York *Times* reporter who after attending a reception there in 1954 wrote that he had 'rarely been in a room more magnificent'. The same care is taken of other halls, such as the Throne Room of St. Andrew. Here approximately twelve hundred delegates to the All-Union Soviet meet, and listen to decrees and resolutions that are read to them from a podium that rests in the exact spot where in former days stood the throne of the Czars.

The apartments of the Czars have also been kept inviolate by the Communists, so that even today, forty years after the revolution, the apartments have the same appearance that they had when Nicholas II and his predecessors used to visit the Kremlin; each detail is meticulously preserved, down to, for instance, the setting of the dining-room table which, with its expensive silverware, silver plate, and gold-edged dishes, each in its proper place and kept sparkling bright by attendants, appears in perfect order as if at any minute the Czar, his family and guests were expected for dinner.

The respect that the Communists have shown for the palaces of the Czars is evident not only in the Kremlin but also in the palaces of Leningrad and its environs; there, too, everything is kept in perfect condition and order, and even the guides, on occasion, speak in awed reverence about the former royal inhabitants and their fabled luxury to sightseers—supplied with felt slippers to make sure they do not scar the expensive floors with their coarse proletarian boots— who pour into the palaces when they are open for inspection. The Soviets have been conscientious in scrupulously preserving the luxurious possessions of the Czars not only because they can show the masses how parasitic and disgusting it was for the royal family to live in such opulence while the common people starved but, as the official guides as well as the official Soviet guidebooks and histories point out, because the Communists by preserving the Czarist treasures—artistic, ecclesiastical and secular—are doing their duty as loyal Russians and as cultured, civilized people. In addition to this self-professed noble purpose, however, they unprofessedly evidence a certain amount of pride in the fact that the Czars, their Little Fathers, lived well and had extravagant tastes, even as some Russians are proud of the fact that their late Stalin, 'their beloved leader', was a modern counterpart of Ivan Grozny.

How many more Ivan Groznys will continue to live and rule in the Kremlin only time will tell. The long, violent story of the Kremlin, its leaders and the people it ruled, does not afford too much hope that the desire for freedom, as distinct from the desire for bread, will effect a change in the basic pattern of Russian tyrannical overlordship. Yet, strangely enough, the history of the Kremlin, as well as the history of Russia itself, tells us, too, that with the Russians anything and everything is possible, and that the Kremlin, which more than anything else in Russia recalls to mind that land's tortured, brutal and tragic history as well as its arrogance, fortitude and steadfastness, may indeed someday become not a citadel of oppression but a citadel of freedom.

BIBLIOGRAPHY

A selected list of books in English

ABBOTT, J. S. C., *The Empire of Russia*, New York, 1872.
AL-GHAZI, A., *A General History of the Turks, Moguls, and Tatars*, London, 1729–30.
ANONYMOUS, *A New and Exact Description of Moscovy*, London, 1698.
BAIN, R. N., *The First Romanovs*, London, 1905.
BAIN, R. N., *The Pupils of Peter the Great*, Westminster, 1897.
BAIN, R. N., *Slavonic Europe*, Cambridge, 1908.
BRYANCHANINOV, N. V., *A History of Russia*, London, 1930.
BUXHOEVEDEN, S. K., *A Cavalier in Muscovy*, London, 1932.
CATHERINE II, *Memoirs of Catherine the Great*, New York, 1927.
CLARK, E. D., *Travels in Russia, Tartary and Turkey*, Edinburgh, 1839.
COXE, W., *Travels into Poland, Russia, Sweden, and Denmark*, London, 1784–90.
CROSS, S. H., *The Russian Primary Chronicle*, Cambridge, 1930.
CRULL, J., *The Antient and Present State of Muscovy*, London, 1698.
CURTIN, J., *The Mongols in Russia*, Boston, 1908.
CUSTINE DE, A. L. L., *Russia*, New York, 1854.
DAVIES, J. E., *Mission to Moscow*, New York, 1941.
DEUTSCHER, I., *Stalin*, New York, 1949.
DOLE, N. H., *Young Folks' History of Russia*, Akron, 1903.
ECKARDT VON, H., *Ivan the Terrible*, New York, 1949.
ECKARDT VON, H., *Russia*, New York, 1932.
FLETCHER, G., *Of the Russe Common Wealth*, London, 1591.
FLORINSKY, M. T., *Russia*, New York, 1953.
FRASER, J. F., *Russia of Today*, New York, 1916.
GAUTIER, T., *A Winter in Russia*, New York, 1874.
GEORGI, J. G., *Russia*, London, 1780.
GIOVIO, P., *Historie* (In Eden, R., ed., *The Decades of the Newe Worlde or West India*), London, 1555.
GORDON, A., *The History of Peter the Great, Emperor of Russia*, Aberdeen, 1755.

GRAHAM, S., *Ivan the Terrible*, New Haven, 1933.

GREENER, W. O., *The Story of Moscow*, London, 1900.

GRUNWALD DE, C., *Peter the Great*, London, 1956.

GUIDE-BOOKS, *Guide to the Soviet Union*, Moscow, 1925.
    Guide to the City of Moscow, Moscow, 1937.
    Moscow, A Short Guide, Moscow, 1955.

HAKLUYT, R., *The Discovery of Muscovy*, London, 1904.

HAMEL, J., *England and Russia, The Voyages of John Tradescant the Elder, Sir Hugh Willoughby, Richard Chancellor, Nelson, and Others*, London, 1854.

HAXTHAUSEN, A., *The Russian Empire*, London, 1856.

HEBERSTEIN VON, S., *Notes Upon Russia*, London, 1851–52.

HOWE, S. E., *Some Russian Heroes, Saints and Sinners*, Philadelphia, 1917.

HOWE, S. E., *The False Dmitri*, New York, 1916.

JENKINSON, A., *et al.*, *Early Voyages and Travels to Russia and Persia*, London, 1886.

KLYUCHEVSKY, V. O., *A History of Russia*, London, 1911–31.

KORB, J. G., *Diary of an Austrian Secretary of Legation at the Court of Czar Peter the Great*, London, 1863.

LAMB, H., *The City and the Tsar*, New York, 1948.

LAMB, H., *The March of the Barbarians*, New York, 1940.

LAMB, H., *The March of Muscovy*, New York, 1948.

LOCKHART, R. H. B., *Memoirs of a British Agent*, New York, 1932.

LOWTH, G. T., *Around the Kremlin*, London, 1868.

LYALL, R., *The Character of the Russians and a Detailed History of Moscow*, London, 1823.

MANLEY, R., *The Russian Imposter*, London, 1677.

MARSDEN, C., *Palmyra of the North*, London, 1943.

MASSON, C. F. P., *Memoirs of Catherine II and the Court of St. Petersburg During Her Reign and That of Paul I*, Paris (*c.* 1900).

MAYNARD, J., *Russia in Flux*, London, 1941.

MAZOUR, A. G., *An Outline of Modern Russian Historiography*, Berkeley, 1939.

MIKHAILOV, N. N., *The Russian Story*, New York, 1945.

MILTON, J., *A Brief History of Moscovia*, London, 1682.

MIRSKY, D. S., *Russia, A Social History*, London, 1931.

MORFILL, W. R., *Russia*, London, 1880.

MOTTLEY, J., *The History of the Life of Peter I, Emperor of Russia*, London, 1739.

NORMAN, H., *All the Russias*, London, 1902.

OLEARIUS, A., *The Voyages and Travels of the Ambassadors from the Duke of Holstein to the Great Duke of Muscovy and the King of Persia*, London, 1662.

PARES, B., *A History of Russia*, New York, 1953.

PASZKIEWICZ, H., *The Origin of Russia*, London, 1954.

PIGOTT, G. W. R., *Savage and Civilized Russia*, London, 1877.

POKROVSKY, M. M., *History of Russia*, New York, 1931.

RAMBAUD, A., *The History of Russia*, London, 1879.

REED, J., *Ten Days That Shook the World*, New York, 1935.

RICHARDSON, W., *Anecdotes of the Russian Empire*, London, 1784.

ROMANOFF, H. C., *Historical Narratives from the Russian*, London, 1871.

SALTUS, E. E., *The Imperial Orgy*, New York, 1920.

SEEGER, E., *The Pageant of Russian History*, New York, 1950.

SUMNER, B. H., *Survey of Russian History*, London, 1944.

TOLSTOY, A., *The Making of Russia*, London, 1945.

TOLSTOY, L., *War and Peace*, New York, 1942.

TOOKE, W., *View of the Russian Empire*, London, 1800.

TYRRELL, H., *History of the Russian Empire*, London, 1859.

VERNADSKY, G. V., *A History of Russia*, New Haven, 1954.

VOLTAIRE DE, F. M. A., *The History of the Russian Empire Under Peter the Great*, London, 1763.

WALISZEWSKI, K., *Peter the Great*, New York, 1897.

WALLACE, D. M., *Russia*, New York, 1877.

WOOD, R. K., *The Tourist's Russia*, London, 1912.

INDEX

INDEX